# Nurturing
## *the Secret Garden*

Also by Barbara Hoi

The Right Brain for the Right Time

Unlock the Dyslexic Potential and Transform
From a Frustrated Reader to an Inspiring Reader

Learning Your Times Tables in Three Bold Steps

Making Multiplications Easy for Visual Learners

90 Shades of Gratitude

A Gratitude Journal with Guided Meditation

# Nurturing
# *the Secret Garden*

## A Manual to THE ONE YEAR SCHOOL

### A Guide to Reading Mastery

## Barbara Hoi

Based on the novel 'the Secret Garden'

By Frances Hodgson Burnett

*based on*

"Nurturing the Secret Garden"

Second edition

Published in October 2020

ISBN: 978-1500187408

Published in July 2014

Visit our websites:
www.sydneydyslexia.com
www.theoneyearschool.com

Contact the author on:
hoi.barbara1@gmail.com

# INDEX

# TERM II

# Foreword

I have worked with many dyslexic clients, children and adults alike – very creative, wonderful and usually visual learners who have become aligned or oriented in a five-day intensive program. They have worked hard to change, to not only learn to read, spell, write and understand literature, but also to transform themselves. What we as facilitators see after a week is a much more confident person, able to master their words and continue to make reading easier and more joyful every day. We also see a person who has let go of some old beliefs that don't serve them any longer and have been replaced with a new outlook and confident self-image.

They have become responsible custodians of their own learning and it is highly rewarding to see the big smile of confidence after a realisation that 'Yes, I can do this and yes, I am bright and able.' In one week we have helped them let go of emotional blocks that often sabotage the success of a program and given them all the tools, shown them the ways to do it and started them on their journey of self-discovery.

We have proven that you can learn to read in twenty hours, with focus and having established new neural pathways that become the foundation to a new way of learning.

However, the journey continues from there – where we have finished the placing of the tools of orientation, of relaxation, of emotional and energetic alignment and of a new way of reading, where every sentence becomes a movie and makes complete sense. They have upgraded the software by opening the neural pathways to different areas of their brain – and now it's time to travel on these pathways every day, at least for three months, ideally for six months.

The five day program has given dyslexic adults the 'know-how', has given mothers a way to support their child and a tutor to help her or his students to achieve their literacy goals.

Unfortunately this is not always easy to do, to remember or to know where to start and how to follow through. Often life gets in the way, unexpected circumstances stop the progress, and sometimes these parents are simply overwhelmed with the task of completing over 200 words – not knowing where to start, how to continue or how to make it meaningful. Yet, the quality of the process of their post-program support either continues to deepen the awareness and knowledge or stops it in its tracks. I cannot emphasise enough the huge role a mother or teacher plays at this point. Miracles are achieved or the opportunity for it is lost forever.

For this reason, the One Year School has created an online platform to facilitate the post-program homework to accompany the students with or without the support of another.

Having been a mother of a dyslexic child who has done a program with another facilitator, I know exactly how it feels and how difficult it is. At the time I wish I had been given a road map – a clear guide as to what I can do and how I can break this seemingly endless list into small bite-size pieces that I can manage to follow through every day.

Out of my own need and the desire to help other mothers and support people on this creative journey, I have compiled this workbook.

# What is Dyslexia?

*(From 'the Right Brain for the Right Time')*

According to Ron Davis, all dyslexics have three traits in common:

a) They think in pictures
b) They become disoriented
c) They have a low threshold for frustration

Thinking in pictures gives them a great awareness of their environment, an inherent curiosity, intuition and insight. They may also show a multidimensional approach to learning, a vivid imagination, creativity, giftedness shown in geniuses like Albert Einstein, Walt Disney, Leonardo da Vinci, Henry Ford and an endless list of great thinkers, politicians, writers, sportsmen and sportswomen, actors and country or industry leaders such as Richard Branson, Winston Churchill or General George Patton.

Dyslexia is a perceptual talent. Perceiving the written or spoken word in pictures affords much more information. However, the downside of multiple images from multiple angles is the difficulty of reigning that mind in and focusing it onto one thing or one page. Some words fail to conjure up the meaning, or picture, needed to comprehend what has been read. Most commonly we see reading, spelling, writing, comprehension or math troubles. The same talent has become a liability, especially in schools, where we still educate our young in a mostly auditory manner, not suitable to visual learners.

When picture thinkers cannot make a picture, a part of their brain experiences confusion. Nobody likes that feeling. The mind tries to find an answer, by moving around an object—or the written word—to make sense of it. When looking at an object, viewing it from different sides has often proven useful in the past. However, try to move around a word and all that happens is a different appearance of letters, like b/d/p/q or words (saw/was …).

The feeling of confusion results in a state of disorientation, caused by a mind searching for meaning. We call disorientation the state of mind, where mental perception does not reflect the reality of the environment. Every one of us experiences disorientation at one time or another, when one of our senses is not in alignment with our body. Let me give you an example:

The other day I drove through a car wash, closed all the windows, and watched from inside my car as the giant bristles moved backwards and forward, washing the sides and roof of my vehicle. Have you ever experienced that sense that your car was in motion just because the outside brushes were? That was my experience and although I knew very well, that my car didn't move an inch, the feeling of disorientation gave the impression of movement. Having the sense of movement or balance out of alignment causes the mind to disorient and record false data.

Daydreaming is a visual, sensory disorientation. The body is present in the classroom or wherever anxiety, panic, confusion or boredom causes the mind to disconnect from it. If a person was forced to read in a state of disorientation, the print on the paper would appear to be blurred or changed in size, shape or appearance. The spaces between words might look like rivers running along the page; the reader might skip lines or words, swap the order of words around, omit or guess words. Additionally, if asked to stand on one leg, they would sway—and that would give away the direction where the mind's eye has moved to.

When I explained to one of my clients that him standing on one leg shows me where his mind is, he told me that he can prove me wrong. Being an excellent sportsman and additionally practising yoga had given him a wonderful sense of balance and he could easily and calmly stay on one leg for a long time. I marvelled at his centeredness and asked if he was able to read a simple text to me while on one leg.

Thinking that this would be an easy task, he was amazed how quickly he lost his balance by reading the sentence from a children's book in front of him. It gave him a real-life example of the material that would cause his mind to disorient.

To be in a state of orientation as opposed to the disorientation would mean that the mind has found the right position to perceive reality. It can be likened to somebody wanting to drive a car, where the right position for it would be to sit in the driver's seat. Disorientation then might be a feeling similar to sitting in the backseat of a car, trying unsuccessfully to manoeuvre a car.

The proper point of observation, which Davis has come to call an Orientation Point, is a position for the Mind's eye above and behind the person's head. The Mind's eye is our visual point of perception. We see images either from memory or imagined.

In these times of visualisation exercises, when we are asked to imagine a future image of self or a desired outcome, we are actually employing our Mind's eye to bring the images forth. When we read and the images are not naturally revealed, confusion can become overwhelming for picture thinkers, leading to frustration.

Confusion and limited comprehension piling up not surprisingly lead to a low threshold for frustration. The level of frustration varies in degree, depending on the "solutions" these children find to cope.

Non-picture words are pronouns, prepositions, some verbs and adverbs, words like "by, for, from, the, so, whether, while …"—you get the picture—or not.

What if I asked you to think of a submarine? Would that picture come up easily? What if I asked you, to picture a submarine, but not a yellow one, please! My guess is, that you can only picture a yellow one … **not** is not a picture. I may have an "x" through the yellow submarine, or a crossed-out picture, but in most cases, the colour of the object will be yellow.

# How do I support my child or student after a correction program?

To continue after a program, with or without support, especially for the next three to six months, is of paramount importance. We have all heard that it takes new neural pathways about three weeks to establish a solid link and become part of self. The amount of time here depends on the individual student and how often they remember using their new tools.

What a support person can do to make this experience fun, creative and enjoyable is the premise of this book. Just ticking off words for the sake of finishing the job as quickly as possible may not do the child any service and most likely make it yet another chore that adds to an already stretched schedule.

The program is only a suggestion and leaves room for you to alter it to your own time frame and circumstances:

- Sit down with your child or student and make an agreement when and how long he or she will be able to work and how that works with your daily schedule. Ask them how quickly they would like to be able to read fluently, make school easier and how much time they can assign and agree to. This includes discussions about what time of day would be most productive and if there is any activity that can be temporarily paused in favour of this literacy project.

- Allocate one area in the house, in the child's room or on a special desk in a study where the materials can remain and be handy to be used at any minute. This 'clay table' can become the hub of creative energy in the house, but should not be a playroom for siblings – as the clay letters and models should only be touched and owned by the client.

- Make it a clean, orderly place that invites to work and play with words, concepts and ideas as well as the words below.

- Have all materials ready to support the work:

  - This book
  - The One Year School Online program (videos)
  - The clay/plasticine alphabet in lower case, usually done already by the child
  - Plasticine for creating models (shouldn't be one that dries out)
  - A plastic cutting tool or a blunt knife
  - A place mat to cut on
  - Tooth picks or a something similar to scratch into the clay
  - A dictionary for spelling words or more definitions of the words below

- Each day has one or two words to model, but it may be too much for some students – or not enough on some days, during school holidays or when the child is particularly motivated.

- Always start with a koosh ball exercise as we have started and explained during the training: The child throws and catches these rubbery stringy balls while standing on one leg, throwing them underhanded, catching them above the head, like an eagle would grab a mouse. Starting off with centred throws, they should then be thrown slightly to the right or left of the other person. This way there is full focus (standing on one leg without shaking makes sure there is good focus), the neural pathways get reinforced (having to catch by crossing the midline with either hand), hand-eye coordination is strengthened, and the child is in a much better mental state to commence the work.

Go through the procedure of mastering each word at the beginning of the passage:

Read the word, the definition and the example sentence. What does the word look like, sound like and most importantly, what is the meaning.

- If you have got access to 'the One Year School', all examples are there as a video version, including grammar tips and video explanations. It really helps to master these words.

- Discuss the meaning and give examples yourself, ask for some by the child until you are certain that the meaning is quite clear.

- Ask the child which example that they have given would be a good choice to show the meaning of that word. A clay model should be memorable, crazy, funny and creative, without being too intricate. Make sure that they model **the definition**, as much as possible – not the example sentence. If a child loves making models, there is a danger that it will take too long and the real message or meaning can get lost in the process. On the other hand, just pushing the same clump of clay around in every model or variation doesn't give the mind the incentive to remember it.

- Arrows, speech bubbles, thinking- or feeling bubbles make it easier to point to a meaning in the model. Arrows can show direction, time or place the attention to the appropriate part in the model. Within the bubbles, place a model, not a word or symbol. No part of the model should be an object from the environment – it's best if everything is in the same light-coloured clay/plasticine.

- It may be good to create a model yourself, maybe a different aspect of the meaning. Creating your own model is a good way to stop yourself from improving their model. No part of their model is yours to touch or manipulate. The ownership has to stay with the child or dyslexic individual.

- Write the word of the model in clay letters underneath the model. The alphabet has to be fully mastered by the child prior. Any letter that may still be a trigger can confuse or cause problems when reading or spelling.

- Ask the child to address the model: "You are 'a', meaning 'one, or one kind of'", then point to the word: "you say 'a'". When the word is more than one letter, say it forwards, backwards, then forwards again.

- The student should then make a mental image of the word while fully oriented and focused. That mental image is very important and should be able to be seen on the mental screen. The words should be able to just show up on that screen of the mind too. When the word can be spelled with ease, forwards – backwards – forwards from that mental screen, the word is fully internalised, mastered and has become part of the visual word bank.

- You may find it useful to have the student write the example sentence underneath each word that helped them to create the model with the meaning. Eventually the increased reading mastery will influence the spelling and writing competency as well and writing down a sentence for each of the words that was completed facilitates this process.

- Have breaks between the models, to give the student time to process the information – instead of quickly rushing through them.

- Words that may still cause confusion later on can always be re-modelled, often with a different meaning (as most words do have more than one meaning) or with the meaning of the word in the reading passage.

The entire process would have been explained to you during the support training session.

- The full version of this Manual, called 'Nurturing the Secret Garden' includes a simpler version of the lovely old story by Frances Hodgson-Burnett, *the Secret Garden*. It should be read out aloud so the parent can help with spelling the words that are not known and check if there is full comprehension of all the material read. Asking the right questions regarding the story is important. Instead of asking, 'What did you read?' It might be more useful to ask more detailed questions about who, where, what, when, how many, which street, what name, how do you think he/she felt?

- Depending on their current reading level, you might just get them to read one word at the time, spell it if they don't know it – and only as the fluency builds, they should be asked to read to a full stop and use the sentence like a slide of a movie, to fully understand it. When reading word by word, it's advisable to go back to the beginning and read the entire sentence again with more fluency for comprehension.

- Spelling words: Use the student's clay to spell difficult words that are not part of this manual. Often it is easier to see a few letters in a group and remember the visual of it, than a long word without a space. Remember that we don't sound out the word. Get your student to say them as you would say the alphabet letters, so there is no guessing, only certainty and mastery. Then they will create an image in their mind of that word, as they see it in lower case alphabet letters. These spelling words do have pictures, so there is no need to add a model. If they don't know the meaning, tell them or get them to look it up in a dictionary.

- Most of all, have fun with it and use this time to create a special bond with your child. Never force a child to work on these words. Instead, make it as much fun, creative and interactive as possible.

# TERM I

## WEEK 1

**Day 1** – Assessment

**Day 2** – Superpower Guide to Dyslexia

**Day 3** – Taking stock: write into your journal, what is currently happening in the student's emotional, physical, mental and academic life. It will be a valuable tool to compare when starting Term 2. Seeing success and changes is very empowering.

We often forget where we started and struggled.

**Day 4** – What is needed:

This book will help

Plasticine, Plastic Cutter, Cutting Board

Koosh balls (2)

Sign up to 'www.theoneyearschool.com'

Journal

Good headphones

You may need to contact a tutor to support you.

**Day 5** - Preparing for week 2

What is different in the program to traditional programs?

How and why do we focus. How to work with the online course.

# WEEK 2

**Day 1** – Explanation of the three tools to focus

- Being relaxed, being centred, being focused – and how the visualisation audios will help in the process

**Day 2** – Video of the 3 Visualisation tools (8 min)

Video on how to develop laser sharp focus (15 min )

**Day 3** – the Alphabet: MODULE on how to create the alphabet, how to make sure there are no triggers that block us from fully understanding and using each letter. Mastering the alphabet forwards and backward

**Day 4** – Cartoon Video on creating the alphabet and mastering it

Explanation on why we learn the alphabet forwards and backwards

**Day 5** – Spelling: using our new self-created alphabet to spell words without sounding them out.

Spelling to remember and starting a spelling journal

# WEEK 3

**Day 1** – Introduction to Koosh balls. Why we play with the Koosh balls, standing on one leg, how we do it and what the aim of it is. Koosh balls help us to reinforce focus and where to keep our mind's eye.

Getting better at throwing and catching these rubbery balls (while on one leg) is brain gym at work.

**Day 2** – Daily visualisation followed by the first grammar lesson:

What are NOUNS? Everything we can see, hear, feel, taste, smell (perceive with our senses) are nouns. Nouns are the most common words.

We choose difficult nouns to learn to spell them. We learn how to spell so we remember the nouns.

**Day 3** – Grammar: PRONOUNS (I, you, he, she, it…)

Using plasticine to create self and others

**Day 4** – Creating models of people and objects

How making models of animals, food, things and people can be fun – and why we do it.

These models will be used throughout the six months' literacy course.

**Day 5** – Cartoon on making people and how to make sure they are standing up like 3D models

# WEEK 4

**Day 1** – Starting the 'sight words' with meaning

Explaining these words and an audio about the meaning of 'a' and 'an'

**Day 2** – A,  AN

**a:**   one; one kind of [I want to buy a book for you.].

...................................................................................................................................

**an:**  one; one kind of [Have you ever seen an elephant?]. Use **"a"** before a word that begins with a consonant sound. Use **"an"** before a word that begins with a vowel sound.

...................................................................................................................................

## Day 3 – THE

**the:** 1 referring to a particular person or thing [I want the cake with the cherry on top.]
   2 that one which is here or which has been mentioned [The day is hot.  The story ended.]

...................................................................................................................................

## Day 4 – OF, OFF

**of:** 1 belonging to; connected to [Three pages of my book are missing.]
   2 about; concerning [Think of me when I'm away.]

...................................................................................................................................

**off:** 1 away; to or at some other place [The button fell off.]
   2 so that it is no longer working or on [Turn the light off.]

...................................................................................................................................

## Day 5 – TO, TOO

**to:** 1 in the direction of [Turn to the right.]
   2 shows the *infinitive form of a verb* [Mary will learn to listen.]

...................................................................................................................................

**too:** 1 in addition; also [He came too.]   2 more than enough [This hat is too big.]

...................................................................................................................................

# WEEK 5

**Day 1** – MODULE 3, explaining PRONOUNS

**Day 2** – I, YOU

**I**:  the person who is speaking [I like sushi. I'm telling you a story.]

..............................................................................................................

**you**:   1 the person or persons that are being spoken to. [You are a good friend.  I saw you both. He borrowed the eggs from you.]

..............................................................................................................

**Day 3** – HE, SHE, IT

**he**:  the man, boy, or male animal that is being talked about [Jim thought he was right.]

..............................................................................................................

**she**:  the woman, girl, or female animal that is being talked about [Annette thought she heard a noise.]

..............................................................................................................

**it**:  the thing or animal that is being talked about [I saw the letter and opened it.]

..............................................................................................................

**Day 4** – WE

**we**: the persons speaking or writing [We like candy.  Are we still friends?]

..............................................................................................................

**Day 5** - THEY

**they**: the people or things being talked about [They loved the present you sent.]

..............................................................................................................

# WEEK 6

## Day 1 – Module 4: Prepositions; IN, INTO

**in**:  1 contained by [There are five fish in the bowl.]  2 living or located at [They are in Chicago.].

.........................................................................................................................

**into**:  1 to the inside of [Let's go into the house.]

2 to the form or condition of [I translated it into English.]

.........................................................................................................................

## Day 2 – FOR, FROM

**for**:  1 meant to be received by or used in [I have got a present for you.].  2 to the distance of; as far as [Every day we walk for two miles.]  3 as long as; through the time of [The movie runs for an hour.]

.........................................................................................................................

**from**:  1 beginning at [They ran from Sydney to Newcastle].  2 made, sent, or said by [I got a letter from my friend in Spain.]  3 out of the whole of [Subtract 2 from 4.]

.........................................................................................................................

## Day 3 – ON, ONTO

**on**:  1 held up by or attached to [a picture on the wall]
   •   Supported by a surface [Put the vase on the table.]
   •   having as its location [a house on Main Street]
   •   in action; working or acting [The radio is on.]

.........................................................................................................................

**onto**:  to a position on [The cat climbed onto the roof.]

.........................................................................................................................

## Day 4 – AT, AS

**at**:  1 on, in, near, or by [Are they at home?]  2 to or toward [Look at her. Aim at the target.]  3 attending [Paul was at the party.]
.........................................................................................................................

**as**: 1 to the same amount or degree; equally [Are you as tall as your brother?]
2 because; since [As I am tired, I'll stay home.] 3  in the role or manner of [He poses as a friend. The table can serve as a desk.]

.........................................................................................................................

## Day 5 – WITH

**with**: 1 in the company of [Come with me.] 2 as part of; into [Mix blue with yellow to get green]

.........................................................................................................................

# WEEK 7

## Day 1 – DO, DOING, DOES

**do**: Do can be both a main verb and a helping verb.
  **do**: (main verb)  1 to carry out or perform [Please do the dishes.]   2 to work at; have as an occupation [What does he do for a living?]

.................................................................................................................

  **do**: (helping verb) 1 to ask a question [Do you want to eat now?]

.................................................................................................................

  **doing**: carrying out; performing [What are you doing here?]

.................................................................................................................

  **does**: he/she/it carries out; performs [She does all the work around here.]

.................................................................................................................

## Day 2 – DID, DONE

  **did**: carried out; performed [I did my homework.]

.................................................................................................................

  **done**: have carried out; have performed [We have done it already.]

.................................................................................................................

## Day 3 – DON'T

  **don't**:  do not [I don't know the answer.]

.................................................................................................................

## Day 4 – WILL, WON'T

**will**:  1 to decide or choose [Let her do as she wills.]
Will is also used with other verbs to show future time. [We will leave next week. Will you please save some dessert for me?]

.................................................................................................................

**won't**:  will not [She won't hire him.]

.................................................................................................................


## Day 5 – EXPLANATION OF TENSES

.................................................................................................................

# WEEK 8

**Day 1** – HAVE (as a helping verb)

**have:** (helping verb) 1 present perfect tense [They have gone to Italy.]

…………………………………………………………………………………………………..

**Day 2** – HAVE (as a main verb), HAVING

**have:**   to be the owner of; possess [We have a new car.]

…………………………………………………………………………………………………..

**having:** being the owner of; possessing; experiencing [Are you having a good time?]

…………………………………………………………………………………………………

**Day 3** – HAS, HAD

**has:** he/she/it is the owner of; possesses [My cat has sharp claws.]

…………………………………………………………………………………………………

**had:** was the owner of; possessed [He had a great smile.]

…………………………………………………………………………………………………

**Day 4** – HAVE TO

**have to:** need to; must [We have to go.]

…………………………………………………………………………………………………..

**Day 5** – MODULE 5: CONCEPT OF TIME, VERBS (changing in time)

…………………………………………………………………………………………………
…………………………………………………………………………………………………
…………………………………………………………………………………………………
…………………………………………………………………………………………………
…………………………………………………………………………………………………
…………………………………………………………………………………………………
…………………………………………………………………………………………………

# WEEK 9

## Day 1 – BE, BEING

**be**:  1 to live or exist [Lincoln will be a doctor. Let it be.]
   2   to stay or continue [I will be here until Monday.]

...............................................................................................................

.... **being**: Present Participle First, Second and Third Person: **being** – living, existing [I'm being polite.]

...............................................................................................................

## Day 2 – I AM;   You/we/they ARE;   He/she/it IS

**am**: First Person singular: **am** – I live [I'm not at home.]

...............................................................................................................

**are**: Second Person singular: **are** – you live [You are my best friend]

...............................................................................................................

   First, Second and Third Person plural: **are** – we/you/they live or exist [We are not welcome. You are all too late. They're my family]

...............................................................................................................

**is**: Third Person singular: **is** – he/she/it lives or exists [He is a great singer. Why is it not produced anymore?]

...............................................................................................................

## Day 3 – WAS, WERE

**was**: Past Tense First and Third Person singular: **was** – lived, existed [She was not feeling well.]

...............................................................................................................

**were**: Second Person singular/ First, Second and Third Person plural: **were** – you, we, they lived/existed [You were right to come along. They were not dressed properly.]

...............................................................................................................

## Day 4 – BEEN

**been**: Past Participle First, Second and Third Person: **been** – have lived/existed

...............................................................................................................

## Day 5 – WE'RE, YOU'RE' THEY'RE

**I'm**: I am [I'm sorry to disappoint you.]

..........................................................................................................................................

**you're**:   you are [You're not a friend of mine.]

..........................................................................................................................................

**he's**: he is [He's a really nice person.] 2 he has [He's got a lot of time.]

..........................................................................................................................................

**she's**:   she is [She's a beautiful girl.]
  2 she has [She's got a lot of time.]

..........................................................................................................................................

**it's:** it is [It's all right; I'm not hurt.]

..........................................................................................................................................

**we're**:   we are. [We're very happy here.]

..........................................................................................................................................

**you're**: you are (plural) [You're the best students.]

..........................................................................................................................................

**they're**:   they are. [They're not fit to play.]

..........................................................................................................................................

# WEEK 10

**Day 1** – MODULE 6: PUNCTUATION MARKS and Exercises

**Day 2** – EITHER, OR

**either**: 1 one or the other of two [You may use either door.]
      2 both one and the other; each [She had a tool in either hand.]

………………………………………………………………………………………………….

**or**: 1 the second of two choices or possibilities [Do you want milk or cocoa?]
   2 the last of a series of choices [Is the light green, yellow, or red?]

…………………………………………………………………………………………………..

**Day 3** – NEITHER, NOR, NOT

**neither**: 1 not one or the other of two; not either [Neither boy went to the park.] 2 not either - often used in phrases with nor [I'll buy neither roses nor tulips.]

…………………………………………………………………………………………………..

**nor**: and not; and not either [I know neither Ben nor Frank.]

………………………………………………………………………………………………….

**not**: in no way; to no degree [Do not talk.  They are not happy.]

…………………………………………………………………………………………………..

**Day 4** – THEY'RE, THERE, THEIR

**they're**: they are. [They're not fit to play.]
………………………………………………………………………………………………………

**there**: 1 at or in that place [Who lives there?]

…………………………………………………………………………………………………..

**their**: done by them or having to do with them [their work; their shoe.]

………………………………………………………………………………………………….

**Day 5** – THERE'S, THEIRS with Punctuation Test and Answers

**there's**: there is [There's a puppy in the room.]

………………………………………………………………………………………………….

**theirs**: belonging to them [The house is theirs.]

…………………………………………………………………………………………………..

# WEEK 11

**Day 1** – ME

**me**:  the form of 'I' as the object 1. After a verb [The dog bit me.]   2 after a preposition [He gave the form to me.]

..................................................................................................................

**Day 2** – HIM, HER

**him**:  The form of 'he' as an object:   1 after certain verbs [The dog bit him.] 2 after prepositions [I came over to talk to him.]

..................................................................................................................

**her**:  The form of 'she' as an object: 1 after verbs [The dog loves her.] 2 after prepositions [The man proposed to her.]

..................................................................................................................

**Day 3** – US, THEM

**us**:  the form of 'we' that is used:   1 after certain verbs [The dog bit us.  He saw us. Tell us the truth.]   2 after prepositions [Tell the story to us.  The song was written by us.] (Object of 'we')

..................................................................................................................

**them**:  the form of they that is used:   1 after certain verbs [The dog bit them. I saw them.]

2 after prepositions [Give it to them.] (Object of 'they')

..................................................................................................................

**Day 4** – THIS, THAT

**this**:   1 the one here [This is Juan.]   2 the thing that is present or nearer [This is prettier than that.]

..................................................................................................................

**that**:   1 the person or thing  being talked about [That man is called Josef.]
- the thing farther away or different in some way [I prefer that dress to this one.]
- *(conjunction)* introduces a result, wish, purpose, reason or clause [He hoped that he would win.]

..................................................................................................................

**Day 5** – THESE, THOSE

**these**: plural of this. [These pills put me to sleep.]

..................................................................................................................

**those**: plural of that. [You can wear those boots instead.]

..................................................................................................................

# WEEK 12

### Day 1 – MY, MINE

**my:** done by me or having to do with me [my work; my shoes]

.................................................................................................

**mine:** the one or the ones that belong to me [I know this book is mine.]

.................................................................................................

### Day 2 – YOUR, YOURS

**your:** done by you or having to do with you [I admire your work.]

.................................................................................................

**yours:** the one or the ones that belong to you [I know that this animal is yours. Yours costs more than ours.]

.................................................................................................

### Day 3 – HIS, ITS, HE'S

**his:** the one or the ones that belong to him [I know that this place is his.]

.................................................................................................
.

**its:** 1 the one or the ones that belong to it [The ribbon of the dress was its.]
2 done by it or having to do with it [Every plant has its particular needs.]

.................................................................................................

**he's:** he is [He's a really nice person.] 2 he has [He's got a lot of time.]

.................................................................................................

### Day 4 – HER, HERS

**her:** done by her or having to do with her [She enjoys her work.]

.................................................................................................

**hers:** the one or the ones that belong to her [I know that this book is hers.]

.................................................................................................

### Day 5 – OUR, OURS

**our:** done by us or having to do with us [our work; our cars]

.................................................................................................

**ours:** the one or the ones that belong to us [The corner block is ours.]

.................................................................................................

## Grammar notes

### Personal Pronouns

| Singular | Subject | Object | Possessive |
|---|---|---|---|
| 1st Person | I | me | my, mine |
| 2nd Person | you | you | your, yours |
| 3rd Person | he, she, it | him, her, it | his, hers, its |

| Plural | Subject | Object | Possessive |
|---|---|---|---|
| 1st Person | we | us | our, ours |
| 2nd Person | you | you | your, yours |
| 3rd Person | they | them | their, theirs |

### Grammar Notes:

Personal pronouns as the object of a sentence: Personal pronouns can either be the subject of a sentence (in action) or the object of a sentence (not in action).

Any part of a sentence that performs the action of a verb is called the subject:

The lovely lady gave me a cake. ("the lovely lady" is the subject)

Any part of a sentence that receives or reacts is called the object:

The lovely lady gave it to me. ('me' is the object)

The subject of the sentence (the lovely lady) can be replaced with a personal pronoun (she) and the object, which is a pronoun (me) can also be a proper noun (a child)

# T E R M  II

## WEEK 1

### Day 1 – ASSESSMENT

What has changed since Term 1 assessment

### Day 2 – JOURNALLING

What has changed emotionally, mentally, academically and continuing to journal throughout Term 2.

### Day 3 – PUBLIC SPEAKING and WRITING TIPS

How to structure a good and memorable speech, how to write it and how to speak with authority, clarity and authenticity.

### Day 4 – WRITING TO READ

Even before writing, it is sometimes a good start to dictate a piece of writing to somebody else, then reading it back, then writing it yourself.

### Day 5 – READING

Video of a reading experience

Module 7: Different steps of reading, depending on the student's abilities and readiness to read.

# WEEK 2

### Day 1 – BY, BUT

**by**:   1 near or beside [Come and sit by the fire.] 2 in or during [We travelled by night.] 3 through the means or work of [I like to travel by car. We've read books by Shakespeare.].

...................................................................................................................

**but**:  1 except; other than [Nobody came but me.]  2 yet; however [The story is long, but it is never dull.]

...................................................................................................................

### Day 2 – HERE, THERE

**here**:  at or in this place [Who lives here?]

...................................................................................................................

**there**:   1 at or in that place [Who lives there?]

...................................................................................................................

### Day 3 – ONE,  NO, NONE

**one**:   1 being a single thing or unit [one vote].   2 one or anything [What can one do about it?]

...................................................................................................................

**no**:  not so; the opposite of yes. [I have no money left.]

...................................................................................................................

**none**:   not one or not any [None of these books is new. None of the cake was eaten.]

...................................................................................................................

### Day 4 – NEVER, NOW

**never**:  at no time; not ever [I never saw her again.]

...................................................................................................................

**now**:  1 at this moment; at the present time [We are eating now.]

...................................................................................................................

### Day 5 - SOME, SAME

**some**:   1 a few; a little [Can you buy me some sweets?]
  2 being a certain group of persons or things that are not named or not known [Some people were playing ball.]

...................................................................................................................

**same**: 1 being the very one [She is the same girl who runs every day.] 2 alike in some way; similar [He has the same bike as Martin.]

...................................................................................................................

# WEEK 3

## Day 1 – WHAT, WHO

**what**:  1 which thing, happening, or condition? [What did he ask? What is your name?]

...........................................................................................................

**who**:  what or which person or persons? [Who helped you? I know who lives here.]

...........................................................................................................

## Day 2 – WHO'S, WHOSE

**who's**:  1 who is [Who's your boss?]  2 who has [Who's got the money?]

...........................................................................................................

**whose**:  the one or the ones that belong to whom [Whose are these cups?]

...........................................................................................................

## Day 3 – WHOM, HOW

**whom**: which person or people? [To whom are you writing?]

...........................................................................................................

**how**:   1 in what way [How do you start the motor?]   2 in what condition [How is your mother today?]

...........................................................................................................

## Day 4 – WHERE, WHEN

**where**:  in or at what place? [Where is the car?]

...........................................................................................................

**when**:  1 at what time? [When did they leave?] 2 at that time [When Mary left home]

...........................................................................................................

## Day 5 - WHICH, WHY

**which**:   1 what person or thing? [Which will you choose?]

...........................................................................................................

**why**:  for what reason, cause, or purpose? [Why did he go?]

...........................................................................................................

# WEEK 4

## Day 1 – OUT, ONLY

**out**:  away from or beyond a certain position, place, or situation [Open the window and look out. Spit it out.]

………………………………………………………………………………………………..

**only**: without any others of the same kind [I am an only child.].

………………………………………………………………………………………………..

## Day 2 – OTHER, OTHERS, OTHERWISE

**other**:   1 not this one or the one just mentioned, but a different one [Stand on one foot and lift the other one.]   2 additional; extra [I have no other shoes.]

………………………………………………………………………………………………..

**others**: (plural of other) different ones [We are staying with the others.]

………………………………………………………………………………………………..

**otherwise**:   1 in some other way; differently [He liked the movie, but I felt otherwise.]
   2 or else [I'm tired; otherwise I would join you.]

………………………………………………………………………………………………..

## Day 3 – ALL, ALSO

**all**: (adjective)  1 the whole of or the whole amount of [He gave her all the money.]   2 every one of [All the students passed the exam.]

………………………………………………………………………………………………

**also**: in addition; too [He could sing and also play the guitar.]

………………………………………………………………………………………………

## Day 4 – UP, DOWN, UPON

**up**:   1 to, in, or on a higher place or position [She climbed up. The sun comes up at dawn.]
   • to a larger amount or size; to a greater degree [Electricity went up in price. My ankle swelled up.]
   • to give up: to surrender; to cease to do or perform [She gave up her position.]

………………………………………………………………………………………………..

**down**:   1 from a higher to a lower place [If you can't jump down, climb down.]
   2 being in a low position or on the ground, floor, or bottom; not up [The sun is down.]

………………………………………………………………………………………………

**upon**:  on or up and on [He put the box upon the table.]

...................................................................................................


## Day 5 – US, USE

**us**:  the form of we that is used:   1 after certain verbs [The dog bit us.  He saw us. Tell us the truth.]   2 after prepositions [Tell the story to us.  The song was written by us.]

...................................................................................................

**use:** take or consume from a limited supply [Can I use your cup?]

...................................................................................................


-----------------------------------------------------------------------------------------------

# WEEK 5

## Day 1 – EACH, EVERY

**each**:  every one of two or more things or people, thought of separately [Each of my pets is special.]

...................................................................................................

**every**:  all or each one of the people or things that are part of a group; each with no exceptions [Every student must take the test.]

...................................................................................................


## Day 2 – EVER, EVEN

**ever**:   1 at any time [Have you ever seen a ghost?]
        2 at all times; always [They lived happily ever after.]

...................................................................................................

**even**:   1 though it may seem unlikely; indeed [Even a child could do it.]
        2 by comparison [She knows even less about music than I do.]
        3 flat, level, or smooth [an even surface].
        4 capable of being divided by two without remainder [2, 4, 6 and 8 are even numbers.]

...................................................................................................

## Day 3 - ABOUT, AGAIN, AGO

**about**:   1 having to do with [Here is a book about cooking. I want to talk about him.]
   2 more or less [She's about nine years old]

..................................................................................................................

**again**: (adverb)   1 once more; a second time [I enjoyed your book so much that I may read it again.]   2 back into a former place or condition; as before [He came to our hotel again.]

..................................................................................................................

**ago**: (adjective) gone by; before now [They were married ten years ago.]   (adverb) in the past [That happened long ago.]

..................................................................................................................
.


## Day 4 – ANY, ANYWAY, ANYHOW

**any**: 1 one, no matter which one, out of three or more;   [Take any fruit you like.]
2 some, no matter how many or what kind [Do you have any roses?]

..................................................................................................................

**anyway**:  no matter what happens; in any case [I'm to London anyway.]

..................................................................................................................

**anyhow**:  no matter what else is true; just the same; anyway [You may know this poem, but study it anyhow.]

..................................................................................................................


## Day 5 – ALMOST, ALWAYS, ALREADY

**almost**: (adverb) 1 very nearly but not completely [Sue is almost six years old.] 2 in addition; too; besides [She sang and also played the piano for us.]

..................................................................................................................

**always**:   1 at all times; at every time [He is always polite.]   2 all the time [Oxygen is always present in the air.]   3 forever [I will always love her.]

..................................................................................................................

**already**: (adverb) 1 by a specified time [The children were already asleep.]                    2
so soon [Are you leaving already?]

..................................................................................................................

34

# WEEK 6

## Day 1 - REALLY, RATHER

**really**: in fact; indeed [She was a really nice girl.]

..................................................................................................................................

**rather**: 1. indicates one's preference in a particular matter [I would rather drink water than wine.] 2. to a certain or significant degree [She was rather tired.]

..................................................................................................................................

## Day 2 - QUITE, VERY, POSSIBLE

**quite:** to the utmost or to a certain extent or degree; fairly; comparatively [Are you quite sure that you want to come?]

..................................................................................................................................

**very:**   1 in a high degree; to a great extent [very cold; very funny; very sad]

..................................................................................................................................

**possible:**  able to be done or achieved, but not certain [Is it possible to learn a new language in three weeks?]

..................................................................................................................................

## Day 3 -CAN, CAN'T, COULD

**can**:  1 know how to [I can speak Russian.]   2 is able to [The baby can walk.]

..................................................................................................................................

**can't**:   cannot [He can't understand you.]

..................................................................................................................................

**could**: - 1 he/she/it was able to or knew how to [She could read every word.]
        2. showing less force or sureness [You could be right.  I could do it tomorrow.]

..................................................................................................................................

**Day 4** - WOULD, LIKE

**would**:  1 past tense of will [They thought they would enjoy the circus, but they didn't like it.]
2 used to [My granny would take me to the movies.]
3 to talk about something that depends on something else [I would have helped if you had asked me.]   2 to ask something in a polite way [Would you please leave?]

………………………………………………………………………………………………………..

**like**:   1 similar to; somewhat the same as [He has hands like claws].  2 fond of or pleased with [I think that they like each other.]

   •   **likes**: (verb) to be fond of or pleased with; enjoy [She likes dogs.]
   •   **liked**: was fond of or pleased with; enjoyed [The girl liked her new room.]
   •   **liking**:  being fond of; enjoying [Are you liking the ice cream?]

………………………………………………………………………………………………………..

………………………………………………………………………………………………………

………………………………………………………………………………………………………

.

**Day 5** - SHALL, SHOULD

**shall**:  Shall is used with other verbs to show future time of 'I' and 'we' [I shall leave tomorrow. Shall we eat?]

………………………………………………………………………………………………………

**should**: 1 something expected [He should be on time for dinner.]
2 to talk about something that one ought to do [I should lose weight.]

………………………………………………………………………………………………………..
-------------------------------------------------------------------------------------------------------.

# WEEK 7

**Day 1** - THEN, THAN

**then**:   1 at that time [We were young then.]   2 after that; next [The party ended, and then we left.]

………………………………………………………………………………………………………..

**than**:   1 compared to.  This word is used before the second part of a comparison [I am taller than you.]  2 besides; except [What could I do other than stop?]

………………………………………………………………………………………………………..

**Day 2** - STILL, IF

**still**: 1 without moving [They stood still for a minute.]
  2 in a greater amount or degree [She became angrier still.]

...................................................................................................................

**if**:  in case that; supposing that: 1 likely [If I like it, I will buy it.]
    2. not likely [If I was rich, I would buy the painting.]
    3. in case I had; not possible [If I had won the lottery, I would have moved to Italy.]

...................................................................................................................


**Day 3** - OVER, SO

**over**:  1 in, at, or to a place above; higher than [Hang the picture over the fireplace.]
    2 so as to cover [Put a blanket over my legs.]  3 in preference to [Hand the child over to her.]

...................................................................................................................

**so**:  1 to the degree or amount that has been expressed [Why are you so late?]
  2 as a result; therefore [He couldn't swim and so was drowned]

...................................................................................................................


**Day 4** - SOON, SEEM

**soon**:  1 in a short time from now [Spring will soon be here.]
  2 fast or quickly [as soon as possible]

...................................................................................................................

**seem**: appear to or giving the impression of being something or having a particular quality [The
children seem to enjoy themselves.]

...................................................................................................................

**Day 5** - SUCH, SURE

**such**:  1 of the same kind or similar [Such rugs are expensive.]
  2 so much or so great [We had such fun that nobody left.]

...................................................................................................................

**sure**:  1 convinced; feeling no doubt [I am sure it will be fun.]
    •    not capable of failing; safe or certain [a sure cure; a sure friend]

...................................................................................................................


------------------------------------------------------------------------------------------------

# WEEK 8

## Day 1 - KNOW - KNEW - KNOWN

**know - knew - known:** to be aware of through observation, inquiry or information [I knew the boy from school.]

......................................................................................................................................

## THROW - THREW - THROWN

**throw:** to send with some force through the air [Don't throw things around.]
   **threw:** past tense of throw [He threw the shoes at her.]

......................................................................................................................................

## THROUGH

**through:** in one side and out the other side of; from end to end of [The nail went through the board. We drove through the tunnel.]

......................................................................................................................................


## Day 2 - THOUGH, ALTHOUGH

**though:** in spite of the fact that; although [Though it rained, we walked.]

......................................................................................................................................

**although:** (conjunction) 1 in spite of the fact that; though [Although it's raining we will go to our picnic] 2 however; and yet [They will probably lose, although nobody seems to think so]

......................................................................................................................................


## Day 3 - THINK - THOUGHT - THOUGHT

**think:** to reason about; reflect on; ponder [What are you thinking about?]

......................................................................................................................................

**thought:** reasoned; pondered [Mary thought this to be unusual.]

......................................................................................................................................

## OUGHT

**ought:** to be forced by what is right, wise or necessary; to be expected to [He ought to do his homework]

......................................................................................................................................

## BUY - BOUGHT - BOUGHT

**buy - bought - bought:** to purchase or obtain in exchange for payment [I bought him a book.]

..............................................................................................................

## Day 4 - CATCH - CAUGHT - CAUGHT

**catch - caught - caught:** capture; intercept and hold [Show me how to catch butterflies!]

..............................................................................................................

## WRITE - WROTE - WRITTEN

**write - wrote - written:** mark words, letters or symbols on a surface [He wrote her a poem.]

..............................................................................................................

..............................................................................................................

## Day 5 - MAKE - MADE - MADE

**make:**   1 to bring into being; build, create, produce, or put together [Let's make a fire.]
- **makes:** he/she/it builds, creates, produces [She makes breakfast for him.]
- **making:** building, creating, producing [We are making plans for Sunday.]
- **made:** built, created, produced [He made plans to go to New Mexico.]

..............................................................................................................

-------------------------------------------------------------------------------------------------

# WEEK 9

## Day 1 - COME - CAME - COME

.**come:**    to move from "there" to "here" [The dogs come to me quickly when I call them.]
 1. **comes:** he/she/it moves, arrives  [She comes home late.]
 2. **coming:** moving from "there" to "here"; arriving [Don't worry, I'm coming]
 3. **came:**  moved from "there" to "here"; arrived [He came too late.]

..............................................................................................................

## BECOME - BECAME - BECOME

**become:**  to come to be [I become ill at the sight of it.]
- **became:** came to be; happened  [What became of that movie star?]
- **becoming:** coming to be [She's becoming quite well known]
- **becomes:** he/she/it comes to be [My sister becomes a lawyer.]

..............................................................................................................

**Day 2** - SEE - SAW - SEEN

**see**:  to be aware of through the eyes; have or use the sense of sight [I don't see very well.]
  **sees**: he/she/it has the sense of sight [My friend sees him all the time.]
  **seeing**: being aware of through the eyes [I am seeing a bird outside.]
  **seen**: have been aware through the eyes [They have seen the horrors of war.]
  **saw**: was aware through the eyes; looked [We saw the movie twice.]

...........................................................................................................

## SAY - SAID - SAID

**say - said - said:** use words to convey information, an opinion or feeling; to voice or speak  [He said that he won't be coming.]

...........................................................................................................

**Day 3** - LET,  LETS, LET'S, LETTING

**let**:  to give permission to; allow [They let me help.]
  **lets**: he/she/it gives permission to [He often lets me work here.]
  **let's**:  let us [Let's go now!]
  **letting**: giving permission to; allowing [We are letting the dogs play outside.]

...........................................................................................................

## LEAVE - LEFT - LEFT

**leave**:   1 to go away from [I always leave the house at 8 a.m.]   2 to let stay or be [Leave the door open.]

- **leaves**: he/she/it goes away from [She leaves the place in a good condition.]
- **leaving**: going away from [Why are you leaving us?]
- **left**: went away from [All children have left the house.]

...........................................................................................................

**Day 4** - GO - WENT- GONE

**go**:  1 to move along or pass from one place, point, or person to another [I must go to the hospital today.]
2. **goes**: he/she/it moves along; belongs [The broom goes in the cupboard.]
3. **went**: moved along; passed from one place to another [He went to New York last night.]
4. **gone**: have moved along; have/has ceased [Is your pain gone?]

...........................................................................................................

**Day 4**

GET - GOT - GOT

**get:** 1 to become the owner of by receiving, buying, or earning; to gain or obtain [We get a new car.] 2 to go and bring [Get your books.]
2. **gets:** he/she/it receives, buys, gets [She gets an allowance.]
3. **got:** received; arrived at; reached [They got home early.]
4. **gotten/got:** have received; have bought; have gained [I've got one hundred dollar.]
5. **getting:** receiving, buying, earning [We are getting a puppy.]

...............................................................................................................................

...............................................................................................................................


**Day 5** - TAKE - TOOK - TAKEN

**take:** 1 to get hold of; grasp [Take my hand as we cross the street.]
  **takes:** gets hold of; grasps [He takes lunch to school.]
  **taking:** getting hold of; grasping; needing [He's taking his time.]
  **took:** got hold of; captured [The soldiers took the town.]

...............................................................................................................................

...............................................................................................................................

-------------------------------------------------------------------------------------------------------------------


# WEEK 10

**Day 1** - AMONG, AROUND

**among:** in the middle of; in the company of [He was among them.]

...............................................................................................................................

**around:** located or situated on every side; to face the opposite direction [They walked around the building twice.]

...............................................................................................................................

## Day 2 - MAY, MIGHT, MAYBE

**may:** 1 can or is likely to [I may stay home. It may rain.] 2 is allowed or has permission to [You may go now.]

……………………………………………………………………………………………………………………..

**might:** (past tense of 'may') expresses a possibility [She might be going overseas.]

……………………………………………………………………………………………………………………..

**maybe:** it may be; perhaps. [Maybe they come over later.]

……………………………………………………………………………………………………………………..


## Day 3 - YET, JUST

**yet:** 1 up to now; so far [He has not gone yet.]

………………………………………………………………………………………………………………………

**just:** 1 right or fair [a just decision]. 2 neither more nor less than; exactly [It's just two o'clock now.] 3 no more than; only [I'm just teasing you.]

………………………………………………………………………………………………………………………


## Day 4 - WHILE, WHETHER

**while:** 1 a period of time [I waited a short while.]
  2 during the time that [I read a book while I waited.]

………………………………………………………………………………………………………………………..
**whether:** 1 if it is true or likely that [I don't know whether I can go.]
2 in either case that [It makes no difference whether he comes or not.]

……………………………………………………………………………………………………………………..


## Day 5 - ANOTHER

**another:** 1 one more [Have another piece of cake.] 2 a different one; not the same [Exchange the movie for another one.]

……………………………………………………………………………………………………………………..

# WEEK 11

## Day 1 - LAST, ELSE

**last:** 1 being or coming after all others [the last month of the year; the last word in an argument]. 2 after all others [Our team came in last.] 3 to go on; continue [The play lasts for only an hour.]

..................................................................................................

**else:** 1 not the same; different or other [I thought you were someone else.]
2 in addition; more [Do you want anything else?]

..................................................................................................

## Day 2 - FULL, BOTH

**full:** holding or containing as much as possible; filled [a full jar]

..................................................................................................

**both:** refers to two people or things, regarded and identified together [Both children were treated equally.]

..................................................................................................

## Day 3 - AWAY, BACK

**away:** 1 from one place to another [The boy ran away from home.]
2 not here; absent [She is away for the day]

..................................................................................................

**back:** 1 at the rear or back [the back wheel of my car].

2 to the place that it came from [Throw the ball back.]

..................................................................................................

## Day 4 - BETWEEN, BECAUSE

**between:** 1 in the space that separates [a lake between the U.S. and Canada].
2 in the time that separates [The doctor has office hours between one and five o'clock.]

..................................................................................................

**because:** for the reason that; since [I'm late because I slept in.]

..................................................................................................

## Day 5 - WITHIN, WITHOUT

**within:** in the inner part of; inside [Stay within the house.]

..................................................................................................

**without:** free from; not having [He only eats food without preservatives.]

..................................................................................................

# WEEK 12

## Day 1 - MANY, MUCH

**many**:  a large number of; not few [many boxes; many times]

..................................................................................................................

**much**:  1 great in amount or degree [Children give me much joy.]  2 to a great degree or extent [I feel much happier.]

..................................................................................................................

## Day 2 - MORE, MOST

**more**:  greater in amount or degree or in number [He has more free time than I do. We need more helpers.]

..................................................................................................................

**most**:  1 superlative of much or many.  2 greatest in amount or degree or in number [Who won the most money? Most people like summer.]

..................................................................................................................

## Day 3 - FEW, LITTLE

**few**:  not many [There are few good men left.]

..................................................................................................................

**little**: small in size, amount or degree [Melany's little sister didn't come along.]

..................................................................................................................

## Day 4 - LESS, LEAST

**less**:  1 a comparative of little.  2 not so much; smaller in size or amount [drink less soda; take less time]

..................................................................................................................

**least**:  1 a superlative of little.  2 smallest in size, amount, or importance [He didn't show the least interest in going.]

..................................................................................................................

## Day 5 - BEFORE, AFTER

**before**: 1 ahead of [The valley stretched before us.]
         2 happening earlier than; previous to [Will you finish before noon?]

..................................................................................................................

**after**: (adverb) 1 behind in place or time; coming next [Please turn left after the petrol station.]   2 behind in time [Shall we meet after school?]

..................................................................................................................

# THE SECRET GARDEN

## CHAPTER ONE

## THERE IS NO ONE LEFT

When Mary Lennox was sent to Misselthwaite to live with her uncle everybody said she was the most disagreeable-looking child ever seen. It was true, too.

She had a little thin face and a little thin body, thin light hair and a sour expression.

Her hair was yellow, and her face was yellow because she had been born in India and had always been ill in one way or another.

Her father had held a position under the English Government and had always been busy and ill himself, and her mother had been a great beauty who cared only to go to parties and amuse herself.

She had not wanted a little girl at all, and when Mary was born she handed her over to the care of an Ayah, who was made to understand that if she wished to please the Mem Sahib she must keep the child out of sight as much as possible.

So when she was a sickly, fretful, ugly little baby she was kept out of the way, and when she became a sickly, fretful, toddling thing she was kept out of the way also.

She never remembered seeing anything familiar but the dark faces of her Ayah and the other native servants, and as they always obeyed her and gave her her own way in everything, because the Mrs. would be angry if she was disturbed by her crying, by the time she was six years old she was as tyrannical and selfish as a little pig.

The young English governess who came to teach her to read and write disliked her so much that she gave up her place in three months, and when other governesses came to try to fill it they always went away in a shorter time than the first one. So if Mary had not chosen to really want to know how to read books she would never have learned her letters at all.

One frightfully hot morning, when she was about nine years old, she awakened feeling very cross, and she became crosser still when she saw that the servant who stood by her bedside was not her Ayah.

"Why did you come?" she said to the strange woman. "I will not let you stay. Send my Ayah to me."

The woman looked frightened, but she only stammered that the Ayah could not come and when Mary threw herself into a passion and beat and kicked her, she looked only more frightened and repeated that it was not possible for the Ayah to come to Missie Sahib.

Mary thought this to be unusual.

There was something mysterious in the air that morning. Nothing was done in its regular order and several of the native servants seemed missing, while those whom Mary saw slunk or hurried about with ashy and scared faces. But no one would tell her anything and her Ayah did not come.

---

*Spelling*
pre.tend
Mem Sahid / Missie Sahib: Mrs Boss / Miss Boss
wandering: walking
wondering: being curious
aw.ful – aw.fully

---

She was wandering alone as the morning went on, and at last she wandered out into the garden and began to play by herself under a tree near the veranda. She pretended that she was making a flower-bed, and she stuck big scarlet hibiscus blossoms into little heaps of earth, all the time growing more and more angry and muttering to herself the things she would *say* and the names she would call Saidie when she returned.

"Pig! Pig! Daughter of Pigs!" she *said*, because to call a native a pig is the worst insult of all.

She was grinding her teeth and *saying* this over and over again when she heard her mother come out on the veranda with someone. She was with a fair young man and they stood talking together in low strange voices. Mary knew the fair young man who looked like a boy. She had heard that he was a very young officer who had just come from England.

The child stared at each of them, but mostly at her mother. She always did this when she had a chance to see her, because the Mem Sahib—Mary used to call her that more often than anything else—was such a tall, slim, pretty person and wore such lovely clothes.

Her hair was like curly silk and she had a delicate little nose which seemed to be disdaining things, and she had large laughing eyes. All her clothes were thin and floating, and Mary said they were "full of lace."

They looked fuller of lace than ever this morning, but her eyes were not laughing at all. They were large and scared and lifted imploringly to the fair boy officer's face

"Is it so very bad? Oh, is it? Who's left?"
Mary heard her say.

"Awfully," the young man answered in a trembling voice. "Awfully, Mrs. Lennox. Whose advice did you follow? You ought to have gone to the hills two weeks ago. Either that or back to England."

The Mem Sahib wrung her hands.

"Oh, I know I ought!" she cried. "I did neither - only stayed to go to that silly dinner party. What a fool I was!"

<table>
<tr><td>

*Spelling*
wail.ing: crying when mourning
app.all.ing: horrible
be.wild.er.ment

</td></tr>
</table>

At that very moment such a loud sound of wailing broke out from the servants' quarters that she clutched the young man's arm, and Mary stood shivering from head to foot. For what seemed like a long time the wailing grew wilder and wilder.

"What is it? Where did that sound come from?" Mrs. Lennox gasped.

"Someone has died," answered the boy officer. "You did not say it had broken out among your servants."

"I couldn't know!" the Mem Sahib cried. "Come with me! Come with me!" and she turned and ran into the house.

After that appalling things happened, and the mysteriousness of the morning was explained to Mary. The cholera had broken out in its most fatal form and people were dying like flies. The Ayah had been taken ill in the night, and it was because she had just died that the servants had wailed in the huts. Before the next day three other servants were dead and others had taken off in terror. There was panic on every side, and dying people in all the bungalows.

Yet during the confusion and bewilderment of the second day Mary hid herself within the nursery and was forgotten by everyone. Nobody thought of her, nobody wanted her, and strange things happened of which she knew nothing. Mary alternately cried and slept through the hours. She only knew that people were ill and that she heard mysterious and frightening sounds.

Once she crept down into the dining-room and found it empty, although a partly finished meal was on the table and chairs and plates looked as if they had been hastily pushed back when the diners rose suddenly for some reason.

The child ate some fruit and biscuits, and being thirsty she drank a glass of wine which stood nearly filled. It was sweet, and she did not know how strong it was. Very soon it made her intensely drowsy, and she went back to her nursery and shut herself in again, frightened by cries she heard in the huts and by the hurrying sound of feet. The wine made her so sleepy that she could scarcely keep her eyes open and she lay down onto her bed and dozed off for a long time.

Many things happened during the hours in which she slept so heavily, but she was neither disturbed by the wails nor the sound of things being carried in and out of the bungalow.

---

*Spelling*
a.waken.ed
frigh.ten - frightened
dis.grace.ful.ly neg.lect.ed

---

When she awakened she lay and stared at the wall until the house was perfectly still. She had never known it to be so silent before. She heard neither voices nor footsteps, and wondered if everybody had got well of the cholera and all the trouble was over.

She wondered also who would take care of her now her Ayah was dead – and whether there would be a new Ayah, and perhaps she would hear some new stories again. Mary had been rather tired of the old ones.

She did not cry because her nurse had died. She was not an affectionate child and had never cared much for anyone.

Even though the noise and hurrying about and wailing over the cholera had frightened her, she had been angrier because no one seemed to remember that she was alive. Everyone was too panic-stricken to think of a little girl no one was fond of. When people had the cholera it seemed that they remembered nothing but themselves. But if everyone had got well again, surely someone would remember and come to look for her.

But no one came, and as she lay waiting the house seemed to grow more and more silent. Just then heard something rustling on the matting and when she looked down she saw a little snake gliding along and watching her with eyes like jewels. She was not frightened or ran away, because he was a harmless little thing who would not hurt her and he seemed in a hurry to get out of the room. He slipped under the door as she watched him.

"How queer and quiet it is," she said. "It sounds as if there was no one in the bungalow but me and the snake."

Almost the next minute she heard footsteps in the compound, and then on the veranda. They were men's footsteps, and the men entered the bungalow and talked in low voices. No one went to meet or speak to them and they seemed to open doors and look into rooms.

"What desolation!" she heard one voice say. "That pretty, pretty woman! I suppose the child, too. I heard there should be a child, though no one ever saw her."

Mary was standing in the middle of the nursery when they opened the door a few minutes later. She looked an ugly, cross little thing and was frowning because she was feeling between hungry and disgracefully neglected. The first man who came in was a large officer she had once seen talking to her father. He looked tired and troubled, but when he saw her he was so startled that he almost jumped back.

> *Spelling*
> bun.ga.low
> chol.era
> self-ab.sorb.ed
> wear — wore- worn
> carry - carried

"Barney!" he cried out. "There is a child here! A child alone! In a place like this! Mercy on us, who is she!"

"I am Mary Lennox," the little girl said, drawing herself up stiffly. She thought the man was very rude to call her father's bungalow "A place like this!" "I fell asleep when everyone had the cholera and I have only just woken up. Why does nobody come?"

"It is the child no one ever saw!" exclaimed the man, turning to his companions. "Unless she has actually been forgotten!"

"Why was I forgotten?" Mary said, stamping her foot. "Why does nobody come?"

The young man whose name was Barney looked at her very sadly. Mary even thought she saw him wink his eyes as if to wink tears away.

"Poor little kid!" he said. "There is nobody left to come."

It was in that strange and sudden way that Mary found out that she had neither father nor mother left; that they had died and been carried away in the night, and that the few native servants who had not died also had left the house as quickly as they could get out of it, none of them even remembering that there was a Missie Sahib.

That was why the place was so quiet. It was true that there was no one in the bungalow but herself and the little rustling snake.

Mary had liked to look at her mother from a distance and she had thought her very pretty, but otherwise she knew very little of her and could scarcely have been expected to love her or to miss her very much when she was gone. She did not miss her at all, in fact, and as she was a self-absorbed child she gave her entire thought to herself, as she had always done. If she had been older she would no doubt have been very anxious at being left alone in the world, but she was very young, and as she had always been taken care of, she supposed she always would be. What she thought was that she would like to know if she was going to nice people, who would be no less polite to her and give her her own way as her Ayah and the other native servants had done.

She knew that she was not going to stay here at the English clergyman's house where she was taken at first. She did not want to stay. The English clergyman was poor and he had five children nearly all the same age and they wore shabby clothes and were always quarrelling and snatching toys from each other.

> *Spelling*
> dis.agree.able
> furi.ous
> im.pud.ent (offensively bold)
> suggest.ion
> con.tra.ry
> de.so.late – deserted; lifeless [He lives in a desolate old house]
>
> stub.born (adjective) [a stubborn girl] – stubbornly

Mary hated their untidy bungalow and was so disagreeable to them that after the first day or two nobody would play with her. By the second day they had given her a nickname which made her furious.

It was Basil who thought of it first. Basil was a little boy with impudent blue eyes and a turned-up nose and Mary hated him. She was playing by herself under a tree, just as she had been playing the day the cholera broke out. She was making heaps of earth and paths for a garden and Basil came and stood near to watch her. Presently he got rather interested and suddenly made a suggestion.

"Why don't you put a heap of stones there and pretend it is a rockery?" he said. "There in the middle," and he leaned over her to point.

"Go away!" cried Mary. "I don't want boys. Go away!"

For a moment Basil looked angry, and then he began to tease. He was always teasing his sisters. He danced round and round her and made faces and sang and laughed.

"Mistress Mary, quite contrary,
How does your garden grow?
With silver bells, and cockle shells,
And marigolds all in a row."

He sang it until the other children heard and laughed, too; and the crosser Mary got, the more they sang "Mistress Mary, quite contrary"; and after that as long as she stayed with them they called her "Mistress Mary Quite Contrary" when they spoke of her to each other, and often when they spoke to her.

"You are going to be sent home," Basil said to her, "at the end of the week. And we're glad that we won't see you again."

"I am glad of it, too," answered Mary. "Where is home?"

"She doesn't know where home is!" said Basil, with seven-year-old scorn. "It's England, of course. Our grandmamma lives there and our sister Mabel was sent to her last year. You are not going to your grandmamma. You have none. You are going to your uncle. His name is Mr. Archibald Craven."

"I don't know anything about him," snapped Mary.

"I know you don't," Basil answered. "You don't know anything. Girls never do. I heard father and mother talking about him. He lives in a great, big, desolate old house in the country and no one goes near him. He's so cross he won't let them, and they wouldn't come if he would let them. He's a hunchback, and he's horrid."

"I don't believe you," said Mary; and she turned her back and stuck her fingers in her ears, because she would not listen any more.

But she thought over it a great deal afterward; and when Mrs. Crawford told her that night that she was going to sail away to England in a few days and go to her uncle,

Mr. Archibald Craven, who lived at Misselthwaite Manor, she looked so stony and stubbornly uninterested that they did not know what to think about her.

*Spelling*

to pity (verb) – pitying [She was pitying you.] – pityingly [She looked at her pityingly]

un.attract.ive

nau.ghty

per.haps – maybe

scarce – scarcely (adverb) [She scarcely ever looked at her.]

voy.age – journey

ab.sorb – ab.sorb.ed

They tried to be kind to her, but she only turned her face away when Mrs. Crawford attempted to kiss her, and held herself stiffly when Mr. Crawford patted her shoulder.

"She is such a plain child," Mrs. Crawford said pityingly, afterward. "And her mother was such a pretty creature. She had a very pretty manner, too, and Mary has the most unattractive ways I ever saw in a child. The children call her 'Mistress Mary Quite Contrary,' and though it's naughty of them, one can't help understanding it."

"Perhaps if her mother had carried her pretty face and her pretty manners more often into the nursery Mary might have learned some pretty ways too. It is very sad, now the poor beautiful thing is gone, to remember that many people never even knew that she had a child at all."

"I believe she scarcely ever looked at her," sighed Mrs. Crawford. "When her Ayah was dead there was no one to give a thought to the little thing. Think of the servants running away and leaving her all alone in that deserted bungalow. Colonel McGrew said he nearly jumped out of his skin when he opened the door and found her standing by herself in the middle of the room."

Mary made the long voyage to England under the care of an officer's wife, who was taking her children to leave them in a boarding school. She was very much absorbed in her own little boy and girl, and was rather glad to hand the child over to the woman Mr. Archibald Craven sent to meet her, in London

## CHAPTER II

## ARRIVAL IN ENGLAND

The woman was his housekeeper at Misselthwaite Manor, and her name was Mrs. Medlock. She was a stout woman, with very red cheeks and sharp black eyes. She wore a very purple dress, a black silk coat with jet fringe on it and a black bonnet with purple velvet flowers which stuck up and trembled when she moved her head.

Mary did not like her at all, but as she very seldom liked people there was nothing remarkable in that; besides which it was very evident Mrs. Medlock did not think much of her.

"My word! She's a plain little piece of goods!" she said. "And we'd heard that her mother was a beauty. She hasn't handed much of it down, has she, ma'am?"

"Perhaps she will improve as she grows older," the officer's wife said good-naturedly. "If she were not so sallow and had a nicer expression, her features are rather good. Children alter so much."

"She'll have to alter a good deal," answered Mrs. Medlock. "And there's nothing likely to improve children at Misselthwaite—if you ask me!"

They thought Mary was not listening because she was standing a little apart from them at the window of the private hotel they had gone to. She was watching the passing buses and cabs, and people, but she heard quite well and was made very curious about her uncle and the place he lived in. What sort of a place was it, and what would he be like? What was a hunchback? She had never seen one. Perhaps there were none in India.

Since she had been living in other people's houses and had had no Ayah, she had begun to feel lonely and to think queer thoughts which were new to her. She had begun to wonder why she had never seemed to belong to anyone even when her

53

father and mother had been alive. Other children seemed to belong to their fathers and mothers, but she had never seemed to really be anyone's little girl.

She had had servants, and food and clothes, but no one had taken any notice of her. She did not know that this was because she was a disagreeable child; but then, of course, she did not know she was disagreeable. She often thought that other people were, but she did not know that she was so herself.

She thought Mrs. Medlock the most disagreeable person she had ever seen, with her common, highly coloured face and her common fine bonnet. When the next day they set out on their journey to Yorkshire, she walked through the station to the railway carriage with her head up and trying to keep as far away from her as she could, because she did not want to seem to belong to her. It would have made her very angry to think people imagined she was her little girl.

But Mrs. Medlock was not in the least disturbed by her and her thoughts. She was the kind of woman who would "stand no nonsense from young ones." At least, that is what she would have said if she had been asked. She had not wanted to go to London just when her sister Maria's daughter was going to be married, but she had a comfortable, well paid place as housekeeper at Misselthwaite Manor and the only way in which she could keep it was to do at once what Mr. Archibald Craven told her to do. She never dared even to ask a question.

"Captain Lennox and his wife died of the cholera," Mr. Craven had said in his short, cold way. "Captain Lennox was my wife's brother and I am their daughter's guardian. The child is to be brought here. You must go to London and bring her yourself."

So she packed her small trunk and made the journey.

Mary sat in her corner of the railway carriage and looked plain and fretful. She had nothing to read or to look at, and she had folded her thin little black-gloved hands in her lap. Her black dress made her look yellower than ever, and her limp light hair straggled from under her black crêpe hat.

*Spelling*

un.resp.on.sive
dis.com.fort – dis.com.fort.ed
app.arant – app.arant.ly
in spite: despite [Mary started listening in spite of herself.]

"A more spoiled-looking young one I never saw in my life," Mrs. Medlock thought. She had never seen a child who sat so still without doing anything; and at last she got tired of watching her and began to talk in a brisk, hard voice.

"I suppose I may as well tell you something about where you are going to," she said. "Do you know anything about your uncle?"

"No," said Mary.

"Never heard your father and mother talk about him?"

"No," said Mary frowning. She frowned because she remembered that her father and mother had never talked to her about anything in particular. Certainly they had never told her things.

"Humph," muttered Mrs. Medlock, staring at her queer, unresponsive little face. She did not say any more for a few moments and then she began again.

"I suppose you might as well be told something—to prepare you. You are going to a queer place."

Mary said nothing at all, and Mrs. Medlock looked rather discomforted by her apparent indifference, but, after taking a breath, she went on.

"Not but that it's a grand big place in a gloomy way, and Mr. Craven's proud of it in his way—and that's gloomy enough, too. The house is six hundred years old and it's on the edge of the moor, and there are nearly a hundred rooms in it, though most of them are shut up and locked. And there are pictures and fine old furniture and things that have been there for ages, and there's a big park round it and gardens and trees with branches trailing to the ground—some of them." She paused and took another breath. "But there's nothing else," she ended suddenly.

Mary had begun to listen in spite of herself. It all sounded so unlike India, and anything new rather attracted her. But she did not intend to look as if she were interested. That was one of her unhappy, disagreeable ways. So she sat still.

"Well," said Mrs. Medlock. "What do you think of it?"

"Nothing," she answered. "I know nothing about such places."

That made Mrs. Medlock laugh a short sort of laugh.

"Eh!" she said, "but you are like an old woman. Don't you care?"

"It doesn't matter," said Mary, "whether I care or not."

"You are right enough there," said Mrs. Medlock. "It doesn't. What you're to be kept at Misselthwaite Manor for I don't know, unless because it's the easiest way. *He's* not going to trouble himself about you, that's sure and certain. He never troubles himself about no one."

She stopped herself as if she had just remembered something in time.

"He's got a crooked back," she said. "That set him wrong. He was a sour young man and got no good of all his money and big place till he was married."

Mary's eyes turned toward her in spite of her intention not to seem to care. She had never thought of the hunchback's being married and she was a trifle surprised. Mrs. Medlock saw this, and as she was a talkative woman she continued with more interest. This was one way of passing some of the time, at any rate.

"She was a sweet, pretty thing and he'd have walked the world over to get her a blade of grass she wanted. Nobody thought she'd marry him, but she did, and people said she married him for his money. But she didn't—she didn't," positively. "When she died—"

Mary gave a little involuntary jump.

"Oh! Did she die!" she exclaimed, quite without meaning to. She had just remembered a French fairy story she had once read called "Riquet à la Houppe." It had been about a poor hunchback and a beautiful princess and it had made her suddenly sorry for Mr. Archibald Craven.

"Yes, she died," Mrs. Medlock answered. "And it made him queerer than ever. He cares about nobody. He won't see people. Most of the time he goes away, and when he is at Misselthwaite he shuts himself up in the West Wing and won't let anyone but Pitcher see him. Pitcher's an old fellow, but he took care of him when he was a child and he knows his ways."

It sounded like something in a book and it did not make Mary feel cheerful. A house with a hundred rooms, nearly all shut up and with their doors locked—a house on the edge of a moor—whatsoever a moor was—sounded dreary.

A man with a crooked back who shut himself up also! She stared out of the window with her lips pinched together, and it seemed quite natural that the rain should have begun to pour down in grey slanting lines and splash and stream down the window-panes.

If the pretty wife had been alive she might have made things cheerful by being something like her own mother and by running in and out and going to parties as she had done in frocks "full of lace." But she was not there anymore.

"You needn't expect to see him, because ten to one you won't," said Mrs. Medlock.

"And you mustn't expect that there will be people to talk to you. You'll have to play about and look after yourself. You'll be told what rooms you can go into and what rooms you're to keep out of. There's gardens enough. But when you're in the house don't go wandering and poking about. Mr. Craven won't have it."

"I shall not want to go poking about," said sour little Mary; and just as suddenly as she had begun to be rather sorry for Mr. Archibald Craven she began to cease to be sorry and to think he was unpleasant enough to deserve all that had happened to him.

And she turned her face toward the streaming panes of the window of the railway carriage and gazed out at the grey rain-storm which looked as if it would go on forever and ever. She watched it so long and steadily that the greyness grew heavier and heavier before her eyes and she fell asleep.

## CHAPTER III

## ACROSS THE MOOR

She slept a long time, and when she awakened Mrs. Medlock had bought a lunch basket at one of the stations and they had some chicken and cold beef, bread and butter and some hot tea. The rain seemed to be streaming down more heavily than ever and everybody in the station wore wet and glistening raincoats. The guard lit the lamps in the carriage, and Mrs. Medlock cheered up very much over her tea and chicken and beef. She ate a great deal and afterward fell asleep herself, and Mary sat and stared at her and watched her fine bonnet slip on one side until she herself fell asleep once more in the corner of the carriage, lulled by the splashing of the rain against the windows. It was quite dark when she awakened again. The train had stopped at a station and Mrs. Medlock was shaking her.

"You have had a sleep!" she said. "It's time to open your eyes! We're at Thwaite Station and we've got a long drive before us."

Mary stood up and tried to keep her eyes open while Mrs. Medlock collected her parcels. The little girl did not offer to help her, because in India native servants always picked up or carried things and it seemed quite proper that other people should wait on one.

The station was a small one and nobody but themselves seemed to be getting out of the train. The station master spoke to Mrs. Medlock in a rough, good-natured way, pronouncing his words in a queer broad fashion which Mary found out afterward was Yorkshire.

"I see you got back," he said. "And you brought this young one with you."

"Aye, that's her," answered Mrs. Medlock, jerking her head over her shoulder toward Mary. "How's your Missus?"

"Well enough. The carriage is waiting outside for you."

A carriage stood on the road before the little outside platform. Mary saw that it was smart and that it was a smart footman who helped her in. His long waterproof coat and the waterproof covering of his hat were shining and dripping with rain as everything was, the burly station-master included.

When he shut the door, mounted the box with the coachman, and they drove off, the little girl found herself seated in a comfortably cushioned corner, but she was not inclined to go to sleep again. She sat and looked out of the window, curious to see something of the road over which she was being driven to the queer place Mrs. Medlock had spoken of. She was not at all a timid child and she was not exactly frightened, but she felt that there was no knowing what might happen in a house with a hundred rooms nearly all shut up—a house standing on the edge of a moor.

"What is a moor?" she said suddenly to Mrs. Medlock.

"Look out of the window in about ten minutes and you'll see," the woman answered. "We've got to drive five miles across Missel Moor before we get to the Manor. You won't see much because it's a dark night, but you can see something."

Mary asked no more questions but waited in the darkness of her corner, keeping her eyes on the window. The carriage lamps cast rays of light a little distance ahead of them and she caught glimpses of the things they passed. After they had left the station they had driven through a tiny village and she had seen whitewashed cottages and the lights of a public house. Then they had passed a church and a little shop-window or so in a cottage with toys and sweets and odd things set out for sale. Then they were on the highroad and she saw hedges and trees. After that there seemed nothing different for a long time—or at least it seemed a long time to her.

At last the horses began to go more slowly, as if they were climbing up-hill, and presently there seemed to be no more hedges and no more trees. She could see nothing, in fact, but a dense darkness on either side. She leaned forward and pressed her face against the window just as the carriage gave a big jolt.

"Eh! We're on the moor now sure enough," said Mrs. Medlock.

---

*Spelling*

ex.pan.se: wide open surface, land or sky

ap.parent.ly: seemingly

part.icu.lar.ly

---

The carriage lamps shed a yellow light on a rough-looking road which seemed to be cut through bushes and low growing things which ended in the great expanse of dark apparently spread out before and around them. A wind was rising and making a singular, wild, low, rushing sound.

"It's—it's not the sea, is it?" said Mary, looking round at her companion.

"No," answered Mrs. Medlock. "Nor is it fields or mountains, it's just miles and miles and miles of wild land that nothing grows on but heather and gorse and broom, and nothing lives on but wild ponies and sheep."

"I feel as if it might be the sea, if there were water on it," said Mary. "It sounds like the sea just now."

"That's the wind blowing through the bushes," Mrs. Medlock said. "It's a wild, dreary enough place to my mind, though there's plenty that likes it—particularly when the heather's in bloom."

On and on they drove through the darkness, and though the rain stopped, the wind rushed by and whistled and made strange sounds. The road went up and down, and several times the carriage passed over a little bridge beneath which water rushed very fast with a great deal of noise. Mary felt as if the drive would never come to an end and that the wide, bleak moor was a wide expanse of black ocean through which she was passing on a strip of dry land.

"I don't like it," she said to herself. "I don't like it," and she pinched her thin lips more tightly together.

The horses were climbing up a hilly piece of road when she first caught sight of a light. Mrs. Medlock saw it as soon as she did and drew a long sigh of relief.

"Eh, I am glad to see that bit of light twinkling," she exclaimed. "It's the light in the lodge window. We shall get a good cup of tea after a bit, at all events."

It was "after a bit," as she said, for when the carriage passed through the park gates there was still two miles of avenue to drive through and the trees (which nearly met overhead) made it seem as if they were driving through a long dark vault.

---

*Spelling*

immense.ly – hugely, vastly

ramble: stroll, roam

hus.ky: dry, croaky

un.cere.moni.ous.ly

---

They drove out of the vault into a clear space and stopped before an immensely long but low-built house which seemed to ramble round a stone court. At first Mary thought that there were no lights at all in the windows, but as she got out of the carriage she saw that one room in a corner up-stairs showed a dull glow.

The entrance door was a huge one made of massive, curiously shaped panels of oak studded with big iron nails and bound with great iron bars. It opened into an enormous hall, which was so dimly lighted that the faces in the portraits on the walls and the figures in the suits of armour made Mary feel that she did not want to look at them. As she stood on the stone floor she looked a very small, odd little black figure, and she felt as small and lost and odd as she looked.

A neat, thin old man stood near the manservant who opened the door for them.

"You are to take her to her room," he said in a husky voice. "He doesn't want to see her. He's going to London in the morning."

"Very well, Mr. Pitcher," Mrs. Medlock answered. "So long as I know what's expected of me, I can manage."

"What's expected of you, Mrs. Medlock," Mr. Pitcher said, "is that you make sure that he's not disturbed and that he doesn't see what he doesn't want to see."

And then Mary Lennox was led up a broad staircase and down a long corridor and up a short flight of steps and through another corridor and another, until a door opened in a wall and she found herself in a room with a fire in it and a supper on a table.

Mrs. Medlock said unceremoniously:

"Well, here you are! This room and the next are where you'll live—and you must keep to them. Don't you forget that!"

It was in this way Mistress Mary arrived at Misselthwaite Manor and she had perhaps never felt quite so contrary in all her life.

*Spelling*

kneel – kneeling

hearth: fireplace [She was kneeling on the hearth-rug]

em.broi.dered

## CHAPTER IV

## MARTHA

When she opened her eyes in the morning it was because a young housemaid had come into her room to light the fire and was kneeling on the hearth-rug raking out the cinders noisily. Mary lay and watched her for a few moments and then began to look about the room. She had never seen a room at all like it and thought it curious and gloomy. The walls were covered with tapestry with a forest scene embroidered on it. There were fantastically dressed people under the trees and in the distance there was a glimpse of the turrets of a castle. There were hunters and horses and dogs and ladies. Mary felt as if she were in the forest with them. Out of a deep window she could see a great climbing stretch of land which seemed to have no trees on it, and to look rather like an endless, dull, purplish sea.

"What is that?" she said, pointing out of the window.

Martha, the young housemaid, who had just risen to her feet, looked and pointed also.

"That there?" she said.

"Yes."

"That's the moor," with a good-natured grin. "Do you like it?"

"No," answered Mary. "I hate it."

"That's because you aren't used to it," Martha said, going back to her hearth. "You thinks it's too big and bare now. But you will like it."

"Do you?" inquired Mary.

"Aye, that I do," answered Martha, cheerfully polishing away at the grate. "I just love it. It's not bare. It's covered with growing things that smell sweet. It's lovely in spring and summer when the gorse and broom and heather are in flower. It smells of honey and there's such a lot of fresh air—and the sky looks so high and the bees and skylarks make such a nice noise humming and singing. Eh! I wouldn't live away from the moor for anything."

---

*Spelling*

sub.missive and serv.ile [Servants are submissive and servile]

pre.sume

haugh.ty – haugh.tily: arrogant

im.per.ious: superior

---

Mary listened to her with a grave, puzzled expression. The native servants she had been used to in India were not in the least like this. They were submissive and servile and did not presume to talk to their masters as if they were their equals. They called their masters "protectors of the poor" and names of that sort. Indian servants were commanded to do things, not asked.

It was not the custom to say "please" and "thank you" and Mary had always slapped her Ayah in the face when she was angry. She wondered a little what this girl would do if one slapped her in the face. She was a round, rosy, good-natured looking creature, but she had a sturdy way which made Mistress Mary wonder if she might not even slap back—if the person who slapped her was only a little girl.

"You are a strange servant," she said from her pillows, rather haughtily.

Martha sat up on her heels, with her blacking-brush in her hand, and laughed, without seeming the least out of temper.

"Eh! I know that," she said. "If there was a grand Missus at Misselthwaite I should never have been even one of the under housemaids. I might have been let to be a kitchen maid but I'd never have been let upstairs. I'm too common and I talk too much. But this is a funny house for all it's so grand. Seems like there's neither Master nor Mistress except Mr. Pitcher and Mrs. Medlock. Mr. Craven, he won't be troubled about anything when he's here, and he's nearly always away. Mrs. Medlock gave me the place out of kindness. She told me she could never have done it if Misselthwaite had been like other big houses."

"Are you going to be my servant?" Mary asked, still in her imperious little Indian way.

Martha began to rub her grate again.

"I'm Mrs. Medlock's servant," she said stoutly. "And she's Mr. Craven's—but I'm to do the housemaid's work up here and wait on you a bit. But you won't need much waiting on."

"Who is going to dress me?" demanded Mary. Martha sat up on her heels again and stared. She spoke in utter amazement.

"Can't you dress yourself?!" she said.

"No," answered Mary, quite indignantly. "I never did in my life. My Ayah dressed me, of course."

"Well," said Martha, evidently not in the least aware that she was impudent, "it's time you should learn. That cannot begin younger. It'll do you good to wait on yourself a bit. My mother always said she couldn't see why grand people's children didn't turn out fair fools—what with nurses and being washed and dressed and taken out to walk as if they were puppies!"

"It is different in India," said Mistress Mary disdainfully. She could scarcely stand this.

But Martha was not at all crushed.

"Eh! I can see it's different," she answered almost sympathetically. "I dare say it's because there's such a lot of blacks there instead of respectable white people. When I heard you were coming from India I thought you were a black too."

Mary sat up in bed furious.

"What!" she said. "What! You thought I was a native. You—you daughter of a pig!"

Martha stared and looked hot.

"Who are you calling names?" she said. "You needn't be so vexed. That's not the way for a young lady to talk. I've nothing against the blacks. When you read about them in tracts they're always very religious. You always read a black as a man and a brother. I've never seen a black and I was fair pleased to think I was going to see one close. When I came in to light your fire this morning I crept up to your bed and pulled the cover back carefully to look at you. And there you were," disappointedly, "no more black than me—for all you're even lighter."

Mary did not even try to control her rage and humiliation.

*Spelling*

un.rest.rain.ed: uncontrolled

vexed: angry

grad.ually cea.sed: slowly stopped [She gradually ceased to cry]

"You thought I was a native! You dared! You don't know anything about natives! They are not people—they're servants who must salaam to you. You know nothing about India. You know nothing about anything!"

She was in such a rage and felt so helpless before the girl's simple stare, and somehow she suddenly felt so horribly lonely and far away from everything she understood and which understood her that she threw herself face downward on the pillows and burst into passionate sobbing. She sobbed so unrestrainedly that good-natured Yorkshire Martha was a little frightened and quite sorry for her. She went to the bed and bent over her.

"Eh! You mustn't cry like that there!" she begged. "You mustn't for sure. I didn't know you'd be vexed. I don't know anything about anything—just like you said. I beg your pardon, Miss. Do stop crying."

There was something comforting and really friendly in her queer speech and sturdy way which had a good effect on Mary. She gradually ceased crying and became quiet. Martha looked relieved.

"It's time for you to get up now," she said. "Mrs. Medlock said I was to carry your breakfast and tea and dinner into the room next to this. It's been made into a nursery for you. I'll help you with your clothes if you get out of bed. If your buttons are at the back you cannot button them up yourself."

When Mary at last decided to get up, the clothes Martha took from the wardrobe were not the ones she had worn when she arrived the night before with Mrs. Medlock.

"Those are not mine," she said. "Mine are black." She looked the thick white wool coat and dress over, and added with cool approval: "Those are nicer than mine."

"These are the ones you must put on," Martha answered. "Mr. Craven ordered Mrs. Medlock to get them in London. He said 'I won't have a child dressed in black wandering about like a lost soul,' he said. 'It'd make the place sadder than it is. Put colour on her.' Mother she said she knew what he meant. Mother always knows what a body means. She doesn't hold with black herself." "I hate black things," said Mary.

---

**Spelling**

an.cest.ors

sub.serv.ient: submissive

---

The dressing process was one which taught them both something. Martha had "buttoned up" her little sisters and brothers but she had never seen a child who stood still and waited for another person to do things for her as if she had neither hands nor feet of her own.

"Why don't you put on your own shoes?" she said when Mary quietly held out her foot.

"My Ayah did it," answered Mary, staring. "It was the custom."

She said that very often—"It was the custom." The native servants were always saying it. If one told them to do a thing their ancestors had not done for a thousand years they gazed at one mildly and said, "It is not the custom" and one knew that was the end of the matter.

It had not been the custom that Mistress Mary should do anything but stand and allow herself to be dressed like a doll, but before she was ready for breakfast she began to suspect that her life at Misselthwaite Manor would end by teaching her a number of things quite new to her—things such as putting on her own shoes and stockings, and picking up things she let fall. If Martha had been a well-trained fine young lady's maid she would have been more subservient and respectful and would have known that it was her business to brush hair, and button boots, and pick things up and lay them away. She was, however, only an untrained Yorkshire rustic who had been brought up in a moorland cottage with a swarm of little brothers and sisters who had never dreamed of doing anything but waiting on themselves and on the younger ones who were either babies in arms or just learning to totter about and tumble over things.

If Mary Lennox had been a child who was ready to be amused she would perhaps have laughed at Martha's readiness to talk, but Mary only listened to her coldly and wondered at her freedom of manner. At first she was not at all interested, but gradually, as the girl rattled on in her good-tempered, homely way, Mary began to notice what she was saying.

"Eh! You should see them all," she said. "There are twelve of us and my father only gets sixteen shillings a week. I can tell you my mother's put to it to get porridge for them all. They tumble about on the moor and play there all day and mother says the air of the moor fattens them.

*Spelling*

sub.stant.ial

in.cred.ulou.sly

in.differ.ence of ig.nor.ance

She says she believes they eat the grass same as the wild ponies do. Our Dickon, he's twelve years old and he's got a young pony he calls his own."

"Where did he get it?" asked Mary.

"He found it on the moor with its mother when it was a little one and he began to make friends with it and give it bits of bread and pluck young grass for it. And it got to like him so it follows him about and it lets him get on its back. Dickon's a kind lad and animals likes him."

Mary had never possessed an animal pet of her own and had always thought she should like one. So she began to feel a slight interest in Dickon, and as she had never before been interested in any one but herself, it was the dawning of a healthy sentiment. When she went into the room which had been made into a nursery for her, she found that it was rather like the one she had slept in. It was not a child's room, but a grown-up person's room, with gloomy old pictures on the walls and heavy old oak chairs. A table in the centre was set with a good substantial breakfast. But she had always had a very small appetite, and she looked with something more than indifference at the first plate Martha set before her.

"I don't want it," she said.

"You don't want your porridge!" Martha exclaimed incredulously.

"No."

"You don't know how good it is. Put a bit of treacle on it or a bit of sugar."

"I don't want it," repeated Mary.

"Eh!" said Martha. "I can't abide to see good victuals go to waste. If our children were at this table they'd clean it bare in five minutes."

"Why?" said Mary coldly.

"Why!" echoed Martha. "Because they hardly ever had their stomachs full in their lives. They're as hungry as young hawks and foxes."

"I don't know what it is to be hungry," said Mary, with the indifference of ignorance.

---

**Spelling**

in.dig.nant

stout.ly: firmly

amuse.ment

---

Martha looked indignant. "Well, it would do you good to try it. I can see that plain enough," she said outspokenly. "I've no patience with folk that sits and just stares at good bread and meat. My word! Don't I wish Dickon and Phil and Jane and the rest of them had what's here."

"Why don't you take it to them?" suggested Mary.

"It's not mine," answered Martha stoutly. "And this isn't my day out. I get my day out once a month same as the rest. Then I go home and clean up for mother and give her a day's rest."

Mary drank some tea and ate a little toast and some marmalade.

"You wrap up warm and run out and play," said Martha. "It'll do you good and give you some stomach for your meat."

Mary went to the window. There were gardens and paths and big trees, but everything looked dull and wintry.

"Out? Why should I go out on a day like this?"

"Well, if you don't go out you'll have to stay in, and what have you got to do?"

Mary glanced about her. There was nothing to do. When Mrs. Medlock had prepared the nursery she had not thought of amusement. Perhaps it would be better to go and see what the gardens were like.

"Who will go with me?" she inquired.

Martha stared.

"You'll go by yourself," she answered. "You'll have to learn to play like other children do when they haven't got sisters and brothers. Our Dickon goes off on the moor by himself and plays for hours. That's how he made friends with the pony. He's got sheep on the moor that know him, and birds that comes and eats out of his hand. However little there is to eat, he always saves a bit of his bread to coax his pets."

*Spelling*

men.tion

hesi.tate

shrubbery

evi.dent.ly

It was really this mention of Dickon which made Mary decide to go out, though she was not aware of it. There would be birds outside though there would not be ponies or sheep. They would be different from the birds in India and it might amuse her to look at them. Martha found her coat and hat for her and a pair of stout little boots and she showed her her way down-stairs.

"If you go round that way you'll come to the gardens," she said, pointing to a gate in a wall of shrubbery. "There are lots of flowers in summer-time, but there's nothing blooming now." She seemed to hesitate a second before she added, "One of the gardens is locked up. No one has been in it for ten years."

"Why?" asked Mary in spite of herself. Here was another locked door added to the hundred in the strange house.

"Mr. Craven had it shut when his wife died so sudden. He won't let no one go inside. It was her garden. He locked the door and dug a hole and buried the key. There's Mrs. Medlock's bell ringing—I must run."

After she was gone Mary turned down the walk which led to the door in the shrubbery. She could not help thinking about the garden which no one had been into for ten years. She wondered what it would look like and whether there were any flowers still alive in it. When she had passed through the shrubbery gate she found herself in great gardens, with wide lawns and winding walks with clipped borders.

There were trees, and flower-beds, and evergreens clipped into strange shapes, and a large pool with an old grey fountain in its midst. But the flower-beds were bare and wintry and the fountain was not playing. This was not the garden which was shut up. How could a garden be shut up? You could always walk into a garden.

She was just thinking this when she saw that, at the end of the path she was following, there seemed to be a long wall, with ivy growing over it. She was not familiar enough with England to know that she was coming upon the kitchen-gardens where the vegetables and fruit were growing. She went toward the wall and found that there was a green door in the ivy, and that it stood open. This was not the closed garden, evidently, and she could go into it.

---

*Spelling*

re.veal.ing

con.tain.ing

myster.ious

---

She went through the door and found that it was a garden with walls all round it and that it was only one of several walled gardens which seemed to open into one another. She saw another open green door, revealing bushes and pathways between beds containing winter vegetables. Fruit trees were trained flat against the wall, and over some of the beds there were glass frames. The place was bare and ugly enough, Mary thought, as she stood and stared about her. It might be nicer in summer when things were green, but there was nothing pretty about it now.

Presently an old man with a spade over his shoulder walked through the door leading from the second garden. He looked startled when he saw Mary, and then touched his cap. He had a surly old face, and did not seem at all pleased to see her—but then she was displeased with his garden and wore her "quite contrary" expression, and certainly did not seem at all pleased to see him.

"What is this place?" she asked.

"One of the kitchen gardens," he answered.

"What is that?" said Mary, pointing through the other green door.

"Another of them," shortly. "There's another on the other side of the wall and there's the orchard at the other side of that."

"Can I go in them?" asked Mary.

"If you like. But there's nothing to see."

Mary made no response. She went down the path and through the second green door. There she found more walls and winter vegetables and glass frames, but in the second wall there was another green door and it was not open. Perhaps it led into the garden which no one had seen for ten years. As she was not at all a timid child and always did what she wanted to do, Mary went to the green door and turned the handle. She hoped the door would not open because she wanted to be sure she had found the mysterious garden—but it did open quite easily and she walked through it and found herself in an orchard. There were walls all round it also and trees trained against them, and there were bare fruit-trees growing in the winter-browned grass—but there was no green door to be seen anywhere.

---

*Spelling*

affect.ion.ate

dread.ful – dread.fully

laugh – laughed - laughing

---

Mary looked for it, and yet when she had entered the upper end of the garden she had noticed that the wall did not seem to end with the orchard but to extend beyond it as if it enclosed a place at the other side. She could see the tops of trees above the wall, and when she stood still she saw a bird with a bright red breast sitting on the topmost branch of one of them, and suddenly he burst into his winter song—almost as if he had caught sight of her and was calling to her.

She stopped and listened to him and somehow his cheerful, friendly little whistle gave her a pleased feeling—even a disagreeable little girl may be lonely, and the big closed house and big bare moor and big bare gardens had made this one feel as if there was no one left in the world but herself. If she had been an affectionate child, who had been used to being loved, she would have broken her heart, but even though she was "Mistress Mary Quite Contrary" she was desolate, and the bright-breasted little bird brought a look into her sour little face which was almost a smile. She listened to him until he flew away. He was not like an Indian bird and she liked him and wondered if she should ever see him again. Perhaps he lived in the mysterious garden and knew all about it.

Perhaps it was because she had nothing whatever to do that she thought so much of the deserted garden. She was curious about it and wanted to see what it was like. Why had Mr. Archibald Craven buried the key? If he had liked his wife so much why did he hate her garden? She wondered if she should ever see him, but she knew that if she did she should not like him, and he would not like her, and that she should only stand and stare at him and say nothing, though she should be wanting dreadfully to ask him why he had done such a queer thing.

"People never like me and I never like people," she thought. "And I never can talk as the Crawford children could. They were always talking and laughing and making noises."

She thought of the robin and of the way he seemed to sing his song at her, and as she remembered the tree-top he perched on she stopped rather suddenly on the path.

"I believe that tree was in the secret garden—I feel sure it was," she said. "There was a wall round the place and there was no door."

---

*Spelling*

grum.py – grum.pily

ex.press.ion

coax.ing; coax – to persuade

---

She walked back into the first kitchen garden she had entered and found the old man digging there. She went and stood beside him and watched him a few moments in her cold little way. He took no notice of her and so at last she spoke to him.

"I have been into the other gardens," she said.

"There was nothing to prevent you," he answered grumpily.

"I went into the orchard."

"There was no dog at the door to bite you," he answered.

"There was no door there into the other garden," said Mary.

"What garden?" he said in a rough voice, stopping his digging for a moment.

"The one on the other side of the wall," answered Mistress Mary. "There are trees there—I saw the tops of them. A bird with a red breast was sitting on one of them and he sang."

To her surprise the surly old weather-beaten face actually changed its expression. A slow smile spread over it and the gardener looked quite different. It made her think that it was curious how much nicer a person looked when he smiled. She had not thought of it before.

He turned about to the orchard side of his garden and began to whistle—a low soft whistle. She could not understand how such a surly man could make such a coaxing sound.

Almost the next moment a wonderful thing happened. She heard a soft little rushing flight through the air—and it was the bird with the red breast flying to them, and he actually alighted on the big clod of earth quite near to the gardener's foot.

"Here he is," chuckled the old man, and then he spoke to the bird as if he were speaking to a child.

"Where have you been, you cheeky little beggar?" he said. "I've not seen you today. Have you begun that courting this early in the season? That's too forward."

---

*Spelling*

fledg.ling: young, unexperienced

con.ceited: proud, vain

---

The bird put his tiny head on one side and looked up at him with his soft bright eye which was like a black dewdrop. He seemed quite familiar and not the least afraid. He hopped about and pecked the earth briskly, looking for seeds and insects.

It actually gave Mary a queer feeling in her heart, because he was so pretty and cheerful and seemed so like a person. He had a tiny plump body and a delicate beak, and slender delicate legs.

"Will he always come when you call him?" she asked almost in a whisper.

"Aye, that he will. I've known him ever since he was a fledgling. He came out of the nest in the other garden and when first he flew over the wall he was too weak to fly back for a few days and we got friendly. When he went over the wall again the rest of the brood was gone and he was lonely and he came back to me."

"What kind of a bird is he?" Mary asked.

"Don't you know? He's a robin redbreast and they're the friendliest, most curious birds alive. They're almost as friendly as dogs—if you know how to get on with them. Watch him pecking about there and looking round at us now and again. He knows we're talking about him."

It was the queerest thing in the world to see the old fellow. He looked at the plump little scarlet-waistcoated bird as if he were both proud and fond of him.

"He's a conceited one," he chuckled. "He likes to hear folk talk about him. And curious—bless me, there never was his like for curiosity and meddling. He's always coming to see what I'm planting. He knows all the things Master Craven never troubles himself to find out. He's the head gardener, he is."

The robin hopped about busily pecking the soil and now and then stopped and looked at them a little.

Mary thought his black dewdrop eyes gazed at her with great curiosity. It really seemed as if he were finding out all about her. The queer feeling in her heart increased.

"Where did the rest of the brood fly to?" she asked.

"There's no knowing. The old ones turn them out of their nest and make them fly and they're scattered before you know it. This one was a knowing one and he knew he was lonely."

Mistress Mary went a step nearer to the robin and looked at him very hard.

"I'm lonely," she said.

She had not known before that this was one of the things which made her feel sour and cross. She seemed to find it out when the robin looked at her and she looked at the robin.

The old gardener pushed his cap back on his bald head and stared at her a minute.

"Aren't you that little lass from India?" he asked.

Mary nodded.

"Then no wonder you're lonely. You'll be lonelier before that's done," he said.

He began to dig again, driving his spade deep into the rich black garden soil while the robin hopped about very busily employed.

"What is your name?" Mary inquired.

He stood up to answer her.

"Ben Weatherstaff," he answered, and then he added with a surly chuckle, "I'm lonely myself except when he's with me," and he jerked his thumb toward the robin. "He's the only friend I've got."

"I have no friends at all," said Mary. "I never had. My Ayah didn't like me and I never played with anyone."

It is a Yorkshire habit to say what you think with blunt frankness, and old Ben Weatherstaff was a Yorkshire moor man.

"Then you and I are a good bit alike," he said. "We were woven out of the same cloth. We're neither of us good looking and we're both of us as sour as we look. We've got the same nasty tempers, both of us, I'll warrant."

This was plain speaking, and Mary Lennox had never heard the truth about herself in her life. Native servants always salaamed and submitted to you, whatever you did. She had never thought much about her looks, but she wondered if she was as unattractive as Ben Weatherstaff and she also wondered if she looked as sour as he had looked before the robin came. She actually began to wonder also if she was "nasty tempered." She felt uncomfortable.

---

*Spelling*

out.right

dar.ned: blasted

laugh.ed

cur.ious

---

Suddenly a clear rippling little sound broke out near her and she turned round. She was standing a few feet from a young apple tree and the robin had flown on to one of its branches and had burst out into a scrap of a song. Ben Weatherstaff laughed outright.

"What did he do that for?" asked Mary.

"He's made up his mind to make friends with you," replied Ben. "Well, I'll be darned if he hasn't taken a fancy to you."

"To me?" said Mary, and she moved toward the little tree softly and looked up.

"Would you make friends with me?" she said to the robin just as if she was speaking to a person. "Would you?" And she did not say it either in her hard little voice or in her imperious Indian voice, but in a tone so soft and eager and coaxing that Ben Weatherstaff was as surprised as she had been when she heard him whistle.

"Why," he cried out, "you've said that as nice and human as if you were a real child instead of a sharp old woman. You said it almost like Dickon talks to his wild things on the moor."

"Do you know Dickon?" Mary asked, turning round rather in a hurry.

"Everybody knows him. Dickon's wandering about everywhere. The very blackberries and heather-bells know him. I'm sure the foxes show him where their cubs lie and the skylarks don't hide their nests from him."

Mary would have liked to ask some more questions. She was almost as curious about Dickon as she was about the deserted garden. But just that moment the robin, who had ended his song, gave a little shake of his wings, spread them and flew away. He had made his visit and had other things to do.

*Spelling*

fly – flew – flown [He has flown over the wall.]

courting: looking for a mate

mum.bled: to mumble is to speak unclearly

un.companion.able: not sociable

daren't: dare not

"He has flown over the wall!" Mary cried out, watching him. "He has flown into the orchard—he has flown across the other wall—into the garden where there is no door!"

"He lives there," said old Ben. "He came out of the egg there. If he's courting, he's making up to some young madam of a robin that lives among the old rose trees there."

"Rose trees," said Mary. "Are there rose trees?"

Ben Weatherstaff took up his spade again and began to dig.

"There were, ten years ago," he mumbled.

"I should like to see them," said Mary. "Where is the green door? There must be a door somewhere."

Ben drove his spade deep and looked as uncompanionable as he had looked when she first saw him.

"That was ten years ago, but that isn't now," he said.

"No door!" cried Mary. "There must be."

"None that anyone can find, and none that is anyone's business. Don't you be a meddlesome wench and poke your nose where it's no cause to go. Here, I must go on with my work. Go and play. I've no more time."

And he actually stopped digging, threw his spade over his shoulder and walked off, without even glancing at her or saying good-bye.

# CHAPTER V

## THE CRY IN THE CORRIDOR

At first each day which passed by for Mary Lennox was exactly like the others. Every morning she awoke in her tapestried room and found Martha kneeling upon the hearth building her fire; every morning she ate her breakfast in the nursery which had nothing amusing in it; and after each breakfast she gazed out of the window across to the huge moor which seemed to spread out on all sides and climb up to the sky, and after she had stared for a while she realized that if she did not go out she would have to stay in and do nothing—and so she went out. She did not know that this was the best thing she could have done, and she did not know that, when she began to walk quickly or even run along the paths and down the avenue, she was stirring her slow blood and making herself stronger by fighting with the wind which swept down from the moor. She ran only to make herself warm, and she hated the wind which rushed at her face and roared and held her back as if it were some giant she could not see.

But the big breaths of rough fresh air blown over the heather filled her lungs with something which was good for her whole thin body and whipped some red colour into her cheeks and brightened her dull eyes when she did not know anything about it.

But after a few days spent almost entirely out of doors she woke up one morning knowing what it was to be hungry, and when she sat down to her breakfast she did not glance disdainfully at her porridge and push it away, but took up her spoon and began to eat it and went on eating it until her bowl was empty.

"You got on well enough with that this morning, didn't you?" said Martha.

"It tastes nice today," said Mary, feeling a little surprised herself.

"It's the air of the moor that's giving you stomach," answered Martha. "It's lucky for you that you've got provisions as well as appetite. There're twelve in our cottage as had the stomach and nothing to put in it. You go on playing outdoors every day and you'll get some flesh on your bones and you won't be so pale."

"I don't play," said Mary. "I have nothing to play with."

"Nothing to play with!" exclaimed Martha.

"Our children play with sticks and stones. They just run about and shout and look at things."

Mary did not shout, but she looked at things. There was nothing else to do. She walked round and round the gardens and wandered about the paths in the park. Sometimes she looked for Ben Weatherstaff, but though several times she saw him at work he was too busy to look at her or was too surly. Once when she was walking toward him he picked up his spade and turned away as if he did it on purpose.

One place she went to more often than to any other. It was the long walk outside the gardens with the walls round them. There were bare flower-beds on either side of it and against the walls ivy grew thickly. There was one part of the wall where the creeping dark green leaves were bushier than elsewhere. It seemed as if for a long time that part had been neglected. The rest of it had been clipped and made to look neat, but at this lower end of the walk it had not been trimmed at all.

A few days after she had talked to Ben Weatherstaff Mary stopped to notice this and wondered why it was so. She had just paused and was looking up at a long spray of ivy swinging in the wind when she saw a gleam of scarlet and heard a brilliant chirp, and there, on the top of the wall, perched Ben Weatherstaff's robin redbreast, tilting forward to look at her with his small head on one side.

"Oh!" she cried out, "is it you—is it you?" And it did not seem at all queer to her that she spoke to him as if she was sure that he would understand and answer her.

He did answer. He twittered and chirped and hopped along the wall as if he were telling her all sorts of things. It seemed to Mistress Mary as if she understood him, too, though he was not speaking in words. It was as if he said:

"Good morning! Isn't the wind nice? Isn't the sun nice? Isn't everything nice? Let us both chirp and hop and twitter. Come on! Come on!"

Mary began to laugh, and as he hopped and took little flights along the wall she ran after him. Poor little thin, sallow, ugly Mary—she actually looked almost pretty for a moment.

"I like you! I like you!" she cried out, pattering down the walk; and she chirped and tried to whistle, which last she did not know how to do in the least. But the robin seemed to be quite satisfied and chirped and whistled back at her. At last he spread his wings and made a darting flight to the top of a tree, where he perched and sang loudly.

That reminded Mary of the first time she had seen him. He had been swinging on a tree-top then and she had been standing in the orchard. Now she was on the other side of the orchard and standing in the path outside a wall—much lower down— and there was the same tree inside.

"It's in the garden no one can go into," she said to herself. "It's the garden without a door. He lives in there. How I wish I could see what it is like!"

She ran up the walk to the green door she had entered the first morning. Then she ran down the path through the other door and then into the orchard, and when she stood and looked up there was the tree on the other side of the wall, and there was the robin just finishing his song and beginning to preen his feathers with his beak.

"It is the garden," she said. "I am sure it is."

She walked round and looked closely at that side of the orchard wall, but she only found what she had found before—that there was no door in it. Then she ran through the kitchen-gardens again and out into the walk outside the long ivy-covered wall, and she walked to the end of it and looked at it, but there was no door; and then she walked to the other end, looking again, but there was no door.

"It's very queer," she said. "Ben Weatherstaff said there was no door and there is no door. But there must have been one ten years ago, because Mr. Craven buried the key."

This gave her so much to think of that she began to be quite interested and feel that she was not sorry that she had come to Misselthwaite Manor. In India she had always felt hot and too languid to care much about anything. The fact was that the fresh wind from the moor had begun to blow the cobwebs out of her young brain and to wake her up a little.

She stayed out of doors nearly all day, and when she sat down to her supper at night she felt hungry and drowsy and comfortable. She did not feel cross when Martha chattered away. She felt as if she rather liked to hear her, and at last she thought she would ask her a question. She asked it after she had finished her supper and had sat down on the hearth-rug before the fire.

"Why did Mr. Craven hate the garden?" she said.

She had made Martha stay with her and Martha had not objected at all. She was very young, and used to a crowded cottage full of brothers and sisters, and she found it dull in the great servants' hall down-stairs where the footman and upper-housemaids made fun of her Yorkshire speech and looked upon her as a common little thing, and sat and whispered among themselves. Martha liked to talk, and the strange child who had lived in India, and been waited upon by "blacks," was novelty enough to attract her.

She sat down on the hearth herself without waiting to be asked.

"Are you thinking about that garden yet?" she said. "I knew you would. That was just the way with me when I first heard about it."

"Why did he hate it?" Mary persisted.

Martha tucked her feet under her and made herself quite comfortable.

"Listen to the wind blowing around the house," she said. "You could barely stand up on the moor if you were out tonight."

Mary listened to that hollow shuddering sort of roar which rushed round and round the house as if the giant no one could see was pounding it and beating at the walls and windows to try to break in. But one knew he could not get in, and somehow it made one feel very safe and warm inside a room with a red coal fire.

"But why did he hate it so?" she asked, after she had listened. She intended to know if Martha did.

Then Martha gave up her store of knowledge.

"Mind," she said, "Mrs. Medlock said it's not to be talked about. There are lots of things in this place that are not to be talked about. That's Mr. Craven's orders. His troubles are no servants' business, he says. But for the garden he wouldn't be like he is. It was Mrs. Craven's garden that she had made when first they were married and she just loved it, and they used to tend the flowers themselves. And none of the gardeners was ever let to go in. He and she used to go in and shut the door and stay there hours and hours, reading and talking. And she was just a bit of a girl and there was an old tree with a branch bent like a seat on it. And she made roses grow over it and she used to sit there. But one day when she was sitting there the branch broke and she fell on the ground and was hurt so badly that on the next day she died. The doctors thought he'd go out of his mind and die, too. That's why he hates it. No one's ever gone in since, and he won't let anyone talk about it."

Mary did not ask any more questions. She looked at the red fire and listened to the wind. It seemed to grow louder than ever.

At that moment a very good thing was happening to her. Four good things had happened to her, in fact, since she came to Misselthwaite Manor. She had felt as if she had understood a robin and that he had understood her; she had run in the wind until her blood had grown warm; she had been healthily hungry for the first time in her life; and she had found out what it was to feel sorry for someone. She was getting on.

But as she was listening to the wind she began to listen to something else. She did not know what it was, because at first she could scarcely distinguish it from the wind itself. It was a curious sound—it seemed almost as if a child were crying somewhere. Sometimes the wind sounded rather like a child crying, but presently Mistress Mary felt quite sure that this sound was inside the house, not outside it. It was far away, but it was inside. She turned round and looked at Martha.

"Do you hear anyone crying?" she said.

Martha suddenly looked confused.

"No," she answered. "It's the wind. Sometimes it sounds like as if someone was lost on the moor and wailing. It's got all sorts of sounds."

"But listen," said Mary. "It's in the house—down one of those long corridors."

And at that very moment a door must have been opened somewhere downstairs; for a great rushing draft blew along the passage and the door of the room they sat in was blown open with a crash, and as they both jumped to their feet the light was blown out and the crying sound was swept down the far corridor so that it was to be heard more plainly than ever.

"There!" said Mary. "I told you so! It is someone crying—and it isn't a grown-up person."

Martha ran and shut the door and turned the key, but before she did it they both heard the sound of a door in some far passage shutting with a bang, and then everything was quiet, for even the wind ceased for a few moments.

"It was the wind," said Martha stubbornly. "And if it wasn't, it was little Betty Butterworth, the scullery-maid. She's had a toothache all day."

But something troubled and awkward in her manner made Mistress Mary stare very hard at her. She did not believe she was speaking the truth.


## CHAPTER VI

## "THERE WAS SOMEONE CRYING—THERE WAS!"

The next day the rain poured down in torrents again, and when Mary looked out of her window the moor was almost hidden by grey mist and cloud. There could be no going out today.

"What do you do in your cottage when it rains like this?" she asked Martha.

"Try to keep from under each other's feet mostly," Martha answered. "Eh! There does seem a lot of us then. Mother's a good-tempered woman but she gets fair tougher. The biggest ones go out in the cow-shed and play there. Dickon he doesn't mind the wet. He goes out just the same as if the sun was shining. He says he sees things on rainy days that don't show when it's fair weather. He once found a little fox cub half drowned in its hole and he brought it home in the bosom of his shirt to keep it warm. Its mother had been killed nearby and the hole was drowned and the rest of the litter was dead. He's got it at home now. He found a half-drowned young crow another time and he brought it home, too, and tamed it. It's named Soot because it's so black, and it hops and flies about with him everywhere."

The time had come when Mary had forgotten to resent Martha's familiar talk. She had even begun to find it interesting and to be sorry when she stopped or went away. The stories she had been told by her Ayah when she lived in India had been quite unlike those Martha had to tell about the moorland cottage which held fourteen people who lived in four little rooms and never had quite enough to eat.

The children seemed to tumble about and amuse themselves like a litter of rough, good-natured collie puppies. Mary was most attracted by the mother and Dickon.

When Martha told stories of what "mother" said or did they always sounded comfortable.

"If I had a raven or a fox cub I could play with it," said Mary. "But I have nothing."

Martha looked perplexed.

"Can't you knit?" she asked.

"No," answered Mary.

"Can't you sew?"

"No."

"Can you read?"

"Yes."

"Then why don't you read something, or learn a bit of spelling? You're old enough to be learning your book a good bit now."

"I haven't got any books," said Mary. "Those I had were left in India."

"That's a pity," said Martha. "If Mrs. Medlock would let you go into the library, there're thousands of books there."

Mary did not ask where the library was, because she was suddenly inspired by a new idea. She made up her mind to go and find it herself. She was not troubled about Mrs. Medlock. Mrs. Medlock seemed always to be in her comfortable housekeeper's sitting room downstairs.

In this queer place one scarcely ever saw anyone at all. In fact, there was no one to see but the servants, and when their master was away they lived a luxurious life below stairs, where there was a huge kitchen hung about with shining brass and pewter, and a large servants' hall where there were four or five abundant meals eaten every day, and where a great deal of lively romping went on when Mrs. Medlock was out of the way.

Mary's meals were served regularly, and Martha waited on her, but no one troubled themselves about her in the least. Mrs. Medlock came and looked at her every day or two, but no one inquired what she did or told her what to do. She supposed that perhaps this was the English way of treating children. In India she had always been attended by her Ayah, who had followed her about and waited on her, hand and foot. She had often been tired of her company. Now she was followed by nobody and was learning to dress herself because Martha looked as though she thought she was silly and stupid when she wanted to have things handed to her and put on.

"Haven't you got good sense?" she said once, when Mary had stood waiting for her to put on her gloves for her. "Our Susan Ann is twice as sharp as you and she's only four years old. Sometimes you looks fair soft in the head."

Mary had worn her contrary scowl for an hour after that, but it made her think several entirely new things.

She stood at the window for about ten minutes this morning after Martha had swept up the hearth for the last time and gone down-stairs. She was thinking over the new idea which had come to her when she heard of the library. She did not care very much about the library itself, because she had read very few books; but to hear of it brought back to her mind the hundred rooms with closed doors.

She wondered if they were all really locked and what she would find if she could get into any of them. Were there a hundred really? Why shouldn't she go and see how many doors she could count? It would be something to do on this morning when she could not go out. She had never been taught to ask permission to do things, and she knew nothing at all about authority, so she would not have thought it necessary to ask Mrs. Medlock if she might walk about the house, even if she had seen her.

She opened the door of the room and went into the corridor, and then she began her wanderings. It was a long corridor and it branched into other corridors and it led her up short flights of steps which mounted to others again. There were doors and doors, and there were pictures on the walls.

Sometimes they were pictures of dark, curious landscapes, but mainly they were portraits of men and women in queer, grand costumes made of satin and velvet. She found herself in one long gallery whose walls were covered with these portraits. She had never thought there could be so many in any house. She walked slowly down this place and stared at the faces which also seemed to stare at her. She felt as if they were wondering what a little girl from India was doing in their house. Some were pictures of children—little girls in thick satin frocks which reached to their feet and stood out about them, and boys with puffed sleeves and lace collars and long hair, or with big ruffs around their necks. She always stopped to look at the children, and wonder what their names were, and where they had gone, and why they wore such odd clothes. There was a stiff, plain little girl rather like herself. She wore a green brocade dress and held a green parrot on her finger. Her eyes had a sharp, curious look.

"Where do you live now?" said Mary aloud to her. "I wish you were here."

Surely no other little girl ever spent such a queer morning. It seemed as if there was no one in all the huge rambling house but her own small self, wandering about up-stairs and down, through narrow passages and wide ones, where it seemed to her that no one but herself had ever walked. Since so many rooms had been built, people must have lived in them, but it all seemed so empty that she could not quite believe it true.

It was not until she climbed to the second floor that she thought of turning the handle of a door. All the doors were shut, as Mrs. Medlock had said they were, but at last she put her hand on the handle of one of them and turned it. She was almost frightened for a moment when she felt that it turned without difficulty and that when she pushed upon the door itself it slowly and heavily opened. It was a massive door and opened into a big bedroom. There were embroidered hangings on the wall, and inlaid furniture such as she had seen in India stood about the room. A broad window with leaded panes looked out upon the moor; and over the mantel was another portrait of the stiff, plain little girl who seemed to stare at her more curiously than ever.

"Perhaps she slept here once," said Mary. "She stares at me so that she makes me feel queer."

After that she opened more doors and more. She saw so many rooms that she became quite tired and began to think that there must be a hundred, though she had not counted them. In all of them there were old pictures or old tapestries with strange scenes worked on them. There were curious pieces of furniture and curious ornaments in nearly all of them.

In one room, which looked like a lady's sitting-room, the hangings were all embroidered velvet, and in a cabinet were about a hundred little elephants made of ivory. They were of different sizes, and some had their mahouts or palanquins on their backs. Some were much bigger than the others and some were so tiny that they seemed only babies. Mary had seen carved ivory in India and she knew all about elephants. She opened the door of the cabinet and stood on a footstool and played with these for quite a long time. When she got tired she set the elephants in order and shut the door of the cabinet.

In all her wanderings through the long corridors and the empty rooms, she had seen nothing alive; but in this room she saw something. Just after she had closed the cabinet door she heard a tiny rustling sound. It made her jump and look around at the sofa by the fireplace, from which it seemed to come. In the corner of the sofa there was a cushion, and in the velvet which covered it there was a hole, and out of the hole peeped a tiny head with a pair of frightened eyes in it.

Mary crept softly across the room to look. The bright eyes belonged to a little grey mouse, and the mouse had eaten a hole into the cushion and made a comfortable nest there. Six baby mice were cuddled up asleep near her. If there was no one else alive in the hundred rooms there were seven mice who did not look lonely at all.

"If they wouldn't be so frightened I would take them back with me," said Mary.

She had wandered about long enough to feel too tired to wander any further, and she turned back. Two or three times she lost her way by turning down the wrong corridor and was obliged to ramble up and down until she found the right one; but at last she reached her own floor again, though she was some distance from her own room and did not know exactly where she was.

"I believe I have taken a wrong turn again," she said, standing still at what seemed the end of a short passage with tapestry on the wall. "I don't know which way to go. How still everything is!"

It was while she was standing here and just after she had said this that the stillness was broken by a sound. It was another cry, but not quite like the one she had heard last night; it was only a short one, a fretful, childish whine muffled by passing through walls.

"It's nearer than it was," said Mary, her heart beating rather faster. "And it *is* crying."

She put her hand accidentally upon the tapestry near her, and then sprang back, feeling quite startled. The tapestry was the covering of a door which fell open and showed her that there was another part of the corridor behind it, and Mrs. Medlock was coming up it with her bunch of keys in her hand and a very cross look on her face.

"What are you doing here?" she said, and she took Mary by the arm and pulled her away. "What did I tell you?"

"I turned round the wrong corner," explained Mary. "I didn't know which way to go and I heard someone crying."

She quite hated Mrs. Medlock at the moment, but she hated her more the next.

"You didn't hear anything of the sort," said the housekeeper. "You come along back to your own nursery or I'll box your ears."

And she took her by the arm and half pushed, half pulled her up one passage and down another until she pushed her in at the door of her own room.

"Now," she said, "you stay where you're told to stay or you'll find yourself locked up. The master had better get you a governess, same as he said he would. You're one that needs someone to look sharp after you. I've got enough to do."

She went out of the room and slammed the door after her, and Mary went and sat on the hearth-rug, pale with rage. She did not cry, but ground her teeth.

"There *was* someone crying—there *was*—there *was*!" she said to herself.

She had heard it twice now, and sometime she would find out. She had found out a great deal this morning. She felt as if she had been on a long journey, and at any rate she had had something to amuse her all the time, and she had played with the ivory elephants and had seen the grey mouse and its babies in their nest in the velvet cushion.

# CHAPTER VII

## THE KEY OF THE GARDEN

Two days after this, when Mary opened her eyes she sat upright in bed immediately, and called to Martha.

"Look at the moor! Look at the moor!"

The rain storm had ended and the grey mist and clouds had been swept away in the night by the wind. The wind itself had ceased and a brilliant, deep blue sky arched high over the moorland. Never, never had Mary dreamed of a sky so blue. In India skies were hot and blazing; this was of a deep cool blue which almost seemed to sparkle like the waters of some lovely bottomless lake, and here and there, high, high in the arched blueness floated small clouds of snow-white fleece. The far-reaching world of the moor itself looked softly blue instead of gloomy purple-black or awful dreary grey.

"Aye," said Martha with a cheerful grin. "The storm's over for a bit. It does like this at this time of the year. It goes off in a night like it was pretending it had never been here and never meant to come again. That's because the springtime's on its way. It's a long way off yet, but it's coming."

"I thought perhaps it always rained or looked dark in England," Mary said.

"Eh! No!" said Martha, sitting up on her heels. "Nothing of the sort!"

"Yorkshire's the sunniest place on earth when it is sunny. I told you that you would like the moor after a bit. Just you wait till you see the gold-coloured gorse blossoms and the blossoms of the broom, and the heather flowering, all purple bells, and hundreds of butterflies fluttering and bees humming and skylarks soaring up and singing. You'll want to get out on it at sunrise and live out on it all day like Dickon does."

"Could I ever get there?" asked Mary wistfully, looking through her window at the far-off blue. It was so new and big and wonderful and such a heavenly colour.

"I don't know," answered Martha. "You never used your legs since you were born, it seems to me. You couldn't walk five miles. It's five miles to our cottage."

"I should like to see your cottage."

Martha stared at her for a moment curiously before she took up her polishing brush and began to rub the grate again. She was thinking that the small plain face did not look quite as sour at this moment as it had done the first morning she saw it. It looked just a trifle like little Susan Ann's when she wanted something very much.

"I'll ask my mother about it," she said. "She's one that nearly always sees a way to do things. It's my day out today and I'm going home. Eh! I am glad. Mrs. Medlock thinks a lot of mother. Perhaps she could talk to her."

"I like your mother," said Mary.

"I should think you would," agreed Martha, polishing away.

"I've never seen her," said Mary.

"No, you haven't," replied Martha.

She sat up on her heels again and rubbed the end of her nose with the back of her hand as if puzzled for a moment, but she ended quite positively.

"Well, she's that sensible and hardworking and good-natured and clean that no one could help liking her whether they'd seen her or not. When I'm going home to her on my day out I just jump for joy when I'm crossing the moor."

"I like Dickon," added Mary. "And I've never seen him."

"Well," said Martha stoutly, "I've told you that the very birds like him and the rabbits and wild sheep and ponies, and the foxes themselves. I wonder," staring at her reflectively, "what Dickon would think of you?"

"He wouldn't like me," said Mary in her stiff, cold little way. "No one does."

Martha looked reflective again.

"How do you like yourself?" she inquired, really quite as if she were curious to know.

Mary hesitated a moment and thought it over.

"Not at all — really," she answered. "But I never thought of that before."

Martha grinned a little as if at some homely recollection.

"Mother said that to me once," she said. "She was at her wash-tub and I was in a bad temper and talking ill of folk, and she turns round on me and says: 'You young vixen! There you stand saying that you don't like this one and you don't like that one. How do you like yourself?' It made me laugh and it brought me to my senses in a minute."

She went away in high spirits as soon as she had given Mary her breakfast. She was going to walk five miles across the moor to the cottage, and she was going to help her mother with the washing and do the week's baking and enjoy herself thoroughly.

Mary felt lonelier than ever when she knew she was no longer in the house. She went out into the garden as quickly as possible, and the first thing she did was to run round and round the fountain flower garden ten times. She counted the times carefully and when she had finished she felt in better spirits. The sunshine made the whole place look different. The high, deep, blue sky arched over Misselthwaite as well as over the moor, and she kept lifting her face and looking up into it, trying to imagine what it would be like to lie down on one of the little snow-white clouds and float about. She went into the first kitchen-garden and found Ben Weatherstaff working there with two other gardeners. The change in the weather seemed to have done him good. He spoke to her of his own accord.

"Springtime's coming," he said. "Can't you smell it?"

Mary sniffed and thought she could.

"I smell something nice and fresh and damp," she said.

"That's the good rich earth," he answered, digging away. "It's in a good humour making ready to grow things. It's glad when planting time comes. It's dull in the winter when it's got nothing to do. In the flower gardens out there things will be stirring down below in the dark. The sun's warming them. You'll see bits of green spikes sticking out of the black earth after a bit."

"What will they be?" asked Mary.

"Crocuses and snowdrops and daffodils. Have you never seen them?"

"No. Everything is hot, and wet, and green after the rains in India," said Mary. "And I think things grow up in a night."

"These won't grow up in a night," said Weatherstaff. "You'll have to wait for them. They'll poke up a bit higher here, and push out a spike more there, and uncurl a leaf this day and another that. You watch them."

"I am going to," answered Mary.

Very soon she heard the soft rustling flight of wings again and she knew at once that the robin had come again. He was very pert and lively, and hopped about so close to her feet, and put his head on one side and looked at her so slyly that she asked Ben Weatherstaff a question.

"Do you think he remembers me?" she said.

"Remembers you!" said Weatherstaff indignantly. "He knows every cabbage stump in the gardens, let alone the people. He's never seen a little wench here before, and he's bent on finding out all about you. There's no need to try to hide anything from *him*."

"Are things stirring down below in the dark in that garden where he lives?" Mary inquired.

"What garden?" grunted Weatherstaff, becoming surly again.

"The one where the old rose trees are." She could not help asking, because she wanted so much to know. "Are all the flowers dead, or do some of them come again in the summer? Are there ever any roses?"

"Ask him," said Ben Weatherstaff, hunching his shoulders toward the robin. "He's the only one who knows. No one else has seen inside it for ten years."

Ten years was a long time, Mary thought. She had been born ten years ago.

She walked away, slowly thinking. She had begun to like the garden just as she had begun to like the robin and Dickon and Martha's mother.

She was beginning to like Martha, too. That seemed a good many people to like—when you were not used to liking. She thought of the robin as one of the people. She went to her walk outside the long, ivy-covered wall over which she could see the tree-tops; and the second time she walked up and down the most interesting and exciting thing happened to her, and it was all through Ben Weatherstaff's robin.

She heard a chirp and a twitter, and when she looked at the bare flower-bed at her left side there he was hopping about and pretending to peck things out of the earth to persuade her that he had not followed her. But she knew he had followed her and the surprise so filled her with delight that she almost trembled a little.

"You do remember me!" she cried out. "You do! You are prettier than anything else in the world!"

She chirped, and talked, and coaxed and he hopped, and flirted his tail and twittered. It was as if he were talking. His red waistcoat was like satin and he puffed his tiny breast out and was so fine and so grand and so pretty that it was really as if he were showing her how important and like a human person a robin could be. Mistress Mary forgot that she had ever been contrary in her life when he allowed her to draw closer and closer to him, and bend down and talk and try to make something like robin sounds.

Oh! To think that he should actually let her come as near to him as that! He knew nothing in the world would make her put out her hand toward him or startle him in the tiniest way. He knew it because he was a real person—only nicer than any other person in the world. She was so happy that she scarcely dared to breathe.

The flower-bed was not quite bare. It was bare of flowers because the perennial plants had been cut down for their winter rest, but there were tall shrubs and low ones which grew together at the back of the bed, and as the robin hopped about under them she saw him hop over a small pile of freshly turned up earth. He stopped on it to look for a worm. The earth had been turned up because a dog had been trying to dig up a mole and he had scratched quite a deep hole.

Mary looked at it, not really knowing why the hole was there, and as she looked she saw something almost buried in the newly-turned soil. It was something like a ring of rusty iron or brass and when the robin flew up into a tree nearby she put out her hand and picked the ring up. It was more than a ring, however; it was an old key which looked as if it had been buried a long time.

Mistress Mary stood up and looked at it with an almost frightened face as it hung from her finger.

"Perhaps it has been buried for ten years," she said in a whisper. "Perhaps it is the key to the garden!"

## CHAPTER VIII

## THE ROBIN WHO SHOWED THE WAY

She looked at the key for a long time. She turned it over and over, and thought about it. As I have said before, she was not a child who had been trained to ask permission or consult her elders about things. All she thought about the key was that if it was the key to the closed garden, and she could find out where the door was, she could perhaps open it and see what was inside the walls, and what had happened to the old rose-trees. It was because it had been shut up so long that she wanted to see it. It seemed as if it must be different from other places and that something strange must have happened to it during ten years. Besides that, if she liked it she could go into it every day and shut the door behind her, and she could make up some play of her own and play it quite alone, because nobody would ever know where she was, but would think the door was still locked and the key buried in the earth. The thought of that pleased her very much.

Living as it were, all by herself in a house with a hundred mysteriously closed rooms and having nothing whatever to do to amuse herself, had set her inactive brain to working and was actually awakening her imagination. There is no doubt that the fresh, strong, pure air from the moor had a great deal to do with it. Just as it had given her an appetite, and fighting with the wind had stirred her blood, so the same things had stirred her mind. In India she had always been too hot and languid and weak to care much about anything, but in this place she was beginning to care and to want to do new things. Already she felt less "contrary," though she did not know why.

She put the key in her pocket and walked up and down her walk. No one but herself ever seemed to come there, so she could walk slowly and look at the wall, or, rather, at the ivy growing on it. The ivy was the baffling thing. However carefully she looked she could see nothing but thickly-growing, glossy, dark green leaves. She was very much disappointed. Something of her contrariness came back to her as she paced the walk and looked over it at the tree-tops inside. It seemed so silly, she said to herself, to be near it and not be able to get in. She took the key in her pocket when she went back to the house, and she made up her mind that she would always carry it with her when she went out, so that if she ever should find the hidden door she would be ready.

Mrs. Medlock had allowed Martha to sleep all night at the cottage, but she was back at her work in the morning with cheeks redder than ever and in the best of spirits.

"I got up at four o'clock," she said. "Eh! It was pretty on the moor with the birds getting up and the rabbits scampering about and the sun rising. I didn't walk all the way. A man gave me a ride in his cart and I can tell you I did enjoy myself."

She was full of stories of the delights of her day out. Her mother had been glad to see her and they had got the baking and washing all out of the way. She had even made each of the children a dough-cake with a bit of brown sugar in it.

"I had them all piping hot when they came in from playing on the moor. And the cottage all smelt of nice, clean hot baking and there was a good fire, and they just shouted for joy. Our Dickon he said our cottage was good enough for a king to live in."

In the evening they had all sat round the fire, and Martha and her mother had sewn patches on torn clothes and mended stockings and Martha had told them about the little girl who had come from India and who had been waited on all her life by what Martha called "blacks" until she didn't know how to put on her own stockings.

"Eh! They did like to hear about you," said Martha. "They wanted to know all about the blacks and about the ship you came in. I couldn't tell them enough."

Mary reflected a little.

"I'll tell you a great deal more before your next day out," she said, "so that you will have more to talk about. I dare say they would like to hear about riding on elephants and camels, and about the officers going to hunt tigers."

"My word!" cried delighted Martha. "It would set them clean off their heads. Would you really do that, Miss? It would be the same as a wild beast show like we heard they had in York once."

"India is quite different from Yorkshire," Mary said slowly, as she thought the matter over. "I never thought of that. Did Dickon and your mother like to hear you talk about me?"

"Why, our Dickon's eyes nearly started out of his head, they got that round," answered Martha. "But mother, she was put out about your seeming to be all by yourself like. She said, 'Hasn't Mr. Craven got a governess for her, or no nurse?' and I said, 'No, he hasn't, though Mrs. Medlock says he will when he thinks of it, but she says he may not think of it for two or three years.'"

"I don't want a governess," said Mary sharply.

"But mother says you ought to be learning your book by this time and you ought to have a woman to look after you, and she says: 'Now, Martha, you just think how you'd feel yourself, in a big place like that, wandering about all alone, and no mother. You do your best to cheer her up,' she says, and I said I would."

Mary gave her a long, steady look.

"You do cheer me up," she said. "I like to hear you talk."

Presently Martha went out of the room and came back with something held in her hands under her apron.

"What do you think," she said, with a cheerful grin. "I've brought you a present."

"A present!" exclaimed Mistress Mary. How could a cottage full of fourteen hungry people give any one a present!

"A man was driving across the moor peddling," Martha explained. "And he stopped his cart at our door. He had pots and pans and odds and ends, but mother had no money to buy anything. Just as he was going away our Elizabeth Ellen called out, 'Mother, he's got skipping-ropes with red and blue handles.' And mother she calls out quite sudden, 'Here, stop, mister! How much are they?' And he says 'Two pence,' and mother began fumbling in her pocket and she says to me, 'Martha, you've brought me your wages like a good lass, and I've got four places to put every penny, but I'm just going to take two pence out of it to buy that child a skipping-rope,' and she bought one and here it is."

She brought it out from under her apron and exhibited it quite proudly. It was a strong, slender rope with a striped red and blue handle at each end, but Mary Lennox had never seen a skipping-rope before. She gazed at it with a mystified expression.

"What is it for?" she asked curiously.

"For!" cried out Martha. "Do you mean that they've not got skipping-ropes in India, for all they've got elephants and tigers and camels? No wonder most of them are black. This is what it's for; just watch me."

And she ran into the middle of the room and, taking a handle in each hand, began to skip, and skip, and skip, while Mary turned in her chair to stare at her, and the queer faces in the old portraits seemed to stare at her, too, and wonder what on earth this common little cottager had the impudence to be doing under their very noses. But Martha did not even see them. The interest and curiosity in Mistress Mary's face delighted her, and she went on skipping and counted as she skipped until she had reached a hundred.

"I could skip longer than that," she said when she stopped. "I've skipped as much as five hundred when I was twelve, but I wasn't as fat then as I am now, and I was in practice."

Mary got up from her chair beginning to feel excited herself.

"It looks nice," she said. "Your mother is a kind woman. Do you think I could ever skip like that?"

"You just try it," urged Martha, handing her the skipping-rope. "You can't skip a hundred at first, but if you practise you'll mount up. That's what mother said. She says, 'Nothing will do her more good than skipping rope. It's the most sensible toy a child can have. Let her play out in the fresh air skipping and it'll stretch her legs and arms and give her some strength in them.'"

It was plain that there was not a great deal of strength in Mistress Mary's arms and legs when she first began to skip. She was not very clever at it, but she liked it so much that she did not want to stop.

"Put on your things and run and skip outdoors," said Martha. "Mother said I must tell you to keep outdoors as much as you could, even when it rains a bit, as long as you wrap up warm."

Mary put on her coat and hat and took her skipping-rope over her arm. She opened the door to go out, and then suddenly thought of something and turned back rather slowly.

"Martha," she said, "they were your wages. It was your two-pence really. Thank you." She said it stiffly because she was not used to thanking people or noticing that they did things for her. "Thank you," she said, and held out her hand because she did not know what else to do.

Martha gave her hand a clumsy little shake, as if she was not accustomed to this sort of thing either. Then she laughed.

"Eh! You are a queer, old-womanish thing," she said. "If you'd been our Elizabeth Ellen you'd have given me a kiss."

Mary looked stiffer than ever.

"Do you want me to kiss you?"

Martha laughed again.

"Nay, not me," she answered. "If you were different, perhaps you'd want to yourself. But you are not. Run off outside and play with your rope."

Mistress Mary felt a little awkward as she went out of the room. Yorkshire people seemed strange, and Martha was always rather a puzzle to her. At first she had disliked her very much, but now she did not.

The skipping-rope was a wonderful thing. She counted and skipped, and skipped and counted, until her cheeks were quite red, and she was more interested than she had ever been since she was born. The sun was shining and a little wind was blowing—not a rough wind, but one which came in delightful little gusts and brought a fresh scent of newly turned earth with it. She skipped round the fountain garden, and up one walk and down another. She skipped at last into the kitchen-garden and saw Ben Weatherstaff digging and talking to his robin, which was hopping about him. She skipped down the walk toward him and he lifted his head and looked at her with a curious expression. She had wondered if he would notice her. She really wanted him to see her skip.

"Well!" he exclaimed. "Upon my word! Perhaps you are a young one, after all, and perhaps you've got child's blood in your veins instead of sour buttermilk. That's skipped red into thy cheeks as sure as my name's Ben Weatherstaff. I wouldn't have believed you could do it."

"I never skipped before," Mary said. "I'm just beginning. I can only go up to twenty."

"You keep on," said Ben. "You do well enough at it for a young one that's lived with heathen. Just see how he's watching you," jerking his head toward the robin. "He followed you yesterday. He'll be at it again today. He'll be bound to find out what the skipping-rope is. He's never seen one. Eh!" shaking his head at the bird, "your curiosity will be the death of you sometime if you don't look sharp."

Mary skipped round all the gardens and round the orchard, resting every few minutes. At length she went to her own special walk and made up her mind to try if she could skip the whole length of it. It was a good long skip and she began slowly, but before she had gone half-way down the path she was so hot and breathless that she was obliged to stop. She did not mind much, because she had already counted up to thirty. She stopped with a little laugh of pleasure, and there, lo and behold, was the robin swaying on a long branch of ivy. He had followed her and he greeted her with a chirp. As Mary had skipped toward him she felt something heavy in her pocket strike against her at each jump, and when she saw the robin she laughed again.

"You showed me where the key was yesterday," she said. "You ought to show me the door today; but I don't believe you know!"

The robin flew from his swinging spray of ivy on to the top of the wall and he opened his beak and sang a loud, lovely trill, merely to show off. Nothing in the world is quite as adorably lovely as a robin when he shows off—and they are nearly always doing it.

Mary Lennox had heard a great deal about Magic in her Ayah's stories, and she always said that what happened almost at that moment was Magic.

One of the nice little gusts of wind rushed down the walk, and it was a stronger one than the rest. It was strong enough to wave the branches of the trees, and it was more than strong enough to sway the trailing sprays of untrimmed ivy hanging from the wall. Mary had stepped close to the robin, and suddenly the gust of wind swung aside some loose ivy trails, and more suddenly still she jumped toward it and caught it in her hand. This she did because she had seen something under it—a round knob which had been covered by the leaves hanging over it. It was the knob of a door.

She put her hands under the leaves and began to pull and push them aside. Thick as the ivy hung, it nearly all was a loose and swinging curtain, though some had crept over wood and iron. Mary's heart began to thump and her hands to shake a little in her delight and excitement. The robin kept singing and twittering away and tilting his head on one side, as if he were as excited as she was. What was this under her hands which was square and made of iron and which her fingers found a hole in?

It was the lock of the door which had been closed ten years and she put her hand in her pocket, drew out the key and found it fitted the keyhole. She put the key in and turned it. It took two hands to do it, but it did turn.

And then she took a long breath and looked behind her up the long walk to see if anyone was coming. No one was coming. No one ever did come, it seemed, and she took another long breath, because she could not help it, and she held back the swinging curtain of ivy and pushed back the door which opened slowly—slowly.

Then she slipped through it, and shut it behind her, and stood with her back against it, looking about her and breathing quite fast with excitement, and wonder, and delight.

She was standing *inside* the secret garden.


## CHAPTER IX

## THE STRANGEST HOUSE ANY ONE EVER LIVED IN

It was the sweetest, most mysterious-looking place any one could imagine. The high walls which shut it in were covered with the leafless stems of climbing roses which were so thick that they were matted together. Mary Lennox knew they were roses because she had seen a great many roses in India. All the ground was covered with grass of a wintry brown and out of it grew clumps of bushes which were surely rose-bushes if they were alive. There were numbers of standard roses which had so spread their branches that they were like little trees. There were other trees in the garden, and one of the things which made the place look strangest and loveliest was that climbing roses had run all over them and swung down long tendrils which made light swaying curtains, and here and there they had caught at each other or at a far-reaching branch and had crept from one tree to another and made lovely bridges of themselves. There were neither leaves nor roses on them now and Mary did not know whether they were dead or alive, but their thin grey or brown branches and sprays looked like a sort of hazy mantle spreading over everything, walls, and trees, and even brown grass, where they had fallen from their fastenings and run along the ground. It was this hazy tangle from tree to tree which made it all look so mysterious.

Mary had thought it must be different from other gardens which had not been left all by themselves so long; and indeed it was different from any other place she had ever seen in her life.

"How still it is!" she whispered. "How still!"

Then she waited a moment and listened at the stillness. The robin, who had flown to his tree-top, was still as all the rest. He did not even flutter his wings; he sat without stirring, and looked at Mary.

"No wonder it is still," she whispered again. "I am the first person who has spoken in here for ten years."

She moved away from the door, stepping as softly as if she were afraid of awakening someone. She was glad that there was grass under her feet and that her steps made no sounds. She walked under one of the fairy-like grey arches between the trees and looked up at the sprays and tendrils which formed them.

"I wonder if they are all quite dead," she said. "Is it all a quite dead garden? I wish it wasn't."

If she had been Ben Weatherstaff she could have told whether the wood was alive by looking at it, but she could only see that there were only grey or brown sprays and branches and none showed any signs of even a tiny leaf-bud anywhere.

But she was *inside* the wonderful garden and she could come through the door under the ivy any time and she felt as if she had found a world all her own.

The sun was shining inside the four walls and the high arch of blue sky over this particular piece of Misselthwaite seemed even more brilliant and soft than it was over the moor. The robin flew down from his tree-top and hopped about or flew after her from one bush to another. He chirped a good deal and had a very busy air, as if he were showing her things. Everything was strange and silent and she seemed to be hundreds of miles away from any one, but somehow she did not feel lonely at all. All that troubled she was her wish that she knew whether all the roses were dead, or if perhaps some of them had lived and might put out leaves and buds as the weather got warmer. She did not want it to be a quite dead garden. If it were a quite alive garden, how wonderful it would be, and what thousands of roses would grow on every side!

Her skipping-rope had hung over her arm when she came in and after she had walked about for a while she thought she would skip round the whole garden, stopping when she wanted to look at things. There seemed to have been grass paths here and there, and in one or two corners there were alcoves of evergreen with stone seats or tall moss-covered flower urns in them.

As she came near the second of these alcoves she stopped skipping. There had once been a flower-bed in it, and she thought she saw something sticking out of the black earth—some sharp little pale green points. She remembered what Ben Weatherstaff had said and she knelt down to look at them.

"Yes, they are tiny growing things and they *might* be crocuses or snowdrops or daffodils," she whispered.

She bent very close to them and sniffed the fresh scent of the damp earth. She liked it very much.

"Perhaps there are some other ones coming up in other places," she said. "I will go all over the garden and look."

She did not skip, but walked. She went slowly and kept her eyes on the ground. She looked in the old border beds and among the grass, and after she had gone round, trying to miss nothing, she had found ever so many more sharp, pale green points, and she had become quite excited again.

"It isn't a quite dead garden," she cried out softly to herself. "Even if the roses are dead, there are other things alive."

She did not know anything about gardening, but the grass seemed so thick in some of the places where the green points were pushing their way through that she thought they did not seem to have room enough to grow. She searched about until she found a rather sharp piece of wood and knelt down and dug and weeded out the weeds and grass until she made nice little clear places around them.

"Now they look as if they could breathe," she said, after she had finished with the first ones. "I am going to do ever so many more. I'll do all I can see. If I haven't time today I can come tomorrow."

She went from place to place, and dug and weeded, and enjoyed herself so immensely that she was led on from bed to bed and into the grass under the trees. The exercise made her so warm that she first threw her coat off, and then her hat, and without knowing it she was smiling down on to the grass and the pale green points all the time.

The robin was tremendously busy. He was very much pleased to see gardening begun on his own estate. He had often wondered at Ben Weatherstaff. Where gardening is done all sorts of delightful things to eat are turned up with the soil. Now here was this new kind of creature who was not half Ben's size and yet had had the sense to come into his garden and begin at once.

Mistress Mary worked in her garden until it was time to go to her midday dinner. In fact, she was rather late in remembering, and when she put on her coat and hat, and picked up her skipping-rope, she could not believe that she had been working two or three hours. She had been actually happy all the time; and dozens and dozens of the tiny, pale green points were to be seen in cleared places, looking twice as cheerful as they had looked before when the grass and weeds had been smothering them.

"I shall come back this afternoon," she said, looking all round at her new kingdom, and speaking to the trees and the rose-bushes as if they heard her.

Then she ran lightly across the grass, pushed open the slow old door and slipped through it under the ivy. She had such red cheeks and such bright eyes and ate such a dinner that Martha was delighted.

"Two pieces of meat and two helpings of rice pudding!" she said. "Eh! Mother will be pleased when I tell her what the skipping-rope's done for you."

In the course of her digging with her pointed stick Mistress Mary had found herself digging up a sort of white root rather like an onion. She had put it back in its place and patted the earth carefully down on it and just now she wondered if Martha could tell her what it was.

"Martha," she said, "what are those white roots that look like onions?"

"They're bulbs," answered Martha. "Lots of spring flowers grow from them. The very little ones are snowdrops and crocuses and the big ones are narcissuses and jonquils. The biggest of all are lilies and purple flags. Eh! They are nice. Dickon's got a whole lot of them planted in our bit of garden."

"Does Dickon know all about them?" asked Mary, a new idea taking possession of her.

"Our Dickon can make a flower grow out of a brick walk. Mother says he just whispers things out of the ground."

"Do bulbs live a long time? Would they live years and years if no one helped them?" inquired Mary anxiously.

"They're things that help themselves," said Martha. "That's why poor folk can afford to have them. If you don't trouble them, most of them will work away underground for a lifetime and spread out and have little ones. There's a place in the park woods here where there's snowdrops by thousands. They're the prettiest sight in Yorkshire when the spring comes. No one knows when they were first planted."

"I wish the spring was here now," said Mary. "I want to see all the things that grow in England."

She had finished her dinner and gone to her favourite seat on the hearth-rug.

"I wish—I wish I had a little spade," she said.

"Whatever do you want a spade for?" asked Martha, laughing. "Are you going to take to digging? I must tell mother that, too."

Mary looked at the fire and pondered a little. She must be careful if she meant to keep her secret kingdom. She wasn't doing any harm, but if Mr. Craven found out about the open door he would be fearfully angry and get a new key and lock it up forevermore. She really could not bear that.

"This is such a big lonely place," she said slowly, as if she were turning matters over in her mind. "The house is lonely, and the park is lonely, and the gardens are lonely. So many places seem shut up. I never did many things in India, but there were more people to look at—natives and soldiers marching by—and sometimes bands playing, and my Ayah told me stories. There is no one to talk to here except you and Ben Weatherstaff. And you have to do your work and Ben Weatherstaff won't speak to me often. I thought if I had a little spade I could dig somewhere as he does, and I might make a little garden if he would give me some seeds."

Martha's face quite lighted up.

"There now!" she exclaimed, "if that wasn't one of the things mother said. She says, 'There's such a lot of room in that big place, why don't they give her a bit for herself, even if she doesn't plant nothing but parsley and radishes? She'd dig and rake away and be right down happy over it.' These were the very words she said."

"Were they?" said Mary. "How many things she knows, doesn't she?"

"Eh!" said Martha. "It's like she says: 'A woman that brings up twelve children learns something besides her A B C. Children are as good as arithmetic to set you finding out things.'"

"How much would a spade cost—a little one?" Mary asked.

"Well," was Martha's reflective answer, "At Thwaite village there's a shop and I saw little garden sets with a spade and a rake and a fork all tied together for two shillings. And they were stout enough to work with, too."

"I've got more than that in my purse," said Mary. "Mrs. Morrison gave me five shillings and Mrs. Medlock gave me some money from Mr. Craven."

"Did he remember you that much?" exclaimed Martha.

"Mrs. Medlock said I was to have a shilling a week to spend. She gives me one every Saturday. I didn't know what to spend it on."

"My word! That's riches," said Martha. "You can buy anything in the world that you want. The rent of our cottage is only one and threepence and it's like pulling eye-teeth to get it. Now I've just thought of something," putting her hands on her hips.

"What?" said Mary eagerly.

"In the shop at Thwaite they sell packages of flower-seeds for a penny each, and our Dickon he knows which the prettiest ones are and how to make them grow. He walks over to Thwaite many a day just for the fun of it. Do you know how to print letters?" suddenly.

"I know how to write," Mary answered.

Martha shook her head.

"Our Dickon can only read printing. If you could print we could write a letter to him and ask him to go and buy the garden tools and the seeds at the same time."

"Oh! You're a good girl!" Mary cried.

"You are, really! I didn't know you were so nice. I know I can print letters if I try. Let's ask Mrs. Medlock for a pen and ink and some paper."

"I've got some of my own," said Martha. "I bought them so I could print a bit of a letter to mother on a Sunday. I'll go and get it."

She ran out of the room, and Mary stood by the fire and twisted her thin little hands together with sheer pleasure.

"If I have a spade," she whispered, "I can make the earth nice and soft and dig up weeds. If I have seeds and can make flowers grow the garden won't be dead at all— it will come alive."

She did not go out again that afternoon because when Martha returned with her pen and ink and paper she was obliged to clear the table and carry the plates and dishes downstairs and when she got into the kitchen Mrs. Medlock was there and told her to do something, so Mary waited for what seemed to her a long time before she came back. Then it was a serious piece of work to write to Dickon. Mary had been taught very little because her governesses had disliked her too much to stay with her. She could not spell particularly well but she found that she could print letters when she tried. This was the letter Martha dictated to her:

"*My Dear Dickon:*
This comes hoping to find you well as it leaves me at present. Miss Mary has plenty of money and will you go to Thwaite and buy her some flower seeds and a set of garden tools to make a flower-bed. Pick the prettiest ones and easy to grow because she has never done it before and lived in India which is different. Give my love to mother and every one of you. Miss Mary is going to tell me a lot more so that on my next day out you can hear about elephants and camels and gentlemen going hunting lions and tigers.

"Your loving sister,
"Martha Phœbe Sowerby."


"We'll put the money in the envelope and I'll get the butcher's boy to take it in his cart. He's a great friend of Dickon's," said Martha.

"How shall I get the things when Dickon buys them?" asked Mary.

"He'll bring them to you himself. He'll like to walk over this way."

"Oh!" exclaimed Mary, "then I shall see him! I never thought I should see Dickon."

"Do you want to see him?" asked Martha suddenly, she had looked so pleased.

"Yes, I do. I never saw a boy foxes and crows loved. I want to see him very much."

Martha gave a little start, as if she suddenly remembered something.

"Now to think," she broke out, "to think of me forgetting that there; and I thought I was going to tell you first thing this morning. I asked mother—and she said she'd ask Mrs. Medlock herself."

"Do you mean—" Mary began.

"What I said Tuesday. Ask her if you might be driven over to our cottage some day and have a bit of mother's hot oat cake, and butter, and a glass of milk."

It seemed as if all the interesting things were happening in one day. To think of going over the moor in the daylight and when the sky was blue! To think of going into the cottage which held twelve children!

"Does she think Mrs. Medlock would let me go?" she asked, quite anxiously.

"Aye, she thinks she would. She knows what a tidy woman mother is and how clean she keeps the cottage."

"If I went I should see your mother as well as Dickon," said Mary, thinking it over and liking the idea very much. "She doesn't seem to be like the mothers in India."

Her work in the garden and the excitement of the afternoon ended by making her feel quiet and thoughtful. Martha stayed with her until tea time, but they sat in comfortable quiet and talked very little. But just before Martha went downstairs for the tea tray, Mary asked a question.

"Martha," she said, "has the scullery-maid had the toothache again today?"

Martha certainly started slightly.

"What makes you ask that?" she said.

"Because when I waited so long for you to come back I opened the door and walked down the corridor to see if you were coming. And I heard that far-off crying again, just as we heard it the other night. There isn't a wind today, so you see it couldn't have been the wind."

"Eh!" said Martha restlessly. "You mustn't go walking about in corridors and listening. Mr. Craven would be that angry there's no knowing what he'd do."

"I wasn't listening," said Mary. "I was just waiting for you—and I heard it. That's three times."

"My word! There's Mrs. Medlock's bell," said Martha, and she almost ran out of the room.

"It's the strangest house any one ever lived in," said Mary drowsily, as she dropped her head on the cushioned seat of the armchair near her. Fresh air, and digging, and skipping rope had made her feel so comfortably tired that she fell asleep.

## CHAPTER X

## DICKON

The sun shone down for nearly a week on the secret garden. The Secret Garden was what Mary called it when she was thinking of it. She liked the name, and she liked still more the feeling that when its beautiful old walls shut her in no one knew where she was. It seemed almost like being shut out of the world in some fairy place. The few books she had read and liked had been fairy story books, and she had read of secret gardens in some of the stories. Sometimes people went to sleep in them for a hundred years, which she had thought must be rather stupid. She had no intention of going to sleep, and, in fact, she was becoming wider awake every day which passed at Misselthwaite. She was beginning to like to be out of doors; she no longer hated the wind, but enjoyed it. She could run faster, and longer, and she could skip up to a hundred. The bulbs in the secret garden must have been much astonished. Such nice clear places were made round them that they had all the breathing space they wanted, and really, if Mistress Mary had known it, they began to cheer up under the dark earth and work tremendously. The sun could get at them and warm them, and when the rain came down it could reach them at once, so they began to feel very much alive.

Mary was an odd, determined little person, and now she had something interesting to be determined about, she was very much absorbed, indeed. She worked and dug and pulled up weeds steadily, only becoming more pleased with her work every hour instead of tiring of it. It seemed to her like a fascinating sort of play. She found many more of the sprouting pale green points than she had ever hoped to find. They seemed to be starting up everywhere and each day she was sure she found tiny new ones, some so tiny that they barely peeped above the earth. There were so many that she remembered what Martha had said about the "snowdrops by the thousands," and about bulbs spreading and making new ones. These had been left to themselves for ten years and perhaps they had spread, like the snowdrops, into thousands. She wondered how long it would be before they showed that they were flowers. Sometimes she stopped digging to look at the garden and try to imagine what it would be like when it was covered with thousands of lovely things in bloom.

During that week of sunshine, she became more intimate with Ben Weatherstaff. She surprised him several times by seeming to start up beside him as if she sprang out of the earth. The truth was that she was afraid that he would pick up his tools and go away if he saw her coming, so she always walked toward him as silently as possible. But, in fact, he did not object to her as strongly as he had at first. Perhaps he was secretly rather flattered by her evident desire for his elderly company. Then, also, she was more civil than she had been. He did not know that when she first saw him she spoke to him as she would have spoken to a native, and had not known that a cross, sturdy old Yorkshire man was not accustomed to salaam to his masters, and be merely commanded by them to do things.

"You're like the robin," he said to her one morning when he lifted his head and saw her standing by him. "I never know when I shall see you or which side you'll come from."

"He's friends with me now," said Mary.

"That's like him," snapped Ben Weatherstaff. "Making up to the women folk just for vanity and flightiness. There's nothing he wouldn't do for the sake of showing off and flirting his tail-feathers. He's as full of pride as an egg's full of meat."

He very seldom talked much and sometimes did not even answer Mary's questions except by a grunt, but this morning he said more than usual. He stood up and rested one hobnailed boot on the top of his spade while he looked her over.

"How long have you been here?" he jerked out.

"I think it's about a month," she answered.

"You're beginning to do Misselthwaite credit," he said. "You're a bit fatter than you were and less pale. You looked like a young plucked crow when you first came into this garden. Was thinking to myself I had never set eyes on an uglier, sourer faced young one."

Mary was not vain and as she had never thought much of her looks she was not greatly disturbed.

"I know I'm fatter," she said. "My stockings are getting tighter. They used to make wrinkles. There's the robin, Ben Weatherstaff."

There, indeed, was the robin, and she thought he looked nicer than ever. His red waistcoat was as glossy as satin and he flirted his wings and tail and tilted his head and hopped about with all sorts of lively graces. He seemed determined to make Ben Weatherstaff admire him. But Ben was sarcastic.

"Aye, there you are!" he said. "You can put up with me for a bit sometimes when you got no one better. You've been reddening up your waistcoat and polishing your feathers these two weeks. I know what you're up to. You're courting some bold young madam somewhere, telling your lies to her about being the finest cock robin on Missel Moor and ready to fight all the rest of them."

"Oh! Look at him!" exclaimed Mary.

The robin was evidently in a fascinating, bold mood. He hopped closer and closer and looked at Ben Weatherstaff more and more engagingly. He flew on to the nearest currant bush and tilted his head and sang a little song right at him.

"Do you thinks you'll get over me by doing that," said Ben, wrinkling his face up in such a way that Mary felt sure he was trying not to look pleased. "You thinks no one can stand out against you —that's what you think."

The robin spread his wings—Mary could scarcely believe her eyes. He flew right up to the handle of Ben Weatherstaff's spade and alighted on the top of it. Then the old man's face wrinkled itself slowly into a new expression. He stood still as if he were afraid to breathe—as if he would not have stirred for the world, lest his robin should start away. He spoke quite in a whisper.

"Well, I'll be dammed!" he said as softly as if he were saying something quite different. "You do know how to get at a chap—don't you? You're fair unearthly, you're so knowing."

And he stood without stirring—almost without drawing his breath—until the robin gave another flirt to his wings and flew away. Then he stood looking at the handle of the spade as if there might be Magic in it, and then he began to dig again and said nothing for several minutes.

But because he kept breaking into a slow grin now and then, Mary was not afraid to talk to him.

"Have you a garden of your own?" she asked.

"No. I'm a bachelor and lodge with Martin at the gate."

"If you had one," said Mary, "what would you plant?"

"Cabbages and potatoes and onions."

"But if you wanted to make a flower garden," persisted Mary, "what would you plant?"

"Bulbs and sweet-smelling things—but mostly roses."

Mary's face lighted up.

"Do you like roses?" she said.

Ben Weatherstaff rooted up a weed and threw it aside before he answered.

"Well, yes, I do. I learned that from a young lady I was gardener to. She had a lot in a place she was fond of, and she loved them like they were children—or robins. I've seen her bend over and kiss them." He dragged out another weed and scowled at it. "That was as much as ten years ago."

Where is she now?" asked Mary, much interested.

"Heaven," he answered, and drove his spade deep into the soil, "According to what people say."

"What happened to the roses?" Mary asked again, more interested than ever.

"They were left to themselves."

Mary was becoming quite excited.

"Did they quite die? Do roses quite die when they are left to themselves?" she ventured.

"Well, I'd got to like them—and I liked her—and she liked them," Ben Weatherstaff admitted reluctantly. "Once or twice a year I'd go and work at them a bit—prune them and dig about the roots. They run wild, but they were in rich soil, so some of them lived."

"When they have no leaves and look grey and brown and dry, how you can tell whether they are dead or alive?" inquired Mary.

"Wait till the spring gets at them—wait till the sun shines and the rain falls and the sun shines and then you will find out."

"How—how?" cried Mary, forgetting to be careful.

"Look along the twigs and branches and if you see a bit of a brown lump swelling here and there, watch it after the warm rain and see what happens." He stopped suddenly and looked curiously at her eager face. "Why do you care so much about roses and such, all of a sudden?" he demanded.

Mistress Mary felt her face grow red. She was almost afraid to answer.

"I—I want to play that—that I have a garden of my own," she stammered. "I—there is nothing for me to do. I have nothing—and no one."

"Well," said Ben Weatherstaff slowly, as he watched her, "that's true. You haven't."

He said it in such an odd way that Mary wondered if he was actually a little sorry for her. She had never felt sorry for herself; she had only felt tired and cross, because she disliked people and things so much. But now the world seemed to be changing and getting nicer. If no one found out about the secret garden, she should enjoy herself always.

She stayed with him for ten or fifteen minutes longer and asked him as many questions as she dared. He answered every one of them in his queer grunting way and he did not seem really cross and did not pick up his spade and leave her.

He said something about roses just as she was going away and it reminded her of the ones he had said he had been fond of.

"Do you go and see those other roses now?" she asked.

"Not been this year. My rheumatism has made me too stiff in the joints."

He said it in his grumbling voice, and then quite suddenly he seemed to get angry with her, though she did not see why he should.

"Now look here!" he said sharply. "Don't ask so many questions. You're the worst wench for asking questions I've ever come across. Go and play. I'm done talking for today."

And he said it so crossly that she knew there was not the least use in staying another minute. She went skipping slowly down the outside walk, thinking him over and saying to herself that, queer as it was, here was another person whom she liked in spite of his crossness. She liked old Ben Weatherstaff. Yes, she did like him. She always wanted to try to make him talk to her. Also she began to believe that he knew everything in the world about flowers.

There was a laurel-hedged walk which curved round the secret garden and ended at a gate which opened into a wood, in the park. She thought she would skip round this walk and look into the wood and see if there were any rabbits hopping about. She enjoyed the skipping very much and when she reached the little gate she opened it and went through because she heard a low, peculiar whistling sound and wanted to find out what it was.

It was a very strange thing indeed. She quite caught her breath as she stopped to look at it. A boy was sitting under a tree, with his back against it, playing on a rough wooden pipe. He was a funny looking boy about twelve. He looked very clean and his nose turned up and his cheeks were as red as poppies and never had Mistress Mary seen such round and such blue eyes in any boy's face. And on the trunk of the tree he leaned against, a brown squirrel was clinging and watching him, and from behind a bush nearby a cock pheasant was delicately stretching his neck to peep out, and quite near him were two rabbits sitting up and sniffing with tremulous noses— and actually it appeared as if they were all drawing near to watch him and listen to the strange low little call his pipe seemed to make.

When he saw Mary he held up his hand and spoke to her in a voice almost as low as and rather like his piping.

"Don't move," he said. "It'd frighten them."

Mary remained motionless. He stopped playing his pipe and began to rise from the ground. He moved so slowly that it scarcely seemed as though he were moving at all, but at last he stood on his feet and then the squirrel scampered back up into the branches of his tree, the pheasant withdrew his head and the rabbits dropped on all fours and began to hop away, though not at all as if they were frightened.

"I'm Dickon," the boy said. "I know you're Miss Mary."

Then Mary realized that somehow she had known at first that he was Dickon. Who else could have been charming rabbits and pheasants as the natives charm snakes in India? He had a wide, red, curving mouth and his smile spread all over his face.

"I got up slow," he explained, "because if you make a quick move it startles them. A body has to move gentle and speak low when wild things are about."

He did not speak to her as if they had never seen each other before but as if he knew her quite well. Mary knew nothing about boys and she spoke to him a little stiffly because she felt rather shy.

"Did you get Martha's letter?" she asked.

He nodded his curly, rust-coloured head.

"That's why I come."

He stooped to pick up something which had been lying on the ground beside him when he piped.

"I've got the garden tools. There's a little spade and rake and a fork and hoe. Eh! They are good ones. There's a trowel, too. And the woman in the shop threw in a packet of white poppy and one of blue larkspur when I bought the other seeds."

"Will you show the seeds to me?" Mary said.

She wished she could talk as he did. His speech was so quick and easy. It sounded as if he liked her and was not the least afraid she would not like him, though he was only a common moor boy, in patched clothes and with a funny face and a rough, rusty-red head. As she came closer to him she noticed that there was a clean fresh scent of heather and grass and leaves about him, almost as if he were made of them. She liked it very much and when she looked into his funny face with the red cheeks and round blue eyes she forgot that she had felt shy.

"Let us sit down on this log and look at them," she said.

They sat down and he took a clumsy little brown paper package out of his coat pocket. He untied the string and inside there were ever so many neater and smaller packages with a picture of a flower on each one.

"There're a lot of mignonette and poppies," he said. "Mignonette's the sweetest smelling thing as grows, and it'll grow wherever you cast it, same as poppies will. They will come up and bloom if you just whistle to them, they're the nicest of all."

He stopped and turned his head quickly, his poppy-cheeked face lighting up.

"Where's that robin that is calling us?" he said.

The chirp came from a thick holly bush, bright with scarlet berries, and Mary thought she knew whose it was.

"Is it really calling us?" she asked.

"Aye," said Dickon, as if it was the most natural thing in the world, "he's calling someone he's friends with. That's the same as saying 'Here I am. Look at me. I want a bit of a chat.' There he is in the bush. Whose is he?"

"He's Ben Weatherstaff's, but I think he knows me a little," answered Mary.

"Aye, he knows you," said Dickon in his low voice again. "And he likes you. He's taken you on. He'll tell me all about you in a minute."

He moved quite close to the bush with the slow movement Mary had noticed before, and then he made a sound almost like the robin's own twitter. The robin listened a few seconds, intently, and then answered quite as if he were replying to a question.

"Aye, he's a friend of yours," chuckled Dickon.

"Do you think he is?" cried Mary eagerly. She did so want to know. "Do you think he really likes me?"

"He wouldn't come near you if he didn't," answered Dickon. "Birds are rare choosers and a robin can flout a body worse than a man. See, he's making up to you now. 'Can't you see a chap?' he's saying."

And it really seemed as if it must be true. He so sidled and twittered and tilted as he hopped on his bush.

"Do you understand everything birds say?" said Mary.

Dickon's grin spread until he seemed all wide, red, curving mouth, and he rubbed his rough head.

"I think I do, and they think I do," he said. "I've lived on the moor with them so long. I've watched them break shell and come out and fledge and learn to fly and begin to sing, till I think I'm one of them. Sometimes I think perhaps I'm a bird, or a fox, or a rabbit, or a squirrel, or even a beetle, and I don't know it."

He laughed and came back to the log and began to talk about the flower seeds again. He told her what they looked like when they were flowers; he told her how to plant them, and watch them, and feed and water them.

"See here," he said suddenly, turning round to look at her. "I'll plant them for you myself. Where is your garden?"

Mary's thin hands clutched each other as they lay on her lap. She did not know what to say, so for a whole minute she said nothing. She had never thought of this. She felt miserable. And she felt as if she went red and then pale.

"You've got a bit of garden, haven't you?" Dickon said.

It was true that she had turned red and then pale. Dickon saw her do it, and as she still said nothing, he began to be puzzled.

"Wouldn't they give you a bit?" he asked. "Haven't you got any yet?"

She held her hands even tighter and turned her eyes toward him.

"I don't know anything about boys," she said slowly. "Could you keep a secret, if I told you one? It's a great secret. I don't know what I should do if anyone found it out. I believe I should die!" She said the last sentence quite fiercely.

Dickon looked more puzzled than ever and even rubbed his hand over his rough head again, but he answered quite good-humouredly.

"I'm keeping secrets all the time," he said. "If I couldn't keep secrets from the other lads, secrets about foxes' cubs, and birds' nests, and wild things' holes, there'd be nothing safe on the moor. Aye, I can keep secrets."

Mistress Mary did not mean to put out her hand and clutch his sleeve but she did it.

"I've stolen a garden," she said very fast. "It isn't mine. It isn't anybody's. Nobody wants it, nobody cares for it, and nobody ever goes into it. Perhaps everything is dead in it already; I don't know."

She began to feel hot and as contrary as she had ever felt in her life.

"I don't care, I don't care! Nobody has any right to take it from me when I care about it and they don't. They're letting it die, all shut in by itself," she ended passionately, and she threw her arms over her face and burst out crying—poor little Mistress Mary.

Dickon's curious blue eyes grew rounder and rounder.

"Eh-h-h!" he said, drawing his exclamation out slowly, and the way he did it meant both wonder and sympathy.

"I've nothing to do," said Mary. "Nothing belongs to me. I found it myself and I got into it myself. I was only just like the robin, and they wouldn't take it from the robin."

"Where is it?" asked Dickon in a dropped voice.

Mistress Mary got up from the log at once. She knew she felt contrary again, and obstinate, and she did not care at all. She was imperious and Indian, and at the same time hot and sorrowful.

"Come with me and I'll show you," she said.

She led him round the laurel path and to the walk where the ivy grew so thickly. Dickon followed her with a queer, almost pitying, look on his face. He felt as if he were being led to look at some strange bird's nest and must move softly. When she stepped to the wall and lifted the hanging ivy he started. There was a door and Mary pushed it slowly open and they passed in together, and then Mary stood and waved her hand round defiantly.

"It's this," she said. "It's a secret garden, and I'm the only one in the world who wants it to be alive."

Dickon looked round and round about it, and round and round again.

"Eh!" he almost whispered, "it is a queer, pretty place! It's like as if a body was in a dream."

## CHAPTER XI

## THE NEST OF THE MISSEL THRUSH

For two or three minutes he stood looking round him, while Mary watched him, and then he began to walk about softly, even more lightly than Mary had walked the first time she had found herself inside the four walls. His eyes seemed to be taking in everything—the grey trees with the grey creepers climbing over them and hanging from their branches, the tangle on the walls and among the grass, the evergreen alcoves with the stone seats and tall flower urns standing in them.

"I never thought I'd see this place," he said at last, in a whisper.

"Did you know about it?" asked Mary.

She had spoken aloud and he made a sign to her.

"We must talk low," he said, "or someone'll hear us and wonder what's to do in here."

"Oh! I forgot!" said Mary, feeling frightened and putting her hand quickly against her mouth. "Did you know about the garden?" she asked again when she had recovered herself.

Dickon nodded.

"Martha told me there was one and no one ever went inside," he answered. "We used to wonder what it was like."

He stopped and looked round at the lovely grey tangle about him, and his round eyes looked queerly happy.

"Eh! The nests will be here come springtime," he said. "It'd be the safest nesting place in England. No one never coming near and tangles of trees and roses to build in. I wonder all the birds on the moor don't build here."

Mistress Mary put her hand on his arm again without knowing it.

"Will there be roses?" she whispered. "Can you tell? I thought perhaps they were all dead."

"Eh! No! Not them—not all of them!" he answered. "Look here!"

He stepped over to the nearest tree—an old, old one with grey lichen all over its bark, but upholding a curtain of tangled sprays and branches. He took a thick knife out of his pocket and opened one of its blades.

"There's lots of dead wood that ought to be cut out," he said. "And there's a lot of old wood, but it made some new last year. This here's a new bit," and he touched a shoot which looked brownish green instead of hard, dry grey.

Mary touched it herself in an eager, reverent way.

"That one?" she said. "Is that one quite alive—quite?"

Dickon curved his wide smiling mouth.

"It's as alive as you or me," he said.

"I'm glad it's alive!" she cried out in her whisper. "I want them all to live. Let us go round the garden and count how many live ones there are."

She quite panted with eagerness, and Dickon was as eager as she was. They went from tree to tree and from bush to bush. Dickon carried his knife in his hand and showed her things which she thought wonderful.

"They've run wild," he said, "but the strongest ones have fair thrived on it. The delicate ones have died out, but the others have grown and grown, and spread and spread, till they'd a wonder. See here!" and he pulled down a thick grey, dry-looking branch. "A body might think this was dead wood, but I don't believe it is—down to the root. I'll cut it low down and see."

He knelt and with his knife cut the lifeless-looking branch through, not far above the earth.

"There!" he said exultantly. "I told you so. There's green in that wood yet. Look at it."

Mary was down on her knees before he spoke, gazing with all her might.

"When it looks a bit greenish and juicy like that, it's alive," he explained. "When the inside is dry and breaks easy, like this piece I've cut off, it's done for. There's a big root here as all this live wood sprung out of, and if the old wood's cut off and it's dug round, an taken care of there'll be—" he stopped and lifted his face to look up at the climbing and hanging sprays above him—"there'll be a fountain of roses here this summer."

They went from bush to bush and from tree to tree. He was very strong and clever with his knife and knew how to cut the dry and dead wood away, and could tell when an unpromising bough or twig had still green life in it. In the course of half an hour Mary thought she could tell too, and when he cut through a lifeless-looking branch she would cry out joyfully under her breath when she caught sight of the least shade of moist green. The spade, and hoe, and fork were very useful. He showed her how to use the fork while he dug about roots with the spade and stirred the earth and let the air in.

They were working industriously round one of the biggest standard roses when he caught sight of something which made him utter an exclamation of surprise.

"Why!" he cried, pointing to the grass a few feet away. "Who did that there?"

It was one of Mary's own little clearings round the pale green points.

"I did it," said Mary.

"Why, I thought you didn't know nothing about gardening," he exclaimed.

"I don't," she answered, "but they were so little, and the grass was so thick and strong, and they looked as if they had no room to breathe. So I made a place for them. I don't even know what they are."

Dickon went and knelt down by them, smiling his wide smile.

"You were right," he said. "A gardener couldn't have told you better. They'll grow now like Jack's bean-stalk. They're crocuses and snowdrops, and these here are narcissuses," turning to another patch, "and here are daffodils. Eh! They will be a sight."

He ran from one clearing to another.

"You have done a lot of work for such a little wench," he said, looking her over.

"I'm growing fatter," said Mary, "and I'm growing stronger. I used always to be tired. When I dig I'm not tired at all. I like to smell the earth when it's turned up."

"It's good for you," he said, nodding his head wisely. "There's nothing as nice as the smell of good clean earth, except the smell of fresh growing things when the rain falls on them. I get out on the moor many a day when it's raining and I lie under a bush and listen to the soft swish of drops on the heather and I just sniff and sniff. My nose end quivers like a rabbit's, mother says."

"Do you never catch cold?" inquired Mary, gazing at him wonderingly. She had never seen such a funny boy, or such a nice one.

"Not me," he said, grinning. "I never caught a cold since I was born. I wasn't brought up posh enough. I've chased about the moor in all weathers same as the rabbits do.

Mother says I've sniffed up too much fresh air for twelve years to ever get to sniffing with cold. I'm as tough as a white-thorn knob stick."

He was working all the time he was talking and Mary was following him and helping him with her fork or the trowel.

"There's a lot of work to do here!" he said once, looking about quite exultantly.

"Will you come again and help me to do it?" Mary begged. "I'm sure I can help, too. I can dig and pull up weeds, and do whatever you tell me. Oh! Do come, Dickon!"

"I'll come every day if you want me, rain or shine," he answered stoutly. "It's the best fun I ever had in my life—shut in here and wakening up a garden."

"If you will come," said Mary, "if you will help me to make it alive I'll—I don't know what I'll do," she ended helplessly. What could you do for a boy like that?

"I'll tell you what you'll do," said Dickon, with his happy grin. "You'll get fat and you'll get as hungry as a young fox and you'll learn how to talk to the robin same as I do. Eh! We'll have a lot of fun."

He began to walk about, looking up in the trees and at the walls and bushes with a thoughtful expression.

"I wouldn't want to make it look like a gardener's garden, all clipped and spick and span, would you?" he said. "It's nicer like this with things running wild, and swinging and catching hold of each other."

"Don't let us make it tidy," said Mary anxiously. "It wouldn't seem like a secret garden if it was tidy."

Dickon stood rubbing his rusty-red head with a rather puzzled look.

"It's a secret garden sure enough," he said, "but seems like someone besides the robin must have been in it since it was shut up ten years ago."

"But the door was locked and the key was buried," said Mary. "No one could get in."

"That's true," he answered. "It's a queer place. Seems to me as if there'd been a bit of pruning done here and there, later than ten years ago."

"But how could it have been done?" said Mary.

He was examining a branch of a standard rose and he shook his head.

"Aye! How could it!" he murmured. "With the door locked and the key buried."

Mistress Mary always felt that however many years she lived she should never forget that first morning when her garden began to grow. Of course, it did seem to begin to grow for her that morning. When Dickon began to clear places to plant seeds, she remembered what Basil had sung at her when he wanted to tease her.

"Are there any flowers that look like bells?" she inquired.

"Lilies of the valley does," he answered, digging away with the trowel, "and there's Canterbury bells, and campanulas."

"Let us plant some," said Mary.

"There are lilies of the valley here already; I saw them. They'll have grown too close and we'll have to separate them, but there are plenty. The other ones take two years to bloom from seed, but I can bring you some bits of plants from our cottage garden. Why do you want them?"

Then Mary told him about Basil and his brothers and sisters in India and of how she had hated them and of their calling her "Mistress Mary Quite Contrary."

"They used to dance round and sing at me. They sang—

'Mistress Mary, quite contrary,

How does your garden grow?

With silver bells, and cockle shells,

And marigolds all in a row.'

I just remembered it and it made me wonder if there were really flowers like silver bells."

She frowned a little and gave her trowel a rather spiteful dig into the earth.

"I wasn't as contrary as they were."

But Dickon laughed.

"Eh!" he said, and as he crumbled the rich black soil she saw he was sniffing up the scent of it, "there doesn't seem to be a need for anyone to be contrary when there're flowers and alike, and lots of friendly wild things running about making homes for themselves, or building nests and singing and whistling, does there?"

Mary, kneeling by him holding the seeds, looked at him and stopped frowning.

"Dickon," she said. "You are as nice as Martha said you were. I like you, and you make the fifth person. I never thought I should like five people."

Dickon sat up on his heels as Martha did when she was polishing the grate. He did look funny and delightful, Mary thought, with his round blue eyes and red cheeks and happy looking turned-up nose.

"Only five folk you like?" he said. "Who are the other four?"

"Your mother and Martha," Mary checked them off on her fingers, "and the robin and Ben Weatherstaff."

Dickon laughed so that he was obliged to stifle the sound by putting his arm over his mouth.

"I know you think I'm a queer lad," he said, "but I think you are the queerest little lass I ever saw."

Then Mary did a strange thing. She leaned forward and asked him a question she had never dreamed of asking anyone before.

"Do you like me?" she said.

"Eh!" he answered heartily, "that I do. I like you wonderful, and so does the robin, I do believe!"

"That's two, then," said Mary. "That's two for me."

And then they began to work harder than ever and more joyfully. Mary was startled and sorry when she heard the big clock in the courtyard strike the hour of her midday dinner.

"I shall have to go," she said mournfully. "And you will have to go too, won't you?"

Dickon grinned.

"My dinner's easy to carry about with me," he said. "Mother always lets me put a bit of something in my pocket."

He picked up his coat from the grass and brought out of a pocket a lumpy little bundle tied up in a quiet clean, coarse, blue and white handkerchief. It held two thick pieces of bread with a slice of something laid between them.

"It's often nothing but bread," he said, "but I've got a fine slice of fat bacon with it today."

Mary thought it looked a queer dinner, but he seemed ready to enjoy it.

"Run on and get your meal," he said. "I'll be done with mine first. I'll get some more work done before I start back home."

He sat down with his back against a tree.

"I'll call the robin up," he said, "and give him the rind of the bacon to peck at. They like a bit of fat wonderful."

Mary could scarcely bear to leave him. Suddenly it seemed as if he might be a sort of wood fairy who might be gone when she came into the garden again. He seemed too good to be true. She went slowly half-way to the door in the wall and then she stopped and went back.

"Whatever happens, you—you never would tell?" she said.

His poppy-coloured cheeks were distended with his first big bite of bread and bacon, but he managed to smile encouragingly.

"If you were a missel thrush and showed me where your nest was, do you think I'd tell anyone? Not me," he said. "You are as safe as a missel thrush."

And she was quite sure she was.

## CHAPTER XII

### "MIGHT I HAVE A BIT OF EARTH?"

Mary ran so fast that she was rather out of breath when she reached her room. Her hair was ruffled on her forehead and her cheeks were bright pink. Her dinner was waiting on the table, and Martha was waiting near it.

"You're a bit late," she said. "Where have you been?"

"I've seen Dickon!" said Mary. "I've seen Dickon!"

"I knew he'd come," said Martha exultantly. "How do you like him?"

"I think—I think he's beautiful!" said Mary in a determined voice.

Martha looked rather taken aback but she looked pleased, too.

"Well," she said, "he's the best lad that has ever was born, but we never thought he was handsome. His nose turns up too much."

"I like it to turn up," said Mary.

"And his eyes are so round," said Martha, a trifle doubtful. "Though they're a nice colour."

"I like them round," said Mary. "And they are exactly the colour of the sky over the moor."

Martha beamed with satisfaction.

"Mother says he made them that colour with always looking up at the birds and the clouds. But he has got a big mouth, hasn't he, now?"

"I love his big mouth," said Mary obstinately. "I wish mine were just like it."

Martha chuckled delightedly.

"It'd look rare and funny in your bit of a face," she said. "But I know it would be that way when you saw him. How did you like the seeds and the garden tools?"

"How did you know he brought them?" asked Mary.

"Eh! I never thought of him not bringing them. He'd be sure to bring them if they were in Yorkshire. He's such a trusty lad."

Mary was afraid that she might begin to ask difficult questions, but she did not. She was very much interested in the seeds and gardening tools, and there was only one moment when Mary was frightened. This was when she began to ask where the flowers were to be planted.

"Who did you ask about it?" she inquired.

"I haven't asked anybody yet," said Mary, hesitating.

"Well, I wouldn't ask the head gardener. He's too grand, Mr. Roach is."

"I've never seen him," said Mary. "I've only seen under-gardeners and Ben Weatherstaff."

"If I were you, I'd ask Ben Weatherstaff," advised Martha. "He's not half as bad as he looks, for all he's so crabbed. Mr. Craven lets him do what he likes because he was here when Mrs. Craven was alive, and he used to make her laugh. She liked him. Perhaps he'd find you a corner somewhere out of the way."

"If it was out of the way and no one wanted it, no one *could* mind my having it, could they?" Mary said anxiously.

"There would be no reason," answered Martha. "You wouldn't do no harm."

Mary ate her dinner as quickly as she could and when she rose from the table she was going to run to her room to put on her hat again, but Martha stopped her.

"I've got something to tell you," she said. "I thought I'd let you eat your dinner first. Mr. Craven came back this morning and I think he wants to see you."

Mary turned quite pale.

"Oh!" she said. "Why! Why! He didn't want to see me when I came. I heard Pitcher say he didn't."

"Well," explained Martha, "Mrs. Medlock says it's because of mother. She was walking to Thwaite village and she met him. She'd never spoken to him before, but Mrs. Craven had been to our cottage two or three times. He'd forgotten, but mother hadn't and she made bold to stop him. I don't know what she said to him about you but she said something that put him in the mind to see you before he goes away again, tomorrow."

"Oh!" cried Mary, "is he going away tomorrow? I am so glad!"

"He's going for a long time. He may not come back till autumn or winter. He's going to travel in foreign places. He's always doing it."

"Oh! I'm so glad—so glad!" said Mary thankfully.

If he did not come back until winter, or even autumn, there would be time to watch the secret garden come alive. Even if he found out then and took it away from her she would have had that much at least.

"When do you think he will want to see—"

She did not finish the sentence, because the door opened, and Mrs. Medlock walked in. She had on her best black dress and cap, and her collar was fastened with a large brooch with a picture of a man's face on it. It was a coloured photograph of Mr. Medlock who had died years ago, and she always wore it when she was dressed up. She looked nervous and excited.

"Your hair's rough," she said quickly. "Go and brush it. Martha, help her to slip on her best dress. Mr. Craven sent me to bring her to him in his study."

All the pink left Mary's cheeks. Her heart began to thump and she felt herself changing into a stiff, plain, silent child again. She did not even answer Mrs. Medlock, but turned and walked into her bedroom, followed by Martha. She said nothing while her dress was changed, and her hair brushed, and after she was quite tidy she followed Mrs. Medlock down the corridors, in silence. What was there for her to say? She was obliged to go and see Mr. Craven and he would not like her, and she would not like him. She knew what he would think of her.

She was taken to a part of the house she had not been into before. At last Mrs. Medlock knocked at a door, and when someone said, "Come in," they entered the room together. A man was sitting in an armchair before the fire, and Mrs. Medlock spoke to him.

"This is Miss Mary, sir," she said.

"You can go and leave her here. I will ring for you when I want you to take her away," said Mr. Craven.

When she went out and closed the door, Mary could only stand waiting, a plain little thing, twisting her thin hands together. She could see that the man in the chair was not so much a hunchback as a man with high, rather crooked shoulders, and he had black hair streaked with white. He turned his head over his high shoulders and spoke to her.

"Come here!" he said.

Mary went to him.

He was not ugly. His face would have been handsome if it had not been so miserable. He looked as if the sight of her worried and fretted him and as if he did not know what in the world to do with her.

"Are you well?" he asked.

"Yes," answered Mary.

"Do they take good care of you?"

"Yes."

He rubbed his forehead fretfully as he looked her over.

"You are very thin," he said.

"I am getting fatter," Mary answered in what she knew was her stiffest way.

What an unhappy face he had! His black eyes seemed as if they scarcely saw her, as if they were seeing something else, and he could hardly keep his thoughts upon her.

"I forgot you," he said. "How could I remember you? I intended to send you a governess or a nurse, or someone of that sort, but I forgot."

"Please," began Mary. "Please—" and then the lump in her throat choked her.

"What do you want to say?" he inquired.

"I am—I am too big for a nurse," said Mary. "And please—please don't make me have a governess yet."

He rubbed his forehead again and stared at her.

"That was what the Sowerby woman said," he muttered absent-mindedly.

Then Mary gathered a scrap of courage.

"Is she—is she Martha's mother?" she stammered.

"Yes, I think so," he replied.

"She knows about children," said Mary. "She has twelve. She knows."

He seemed to rouse himself.

"What do you want to do?"

"I want to play out of doors," Mary answered, hoping that her voice did not tremble. "I never liked it in India. It makes me hungry here, and I am getting fatter."

He was watching her.

"Mrs. Sowerby said it would do you good. Perhaps it will," he said. "She thought you had better get stronger before you had a governess."

"It makes me feel strong when I play and the wind comes over the moor," argued Mary.

"Where do you play?" he asked next.

"Everywhere," gasped Mary. "Martha's mother sent me a skipping-rope. I skip and run—and I look about to see if things are beginning to stick up out of the earth. I don't do any harm."

"Don't look so frightened," he said in a worried voice. "You could not do any harm, a child like you! You may do what you like."

Mary put her hand up to her throat because she was afraid he might see the excited lump which she felt jump into it. She came a step nearer to him.

"May I?" she said tremulously.

Her anxious little face seemed to worry him more than ever.

"Don't look so frightened," he exclaimed. "Of course you may. I am your guardian, though I am a poor one for any child. I cannot give you time or attention. I am too ill, and wretched and distracted; but I wish you to be happy and comfortable. I don't know anything about children, but Mrs. Medlock is to see that you have all you need. I sent for you today because Mrs. Sowerby said I ought to see you. Her daughter had talked about you. She thought you needed fresh air and freedom and running about."

"She knows all about children," Mary said again in spite of herself.

"She ought to," said Mr. Craven. "I thought her rather bold to stop me on the moor, but she said—Mrs. Craven had been kind to her." It seemed hard for him to speak his dead wife's name. "She is a respectable woman. Now I have seen you I think she said sensible things. Play out of doors as much as you like. It's a big place and you may go where you like and amuse yourself as you like. Is there anything you want?" as if a sudden thought had struck him. "Do you want toys, books, dolls?"

"Might I," quavered Mary, "might I have a bit of earth?"

In her eagerness she did not realize how queer the words would sound and that they were not the ones she had meant to say. Mr. Craven looked quite startled.

"Earth!" he repeated. "What do you mean?"

"To plant seeds in—to make things grow—to see them come alive," Mary faltered.

He gazed at her a moment and then passed his hand quickly over his eyes.

"Do you—care about gardens so much," he said slowly.

"I didn't know about them in India," said Mary. "I was always ill and tired and it was too hot. I sometimes made little beds in the sand and stuck flowers in them. But here it is different."

Mr. Craven got up and began to walk slowly across the room.

"A bit of earth," he said to himself, and Mary thought that somehow she must have reminded him of something. When he stopped and spoke to her his dark eyes looked almost soft and kind.

"You can have as much earth as you want," he said. "You remind me of someone else who loved the earth and things that grow. When you see a bit of earth you want," with something like a smile, "take it, child, and make it come alive."

"May I take it from anywhere—if it's not wanted?"

"Anywhere," he answered. "There! You must go now, I am tired." He touched the bell to call Mrs. Medlock. "Good-bye. I shall be away all summer."

Mrs. Medlock came so quickly that Mary thought she must have been waiting in the corridor.

"Mrs. Medlock," Mr. Craven said to her, "now I have seen the child I understand what Mrs. Sowerby meant. She must be less delicate before she begins lessons. Give her simple, healthy food. Let her run wild in the garden. Don't look after her too much. She needs liberty and fresh air and romping about. Mrs. Sowerby is to come and see her now and then and she may sometimes go to the cottage."

Mrs. Medlock looked pleased. She was relieved to hear that she need not "look after" Mary too much. She had felt her a tiresome charge and had indeed seen as little of her as she dared. In addition to this she was fond of Martha's mother.

"Thank you, sir," she said. "Susan Sowerby and me went to school together and she's as sensible and good-hearted a woman as you'd find in a day's walk. I never had any children myself and she's had twelve, and there never were healthier or better ones. Miss Mary can get no harm from them. I'd always take Susan Sowerby's advice about children myself. She's what you might call healthy-minded—if you understand me."

"I understand," Mr. Craven answered. "Take Miss Mary away now and send Pitcher to me."

When Mrs. Medlock left her at the end of her own corridor Mary flew back to her room. She found Martha waiting there. Martha had, in fact, hurried back after she had removed the dinner service.

"I can have my garden!" cried Mary. "I may have it where I like! I am not going to have a governess for a long time! Your mother is coming to see me and I may go to your cottage! He says a little girl like me could not do any harm and I may do what I like—anywhere!"

"Eh!" said Martha delightedly, "that was nice of him wasn't it?"

"Martha," said Mary solemnly, "he is really a nice man, only his face is so miserable and his forehead is all drawn together."

She ran as quickly as she could to the garden. She had been away so much longer than she had thought she should and she knew Dickon would have to set out early on his five-mile walk. When she slipped through the door under the ivy, she saw he was not working where she had left him. The gardening tools were laid together under a tree. She ran to them, looking all round the place, but there was no Dickon to be seen. He had gone away and the secret garden was empty—except for the robin who had just flown across the wall and sat on a standard rose-bush watching her.

"He's gone," she said woefully. "Oh! Was he—was he—was he only a wood fairy?"

Something white fastened to the standard rose-bush caught her eye. It was a piece of paper—in fact, it was a piece of the letter she had printed for Martha to send to Dickon. It was fastened on the bush with a long thorn, and in a minute she knew Dickon had left it there. There were some roughly printed letters on it and a sort of picture. At first she could not tell what it was. Then she saw it was meant for a nest with a bird sitting on it. Underneath were the printed letters and they said:

"I will come back."

## CHAPTER XIII

## "I AM COLIN"

Mary took the picture back to the house when she went to her supper and she showed it to Martha.

"Eh!" said Martha with great pride. "I never knew our Dickon was as clever as that. That there's a picture of a missel thrush on her nest, as large as life and twice as natural."

Then Mary knew Dickon had meant the picture to be a message. He had meant that she might be sure he would keep her secret. Her garden was her nest and she was like a missel thrush. Oh, how she did like that queer, common boy!

She hoped he would come back the very next day and she fell asleep looking forward to the morning.

But you never know what the weather will do in Yorkshire, particularly in the springtime. She was awakened in the night by the sound of rain beating with heavy drops against her window. It was pouring down in torrents and the wind was "wuthering" round the corners and in the chimneys of the huge old house. Mary sat up in bed and felt miserable and angry.

"The rain is as contrary as I ever was," she said. "It came because it knew I did not want it."

She threw herself back on her pillow and buried her face. She did not cry, but she lay and hated the sound of the heavily beating rain, she hated the wind and its "wuthering." She could not go to sleep again. The mournful sound kept her awake because she felt mournful herself. If she had felt happy it would probably have lulled her to sleep. How it "wuthered" and how the big rain-drops poured down and beat against the pane!

"It sounds just like a person lost on the moor and wandering on and on crying," she said.

She had been lying awake turning from side to side for about an hour, when suddenly something made her sit up in bed and turn her head toward the door listening. She listened and she listened.

"It isn't the wind now," she said in a loud whisper. "That isn't the wind. It is different. It is that crying I heard before."

The door of her room was ajar and the sound came down the corridor, a far-off faint sound of fretful crying. She listened for a few minutes and each minute she became more and surer. She felt as if she must find out what it was. It seemed even stranger than the secret garden and the buried key. Perhaps the fact that she was in a rebellious mood made her bold. She put her foot out of bed and stood on the floor.

"I am going to find out what it is," she said. "Everybody is in bed and I don't care about Mrs. Medlock—I don't care!"

There was a candle by her bedside and she took it up and went softly out of the room. The corridor looked very long and dark, but she was too excited to mind that. She thought she remembered the corners she must turn to find the short corridor with the door covered with tapestry—the one Mrs. Medlock had come through the day she lost herself. The sound had come up that passage. So she went on with her dim light, almost feeling her way, her heart beating so loud that she fancied she could hear it. The far-off faint crying went on and led her. Sometimes it stopped for a moment or so and then began again. Was this the right corner to turn? She stopped and thought. Yes it was. Down this passage and then to the left, and then up two broad steps, and then to the right again. Yes, there was the tapestry door.

She pushed it open very gently and closed it behind her, and she stood in the corridor and could hear the crying quite plainly, though it was not loud. It was on the other side of the wall at her left and a few yards farther on there was a door. She could see a glimmer of light coming from beneath it. Someone was crying in that room, and it was quite a young someone.

So she walked to the door and pushed it open, and there she was standing in the room!

It was a big room with ancient, handsome furniture in it. There was a low fire glowing faintly on the hearth and a night light burning by the side of a carved four-posted bed hung with brocade, and on the bed was lying a boy, crying fretfully.

Mary wondered if she was in a real place or if she had fallen asleep again and was dreaming without knowing it.

The boy had a sharp, delicate face the colour of ivory and he seemed to have eyes too big for it. He had also a lot of hair which tumbled over his forehead in heavy locks and made his thin face seem smaller. He looked like a boy who had been ill, but he was crying more as if he were tired and cross than as if he were in pain.

Mary stood near the door with her candle in her hand, holding her breath. Then she crept across the room, and as she drew nearer the light attracted the boy's attention and he turned his head on his pillow and stared at her, his grey eyes opening so wide that they seemed immense.

### "'WHO ARE YOU?—ARE YOU A GHOST?'"—

"Who are you?" he said at last in a half-frightened whisper. "Are you a ghost?"

"No, I am not," Mary answered, her own whisper sounding half frightened. "Are you one?"

He stared and stared and stared. Mary could not help noticing what strange eyes he had. They were agate grey and they looked too big for his face because they had black lashes all round them.

"No," he replied after waiting a moment or so. "I am Colin."

"Who is Colin?" she faltered.

"I am Colin Craven. Who are you?"

"I am Mary Lennox. Mr. Craven is my uncle."

"He is my father," said the boy.

"Your father!" gasped Mary. "No one ever told me he had a boy! Why didn't they?"

"Come here," he said, still keeping his strange eyes fixed on her with an anxious expression.

She came close to the bed and he put out his hand and touched her.

"You are real, aren't you?" he said. "I have such real dreams very often. You might be one of them."

Mary had slipped on a woollen wrapper before she left her room and she put a piece of it between his fingers.

"Rub that and see how thick and warm it is," she said. "I will pinch you a little if you like, to show you how real I am. For a minute I thought you might be a dream too."

"Where did you come from?" he asked.

"From my own room. The wind wuthered so I couldn't go to sleep and I heard someone crying and wanted to find out who it was. What were you crying for?"

"Because I couldn't go to sleep either and my head ached. Tell me your name again."

"Mary Lennox. Did no one ever tell you I had come to live here?"

He was still fingering the fold of her wrapper, but he began to look a little more as if he believed in her reality.

"No," he answered. "They daren't."

"Why?" asked Mary.

"Because I should have been afraid you would see me. I won't let people see me and talk me over."

"Why?" Mary asked again, feeling more mystified every moment.

"Because I am like this always, ill and having to lie down. My father won't let people talk me over either. The servants are not allowed to speak about me. If I live I may be a hunchback, but I shan't live. My father hates to think I may be like him."

"Oh, what a queer house this is!" Mary said. "What a queer house! Everything is a kind of secret. Rooms are locked up and gardens are locked up—and you! Have you been locked up?"

"No. I stay in this room because I don't want to be moved out of it. It tires me too much."

"Does your father come and see you?" Mary ventured.

"Sometimes. Generally when I am asleep. He doesn't want to see me."

"Why?" Mary could not help asking again.

A sort of angry shadow passed over the boy's face.

"My mother died when I was born and it makes him wretched to look at me. He thinks I don't know, but I've heard people talking. He almost hates me."

"He hates the garden, because she died," said Mary half speaking to herself.

"What garden?" the boy asked.

"Oh! Just—just a garden she used to like," Mary stammered. "Have you been here always?"

"Nearly always. Sometimes I have been taken to places at the seaside, but I won't stay because people stare at me. I used to wear an iron thing to keep my back straight, but a grand doctor came from London to see me and said it was stupid. He told them to take it off and keep me out in the fresh air. I hate fresh air and I don't want to go out."

"I didn't when first I came here," said Mary. "Why do you keep looking at me like that?"

"Because of the dreams that are so real," he answered rather fretfully. "Sometimes when I open my eyes I don't believe I'm awake."

"We're both awake," said Mary. She glanced round the room with its high ceiling and shadowy corners and dim firelight. "It looks quite like a dream, and it's the middle of the night, and everybody in the house is asleep—everybody but us. We are wide awake."

"I don't want it to be a dream," the boy said restlessly.

Mary thought of something all at once.

"If you don't like people to see you," she began, "do you want me to go away?"

He still held the fold of her wrapper and he gave it a little pull.

"No," he said. "I should be sure you were a dream if you went. If you are real, sit down on that big footstool and talk. I want to hear about you."

Mary put down her candle on the table near the bed and sat down on the cushioned stool. She did not want to go away at all. She wanted to stay in the mysterious hidden-away room and talk to the mysterious boy.

"What do you want me to tell you?" she said.

He wanted to know how long she had been at Misselthwaite; he wanted to know which corridor her room was on; he wanted to know what she had been doing; if she disliked the moor as he disliked it; where she had lived before she came to Yorkshire. She answered all these questions and many more and he lay back on his pillow and listened. He made her tell him a great deal about India and about her voyage across the ocean. She found out that because he had been an invalid he had not learned things as other children had. One of his nurses had taught him to read when he was quite little and he was always reading and looking at pictures in splendid books.

Though his father rarely saw him when he was awake, he was given all sorts of wonderful things to amuse himself with. He never seemed to have been amused, however. He could have anything he asked for and was never made to do anything he did not like to do.

"Everyone is obliged to do what pleases me," he said indifferently. "It makes me ill to be angry. No one believes I shall live to grow up."

He said it as if he was so accustomed to the idea that it had ceased to matter to him at all. He seemed to like the sound of Mary's voice. As she went on talking he listened in a drowsy, interested way. Once or twice she wondered if he were not gradually falling into a doze. But at last he asked a question which opened up a new subject.

"How old are you?" he asked.

"I am ten," answered Mary, forgetting herself for the moment, "and so are you."

"How do you know that?" he demanded in a surprised voice.

"Because when you were born the garden door was locked and the key was buried. And it has been locked for ten years."

Colin half sat up, turning toward her, leaning on his elbows.

"What garden door was locked? Who did it? Where was the key buried?" he exclaimed as if he were suddenly very much interested.

"It—it was the garden Mr. Craven hates," said Mary nervously. "He locked the door. No one—no one knew where he buried the key."

"What sort of a garden is it?" Colin persisted eagerly.

"No one has been allowed to go into it for ten years," was Mary's careful answer.

But it was too late to be careful. He was too much like herself. He too had had nothing to think about and the idea of a hidden garden attracted him as it had attracted her. He asked question after question. Where was it? Had she never looked for the door? Had she never asked the gardeners?

"They won't talk about it," said Mary. "I think they have been told not to answer questions."

"I would make them," said Colin.

"Could you?" Mary faltered, beginning to feel frightened. If he could make people answer questions, who knew what might happen!

"Everyone is obliged to please me. I told you that," he said. "If I were to live, this place would sometime belong to me. They all know that. I would make them tell me."

Mary had not known that she herself had been spoiled, but she could see quite plainly that this mysterious boy had been. He thought that the whole world belonged to him. How peculiar he was and how coolly he spoke of not living.

"Do you think you won't live?" she asked, partly because she was curious and partly in hope of making him forget the garden.

"I don't suppose I shall," he answered as indifferently as he had spoken before. "Ever since I remember anything I have heard people say I shan't. At first they thought I was too little to understand and now they think I don't hear. But I do. My doctor is my father's cousin. He is quite poor and if I die he will have all Misselthwaite when my father is dead. I should think he wouldn't want me to live."

"Do you want to live?" inquired Mary.

"No," he answered, in a cross, tired fashion. "But I don't want to die. When I feel ill I lie here and think about it until I cry and cry."

"I have heard you crying three times," Mary said, "but I did not know who it was. Were you crying about that?" She did so want him to forget the garden.

"I dare say," he answered. "Let us talk about something else. Talk about that garden. Don't you want to see it?"

"Yes," answered Mary, in quite a low voice.

"I do," he went on persistently. "I don't think I ever really wanted to see anything before, but I want to see that garden. I want the key dug up. I want the door unlocked. I would let them take me there in my chair. That would be getting fresh air. I am going to make them open the door."

He had become quite excited and his strange eyes began to shine like stars and looked more immense than ever.

"They have to please me," he said. "I will make them take me there and I will let you go, too."

Mary's hands clutched each other. Everything would be spoiled—everything! Dickon would never come back. She would never again feel like a missel thrush with a safe-hidden nest.

"Oh, don't—don't—don't—don't do that!" she cried out.

He stared as if he thought she had gone crazy!

"Why?" he exclaimed. "You said you wanted to see it."

"I do," she answered almost with a sob in her throat, "but if you make them open the door and take you in like that it will never be a secret again."

He leaned still farther forward.

"A secret," he said. "What do you mean? Tell me."

Mary's words almost tumbled over one another.

"You see—you see," she panted, "if no one knows but ourselves—if there was a door, hidden somewhere under the ivy—if there was—and we could find it; and if we could slip through it together and shut it behind us, and no one knew any one was inside and we called it our garden and pretended that—that we were missel thrushes and it was our nest, and if we played there almost every day and dug and planted seeds and made it all come alive—"

"Is it dead?" he interrupted her.

"It soon will be if no one cares for it," she went on. "The bulbs will live but the roses—"

He stopped her again as excited as she was herself.

"What are bulbs?" he put in quickly.

"They are daffodils and lilies and snowdrops. They are working in the earth now—pushing up pale green points because the spring is coming."

"Is the spring coming?" he said. "What is it like? You don't see it in rooms if you are ill."

"It is the sun shining on the rain and the rain falling on the sunshine, and things pushing up and working under the earth," said Mary. "If the garden was a secret and we could get into it we could watch the things grow bigger every day, and see how many roses are alive. Don't you see? Oh, don't you see how much nicer it would be if it was a secret?"

He dropped back on his pillow and lay there with an odd expression on his face.

"I never had a secret," he said, "except that one about not living to grow up. They don't know I know that, so it is a sort of secret. But I like this kind better."

"If you won't make them take you to the garden," pleaded Mary, "perhaps—I feel almost sure I can find out how to get in sometime. And then—if the doctor wants you to go out in your chair, and if you can always do what you want to do, perhaps—perhaps we might find some boy who would push you, and we could go alone and it would always be a secret garden."

"I should—like—that," he said very slowly, his eyes looking dreamy. "I should like that. I should not mind fresh air in a secret garden."

Mary began to recover her breath and feel safer because the idea of keeping the secret seemed to please him. She felt almost sure that if she kept on talking and could make him see the garden in his mind as she had seen it he would like it so much that he could not bear to think that everybody might tramp into it when they chose.

"I'll tell you what I *think* it would be like, if we could go into it," she said. "It has been shut up so long things have grown into a tangle perhaps."

He lay quite still and listened while she went on talking about the roses which *might* have clambered from tree to tree and hung down—about the many birds which *might* have built their nests there because it was so safe. And then she told him about the robin and Ben Weatherstaff, and there was so much to tell about the robin and it was so easy and safe to talk about it that she ceased to feel afraid. The robin pleased him so much that he smiled until he looked almost beautiful, and at first Mary had thought that he was even plainer than herself, with his big eyes and heavy locks of hair.

"I did not know birds could be like that," he said. "But if you stay in a room you never see things. What a lot of things you know. I feel as if you had been inside that garden."

She did not know what to say, so she did not say anything. He evidently did not expect an answer and the next moment he gave her a surprise.

"I am going to let you look at something," he said. "Do you see that rose-coloured silk curtain hanging on the wall over the mantel-piece?"

Mary had not noticed it before, but she looked up and saw it. It was a curtain of soft silk hanging over what seemed to be some picture.

"Yes," she answered.

"There is a cord hanging from it," said Colin. "Go and pull it."

Mary got up, much mystified, and found the cord. When she pulled it the silk curtain ran back on rings and when it ran back it uncovered a picture. It was the picture of a girl with a laughing face. She had bright hair tied up with a blue ribbon and her gay, lovely eyes were exactly like Colin's unhappy ones, agate grey and looking twice as big as they really were because of the black lashes all round them.

"She is my mother," said Colin complainingly. "I don't see why she died. Sometimes I hate her for doing it."

"How queer!" said Mary.

"If she had lived I believe I should not have been ill always," he grumbled. "I dare say I should have lived, too. And my father would not have hated to look at me. I dare say I should have had a strong back. Draw the curtain again."

Mary did as she was told and returned to her footstool.

"She is much prettier than you," she said, "but her eyes are just like yours—at least they are the same shape and colour. Why is the curtain drawn over her?"

He moved uncomfortably.

"I made them do it," he said. "Sometimes I don't like to see her looking at me. She smiles too much when I am ill and miserable. Besides, she is mine and I don't want everyone to see her."

There were a few moments of silence and then Mary spoke.

"What would Mrs. Medlock do if she found out that I had been here?" she inquired.

"She would do as I told her to do," he answered. "And I should tell her that I wanted you to come here and talk to me every day. I am glad you came."

"So am I," said Mary. "I will come as often as I can, but"—she hesitated—"I shall have to look every day for the garden door."

"Yes, you must," said Colin, "and you can tell me about it afterward."

He lay thinking a few minutes, as he had done before, and then he spoke again.

"I think you shall be a secret, too," he said. "I will not tell them until they find out. I can always send the nurse out of the room and say that I want to be by myself. Do you know Martha?"

"Yes, I know her very well," said Mary. "She waits on me."

He nodded his head toward the outer corridor.

"She is the one who is asleep in the other room. The nurse went away yesterday to stay all night with her sister and she always makes Martha attend to me when she wants to go out. Martha shall tell you when to come here."

Then Mary understood Martha's troubled look when she had asked questions about the crying.

"Martha knew about you all the time?" she said.

"Yes; she often attends to me. The nurse likes to get away from me and then Martha comes."

"I have been here a long time," said Mary. "Shall I go away now? Your eyes look sleepy."

"I wish I could go to sleep before you leave me," he said rather shyly.

"Shut your eyes," said Mary, drawing her footstool closer, "and I will do what my Ayah used to do in India. I will pat your hand and stroke it and sing something quite low."

"I should like that perhaps," he said drowsily.

Somehow she was sorry for him and did not want him to lie awake, so she leaned against the bed and began to stroke and pat his hand and sing a very low little chanting song in Hindustani.

"That is nice," he said more drowsily still, and she went on chanting and stroking, but when she looked at him again his black lashes were lying close against his cheeks, for his eyes were shut and he was fast asleep. So she got up softly, took her candle and crept away without making a sound.

# CHAPTER XIV

## A YOUNG RAJAH

The moor was hidden in mist when the morning came and the rain had not stopped pouring down. There could be no going out of doors. Martha was so busy that Mary had no opportunity of talking to her, but in the afternoon she asked her to come and sit with her in the nursery. She came bringing the stocking she was always knitting when she was doing nothing else.

"What's the matter with you?" she asked as soon as they sat down. "You look as if you'd something to say."

"I have. I have found out what the crying was," said Mary.

Martha let her knitting drop on her knee and gazed at her with startled eyes.

"You haven't!" she exclaimed. "Never!"

"I heard it in the night," Mary went on. "And I got up and went to see where it came from. It was Colin. I found him."

Martha's face became red with fright.

"Eh! Miss Mary!" she said half crying.

"You shouldn't have done it— you shouldn't! You'll get me in trouble. I never told you anything about him—but you'll get me in trouble. I shall lose my place and what'll mother do!"

"You won't lose your place," said Mary. "He was glad I came. We talked and talked and he said he was glad I came."

"Was he?" cried Martha. "Are you sure? You don't know what he's like when anything vexes him. He's a big boy to cry like a baby, but when he's in a passion he'll fair scream just to frighten us. He knows we daren't call our souls our own."

"He wasn't vexed," said Mary. "I asked him if I should go away and he made me stay. He asked me questions and I sat on a big footstool and talked to him about India and about the robin and gardens. He wouldn't let me go. He let me see his mother's picture. Before I left him I sang him to sleep."

Martha fairly gasped with amazement.

"I can scarcely believe you!" she protested. "It's as if you'd walked straight into a lion's den. If he'd been like he is most times he'd have thrown himself into one of his tantrums and roused the house. He won't let strangers look at him."

"He let me look at him. I looked at him all the time and he looked at me. We stared!" said Mary.

"I don't know what to do!" cried agitated Martha. "If Mrs. Medlock finds out, she'll think I broke orders and told you and I shall be packed back to mother."

"He is not going to tell Mrs. Medlock anything about it yet. It's to be a sort of secret just at first," said Mary firmly. "And he says everybody is obliged to do as he pleases."

"Aye, that's true enough—the bad lad!" sighed Martha, wiping her forehead with her apron.

"He says Mrs. Medlock must. And he wants me to come and talk to him every day. And you are to tell me when he wants me."

"Me!" said Martha; "I shall lose my place—I shall for sure!"

"You can't if you are doing what he wants you to do and everybody is ordered to obey him," Mary argued.

"Do you mean to say," cried Martha with wide open eyes, "that he was nice to you!"

"I think he almost liked me," Mary answered.

"Then you must have bewitched him!" decided Martha, drawing a long breath.

"Do you mean Magic?" inquired Mary. "I've heard about Magic in India, but I can't make it. I just went into his room and I was so surprised to see him I stood and stared. And then he turned round and stared at me. And he thought I was a ghost or a dream and I thought perhaps he was. And it was so queer being there alone together in the middle of the night and not knowing about each other. And we began to ask each other questions. And when I asked him if I must go away he said I must not."

"Your world's coming to an end!" gasped Martha.

"What is the matter with him?" asked Mary.

"Nobody knows for sure and certain," said Martha. "Mr. Craven went off his head like when he was born. The doctors thought he'd have to be put in an asylum. It was because Mrs. Craven died like I told you. He wouldn't set eyes on the baby. He just raved and said it'd be another hunchback like him and it'd better die."

"Is Colin a hunchback?" Mary asked. "He didn't look like one."

"He isn't yet," said Martha. "But he began all wrong. Mother said that there was enough trouble and raging in the house to set any child wrong. They were afraid his back was weak and they've always been taking care of it—keeping him lying down and not letting him walk. Once they made him wear a brace but he fretted so he was downright ill. Then a big doctor came to see him and made them take it off. He talked to the other doctor quite rough—in a polite way. He said there'd been too much medicine and too much letting him have his own way."

"I think he's a very spoiled boy," said Mary.

"He's the worst young one that ever was!" said Martha. "I won't say as he hasn't been ill a good bit. He's had coughs and colds that have nearly killed him two or three times. Once he had rheumatic fever and once he had typhoid. Eh! Mrs. Medlock did get a fright then. He'd been out of his head and she was talking to the nurse, thinking he didn't know anything, and she said, 'He'll die this time sure enough, and best thing for him and for everybody.' And she looked at him and there he was with his big eyes open, staring at her as sensible as she was herself. She didn't know what had happened but he just stared at her and said, 'You give me some water and stop talking.'"

"Do you think he will die?" asked Mary.

"Mother says there's no reason why any child should live that gets no fresh air and doesn't do nothing but lie on his back and read picture-books and take medicine. He's weak and hates the trouble of being taken out of doors, and he gets cold so easy he says it makes him ill."

Mary sat and looked at the fire.

"I wonder," she said slowly, "if it would not do him good to go out into a garden and watch things growing. It did me good."

"One of the worst fits he ever had," said Martha, "was one time they took him out where the roses are by the fountain. He'd been reading in a paper about people getting something he called 'rose cold' and he began to sneeze and said he'd got it and then a new gardener that didn't know the rules passed by and looked at him curious. He threw himself into a passion and he said he'd looked at him because he was going to be a hunchback. He cried himself into a fever and was ill all night."

"If he ever gets angry at me, I'll never go and see him again," said Mary.

"He'll have you if he wants you," said Martha. "You may as well know that at the start."

Very soon afterward a bell rang and she rolled up her knitting.

"I dare say the nurse wants me to stay with him a bit," she said. "I hope he's in a good temper."

She was out of the room about ten minutes and then she came back with a puzzled expression.

"Well, you have bewitched him," she said. "He's up on his sofa with his picture-books. He's told the nurse to stay away until six o'clock. I'm to wait in the next room. The minute she was gone he called me to him and says, 'I want Mary Lennox to come and talk to me, and remember you're not to tell anyone.' You'd better go as quickly as you can."

Mary was quite willing to go quickly. She did not want to see Colin as much as she wanted to see Dickon, but she wanted to see him very much.

There was a bright fire on the hearth when she entered his room, and in the daylight she saw it was a very beautiful room indeed. There were rich colours in the rugs and hangings and pictures and books on the walls which made it look glowing and comfortable even in spite of the grey sky and falling rain. Colin looked rather like a picture himself. He was wrapped in a velvet dressing-gown and sat against a big brocaded cushion. He had a red spot on each cheek.

"Come in," he said. "I've been thinking about you all morning."

"I've been thinking about you, too," answered Mary. "You don't know how frightened Martha is. She says Mrs. Medlock will think she told me about you and then she will be sent away."

He frowned.

"Go and tell her to come here," he said. "She is in the next room."

Mary went and brought her back. Poor Martha was shaking in her shoes. Colin was still frowning.

"Have you to do what I please or have you not?" he demanded.

"I have to do what you please, sir," Martha faltered, turning quite red.

"Has Medlock to do what I please?"

"Everybody has, sir," said Martha.

"Well, then, if I order you to bring Miss Mary to me, how can Medlock send you away if she finds it out?"

"Please don't let her, sir," pleaded Martha.

"I'll send *her* away if she dares to say a word about such a thing," said Master Craven grandly. "She wouldn't like that, I can tell you."

"Thank you, sir," bobbing a curtsy, "I want to do my duty, sir."

"What I want is your duty," said Colin more grandly still. "I'll take care of you. Now go away."

When the door closed behind Martha, Colin found Mistress Mary gazing at him as if he had set her wondering.

"Why do you look at me like that?" he asked her. "What are you thinking about?"

"I am thinking about two things."

"What are they? Sit down and tell me."

"This is the first one," said Mary, seating herself on the big stool. "Once in India I saw a boy who was a Rajah. He had rubies and emeralds and diamonds stuck all over him. He spoke to his people just as you spoke to Martha. Everybody had to do everything he told them—in a minute. I think they would have been killed if they hadn't."

"I shall make you tell me about Rajahs presently," he said, "but first tell me what the second thing was."

"I was thinking," said Mary, "how different you are from Dickon."

"Who is Dickon?" he said. "What a queer name!"

She might as well tell him, she thought. She could talk about Dickon without mentioning the secret garden. She had liked to hear Martha talk about him. Besides, she longed to talk about him. It would seem to bring him nearer.

"He is Martha's brother. He is twelve years old," she explained. "He is not like anyone else in the world. He can charm foxes and squirrels and birds just as the natives in India charm snakes. He plays a very soft tune on a pipe and they come and listen."

There were some big books on a table at his side and he dragged one suddenly toward him.

"There is a picture of a snake-charmer in this," he exclaimed. "Come and look at it."

The book was a beautiful one with superb coloured illustrations and he turned to one of them.

"Can he do that?" he asked eagerly.

"He played on his pipe and they listened," Mary explained. "But he doesn't call it Magic. He says it's because he lives on the moor so much and he knows their ways. He says he feels sometimes as if he was a bird or a rabbit himself, he likes them so. I think he asked the robin questions. It seemed as if they talked to each other in soft chirps."

Colin lay back on his cushion and his eyes grew larger and larger and the spots on his cheeks burned.

"Tell me some more about him," he said.

"He knows all about eggs and nests," Mary went on. "And he knows where foxes and badgers and otters live. He keeps them secret so that other boys won't find their holes and frighten them. He knows about everything that grows or lives on the moor."

"Does he like the moor?" said Colin. "How can he when it's such a great, bare, dreary place?"

"It's the most beautiful place," protested Mary. "Thousands of lovely things grow on it and there are thousands of little creatures all busy building nests and making holes and burrows or singing or squeaking to each other. They are so busy and having such fun under the earth or in the trees or heather. It's their world."

"How do you know all that?" said Colin, turning on his elbow to look at her.

"I have never been there once, really," said Mary suddenly remembering. "I only drove over it in the dark. I thought it was hideous. Martha told me about it first and then Dickon. When Dickon talks about it you feel as if you saw things and heard them and as if you were standing in the heather with the sun shining and the gorse smelling like honey—and all full of bees and butterflies."

"You never see anything if you are ill," said Colin restlessly. He looked like a person listening to a new sound in the distance and wondering what it was.

"You can't if you stay in a room," said Mary.

"I couldn't go on the moor," he said in a resentful tone.

Mary was silent for a minute and then she said something bold.

"You might—sometime."

He moved as if he were startled.

"Go on the moor! How could I? I am going to die."

"How do you know?" said Mary unsympathetically. She didn't like the way he had of talking about dying. She did not feel very sympathetic. She felt rather as if he almost boasted about it.

"Oh, I've heard it ever since I remember," he answered crossly. "They are always whispering about it and thinking I don't notice. They wish I would, too."

Mistress Mary felt quite contrary. She pinched her lips together.

"If they wished I would," she said, "I wouldn't. Who wishes you would?"

"The servants—and of course Dr. Craven because he would get Misselthwaite and be rich instead of poor. He daren't say so, but he always looks cheerful when I am worse. When I had typhoid fever his face got quite fat. I think my father wishes it, too."

"I don't believe he does," said Mary quite obstinately.

That made Colin turn and look at her again.

"Don't you?" he said.

And then he lay back on his cushion and was still, as if he were thinking. And there was quite a long silence. Perhaps they were both of them thinking strange things children do not usually think of.

"I like the grand doctor from London, because he made them take the iron thing off," said Mary at last. "Did he say you were going to die?"

"No."

"What did he say?"

"He didn't whisper," Colin answered. "Perhaps he knew I hated whispering. I heard him say one thing quite aloud. He said, 'The lad might live if he would make up his mind to it. Put him in the humour.' It sounded as if he was in a temper."

"I'll tell you who would put you in the humour, perhaps," said Mary reflecting. She felt as if she would like this thing to be settled one way or the other. "I believe Dickon would. He's always talking about live things. He never talks about dead things or things that are ill. He's always looking up in the sky to watch birds flying—or looking down at the earth to see something growing. He has such round blue eyes and they are so wide open with looking about. And he laughs such a big laugh with his wide mouth—and his cheeks are as red—as red as cherries."

She pulled her stool nearer to the sofa and her expression quite changed at the remembrance of the wide curving mouth and wide open eyes.

"See here," she said. "Don't let us talk about dying; I don't like it. Let us talk about living. Let us talk and talk about Dickon. And then we will look at your pictures."

It was the best thing she could have said. To talk about Dickon meant to talk about the moor and about the cottage and the fourteen people who lived in it on sixteen shillings a week—and the children who got fat on the moor grass like the wild ponies. And about Dickon's mother—and the skipping-rope—and the moor with the sun on it—and about pale green points sticking up out of the black sod. And it was all so alive that Mary talked more than she had ever talked before—and Colin both talked and listened as he had never done either before. And they both began to laugh over nothing as children will when they are happy together. And they laughed so that in the end they were making as much noise as if they had been two

137

ordinary healthy natural ten-year-old creatures—instead of a hard, little, unloving girl and a sickly boy who believed that he was going to die.

They enjoyed themselves so much that they forgot the pictures and they forgot about the time. They had been laughing quite loudly over Ben Weatherstaff and his robin and Colin was actually sitting up as if he had forgotten about his weak back when he suddenly remembered something.

"Do you know there is one thing we have never once thought of," he said. "We are cousins."

It seemed so queer that they had talked so much and never remembered this simple thing that they laughed more than ever, because they had got into the humour to laugh at anything. And in the midst of the fun the door opened and in walked Dr. Craven and Mrs. Medlock.

Dr. Craven started in actual alarm and Mrs. Medlock almost fell back because he had accidentally bumped against her.

"Good Lord!" exclaimed poor Mrs. Medlock, with her eyes almost starting out of her head. "Good Lord!"

"What is this?" said Dr. Craven, coming forward. "What does it mean?"

Then Mary was reminded of the boy Rajah again. Colin answered as if neither the doctor's alarm nor Mrs. Medlock's terror were of the slightest consequence. He was as little disturbed or frightened as if an elderly cat and dog had walked into the room.

"This is my cousin, Mary Lennox," he said. "I asked her to come and talk to me. I like her. She must come and talk to me whenever I send for her."

Dr. Craven turned reproachfully to Mrs. Medlock.

"Oh, sir," she panted. "I don't know how it's happened. There's not a servant on the place that'd dare to talk—they all have their orders."

"Nobody told her anything," said Colin, "she heard me crying and found me herself. I am glad she came. Don't be silly, Medlock."

Mary saw that Dr. Craven did not look pleased, but it was quite plain that he dare not oppose his patient. He sat down by Colin and felt his pulse.

"I am afraid there has been too much excitement. Excitement is not good for you, my boy," he said.

"I should be excited if she kept away," answered Colin, his eyes beginning to look dangerously sparkling. "I am better. She makes me better. The nurse must bring up her tea with mine. We will have tea together."

Mrs. Medlock and Dr. Craven looked at each other in a troubled way, but there was evidently nothing to be done.

"He does look rather better, sir," ventured Mrs. Medlock. "But"—thinking the matter over—"he looked better this morning before she came into the room."

"She came into the room last night. She stayed with me a long time. She sang a Hindustani song to me and it made me go to sleep," said Colin. "I was better when I wakened up. I wanted my breakfast. I want my tea now. Tell nurse, Medlock."

Dr. Craven did not stay very long. He talked to the nurse for a few minutes when she came into the room and said a few words of warning to Colin. He must not talk too much; he must not forget that he was ill; he must not forget that he was very easily tired. Mary thought that there seemed to be a number of uncomfortable things he was not to forget.

Colin looked fretful and kept his strange black-lashed eyes fixed on Dr. Craven's face.

"I *want* to forget it," he said at last. "She makes me forget it. That is why I want her."

Dr. Craven did not look happy when he left the room. He gave a puzzled glance at the little girl sitting on the large stool. She had become a stiff, silent child again as soon as he entered and he could not see what the attraction was. The boy actually did look brighter, however—and he sighed rather heavily as he went down the corridor.

"They are always wanting me to eat things when I don't want to," said Colin, as the nurse brought in the tea and put it on the table by the sofa. "Now, if you'll eat I will. Those muffins look so nice and hot. Tell me about Rajahs. "

## CHAPTER XV

## NEST BUILDING

After another week of rain the high arch of blue sky appeared again and the sun which poured down was quite hot. Though there had been no chance to see either the secret garden or Dickon, Mistress Mary had enjoyed herself very much. The week had not seemed long. She had spent hours of every day with Colin in his room, talking about Rajahs or gardens or Dickon and the cottage on the moor. They had looked at the splendid books and pictures and sometimes Mary had read things to Colin, and sometimes he had read a little to her. When he was amused and interested she thought he scarcely looked like an invalid at all, except that his face was so colourless and he was always on the sofa.

"You are a sly young one to listen and get out of your bed to go following things up like you did that night," Mrs. Medlock said once. "But there's no saying it's not been a sort of blessing to the lot of us. He's not had a tantrum or a whining fit since you made friends. The nurse was just going to give up the case because she was so sick of him, but she says she doesn't mind staying now you've gone on duty with her," laughing a little.

In her talks with Colin, Mary had tried to be very cautious about the secret garden. There were certain things she wanted to find out from him, but she felt that she must find them out without asking him direct questions. In the first place, as she began to like to be with him, she wanted to discover whether he was the kind of boy you could tell a secret to. He was not in the least like Dickon, but he was evidently so pleased with the idea of a garden no one knew anything about that she thought perhaps he could be trusted. But she had not known him long enough to be sure. The second thing she wanted to find out was this: If he could be trusted—if he really could—wouldn't it be possible to take him to the garden without having any one find it out? The grand doctor had said that he must have fresh air and Colin had said that he would not mind fresh air in a secret garden. Perhaps if he had a great deal of fresh air and knew Dickon and the robin and saw things growing he might not think so much about dying. Mary had seen herself in the glass sometimes lately when she had realized that she looked quite a different creature from the child she had seen when she arrived from India. This child looked nicer. Even Martha had seen a change in her.

"The air from the moor has done you good already," she had said. "You aren't nearly as pale and not nearly as scrawny. Even your hair doesn't slump down on your head so flat. It's got some life in it so as it sticks out a bit."

"It's like me," said Mary. "It's growing stronger and fatter. I'm sure there's more of it."

"It looks it, for sure," said Martha, ruffling it up a little round her face. "You aren't half as ugly when it's that way and there's a bit of red in your cheeks."

If gardens and fresh air had been good for her perhaps they would be good for Colin. But then, if he hated people to look at him, perhaps he would not like to see Dickon.

"Why does it make you angry when you are looked at?" she inquired one day.

"I always hated it," he answered, "even when I was very little. Then when they took me to the seaside and I used to lie in my carriage everybody used to stare and ladies would stop and talk to my nurse and then they would begin to whisper and I knew then they were saying I shouldn't live to grow up. Then sometimes the ladies would pat my cheeks and say 'Poor child!' Once when a lady did that I screamed out loud and bit her hand. She was so frightened she ran away."

"She thought you had gone mad like a dog," said Mary, not at all admiringly.

140

"I don't care what she thought," said Colin, frowning.

"I wonder why you didn't scream and bite me when I came into your room?" said Mary. Then she began to smile slowly.

"I thought you were a ghost or a dream," he said. "You can't bite a ghost or a dream, and if you scream they don't care."

"Would you hate it if—if a boy looked at you?" Mary asked uncertainly.

He lay back on his cushion and paused thoughtfully.

"There's one boy," he said quite slowly, as if he were thinking over every word, "there's one boy I believe I shouldn't mind. It's that boy who knows where the foxes live—Dickon."

"I'm sure you wouldn't mind him," said Mary.

"The birds don't and other animals," he said, still thinking it over, "perhaps that's why I shouldn't. He's a sort of animal charmer and I am a boy animal."

Then he laughed and she laughed too; in fact it ended in their both laughing a great deal and finding the idea of a boy animal hiding in his hole very funny indeed.

What Mary felt afterward was that she need not fear about Dickon.

On that first morning when the sky was blue again Mary wakened very early. The sun was pouring in slanting rays through the blinds and there was something so joyous in the sight of it that she jumped out of bed and ran to the window. She drew up the blinds and opened the window itself and a great waft of fresh, scented air blew in upon her. The moor was blue and the whole world looked as if something Magic had happened to it. There were tender little fluting sounds here and there and everywhere, as if scores of birds were beginning to tune up for a concert. Mary put her hand out of the window and held it in the sun.

"It's warm—warm!" she said. "It will make the green points push up and up and up, and it will make the bulbs and roots work and struggle with all their might under the earth."

She kneeled down and leaned out of the window as far as she could, breathing big breaths and sniffing the air until she laughed because she remembered what Dickon's mother had said about the end of his nose quivering like a rabbit's.

"It must be very early," she said. "The little clouds are all pink and I've never seen the sky look like this. No one is up. I don't even hear the stable boys."

A sudden thought made her scramble to her feet.

"I can't wait! I am going to see the garden!"

She had learned to dress herself by this time and she put on her clothes in five minutes. She knew a small side door which she could unbolt herself and she flew down-stairs in her stocking feet and put on her shoes in the hall. She unchained and unbolted and unlocked and when the door was open she sprang across the step with one bound, and there she was standing on the grass, which seemed to have turned green, and with the sun pouring down on her and warm sweet wafts about her and the fluting and twittering and singing coming from every bush and tree. She clasped her hands for pure joy and looked up in the sky and it was so blue and pink and pearly and white and flooded with springtime light that she felt as if she must flute and sing aloud herself and knew that thrushes and robins and skylarks could not possibly help it. She ran around the shrubs and paths toward the secret garden.

"It is all different already," she said. "The grass is greener and things are sticking up everywhere and things are uncurling and green buds of leaves are showing. This afternoon I am sure Dickon will come."

The long warm rain had done strange things to the herbaceous beds which bordered the walk by the lower wall. There were things sprouting and pushing out from the roots of clumps of plants and there were actually here and there glimpses of royal purple and yellow unfurling among the stems of crocuses. Six months before Mistress Mary would not have seen how the world was waking up, but now she missed nothing.

When she had reached the place where the door hid itself under the ivy, she was startled by a curious loud sound. It was the caw—caw of a crow and it came from the top of the wall, and when she looked up, there sat a big glossy-plumaged blue-black bird, looking down at her very wisely indeed. She had never seen a crow so close before and he made her a little nervous, but the next moment he spread his wings and flapped away across the garden. She hoped he was not going to stay inside and she pushed the door open wondering if he would. When she got fairly into the garden she saw that he probably did intend to stay because he had alighted on a dwarf apple-tree, and under the apple-tree was lying a little reddish animal with a bushy tail, and both of them were watching the stooping body and rust-red head of Dickon, who was kneeling on the grass working hard.

Mary flew across the grass to him.

"Oh, Dickon! Dickon!" she cried out. "How could you get here so early? How could you! The sun has only just got up!"

He got up himself, laughing and glowing, and tousled; his eyes like a bit of the sky.

"Eh!" he said. "I was up long before him. How could I have stayed in bed! The world's all fair begun again this morning, it has. And it's working and humming and scratching and piping and nest-building and breathing out scents, till you've got to be out on it instead of lying on your back. When the sun did jump up, the moor went mad for joy, and I was in the midst of the heather, and I run like mad myself,

142

shouting and singing. And I come straight here. I couldn't have stayed away. Why, the garden was lying here waiting!"

Mary put her hands on her chest, panting, as if she had been running herself.

"Oh, Dickon! Dickon!" she said. "I'm so happy I can scarcely breathe!"

Seeing him talking to a stranger, the little bushy-tailed animal rose from its place under the tree and came to him, and the rook, cawing once, flew down from its branch and settled quietly on his shoulder.

"This is the little fox cub," he said, rubbing the little reddish animal's head. "It's named Captain. And this here's Soot. Soot he flew across the moor with me and Captain ran as if the hounds had been after him. They both felt the same as I did."

Neither of the creatures looked as if he were the least afraid of Mary. When Dickon began to walk about, Soot stayed on his shoulder and Captain trotted quietly close to his side.

"See here!" said Dickon. "See how these have pushed up, and these and these! And Eh! Look at these here!"

He threw himself upon his knees and Mary went down beside him. They had come upon a whole clump of crocuses burst into purple and orange and gold. Mary bent her face down and kissed and kissed them.

"You never kiss a person in that way," she said when she lifted her head. "Flowers are so different."

He looked puzzled but smiled.

"Eh!" he said, "I've kissed mother many a time that way when I come in from the moor after a day's roaming and she stood there at the door in the sun, looking so glad and comfortable."

They ran from one part of the garden to another and found so many wonders that they were obliged to remind themselves that they must whisper or speak low. He showed her swelling leaf-buds on rose branches which had seemed dead. He showed her ten thousand new green points pushing through the mould. They put their eager young noses close to the earth and sniffed its warmed springtime breathing; they dug and pulled and laughed low with rapture until Mistress Mary's hair was as tumbled as Dickon's and her cheeks were almost as poppy red as his.

There was every joy on earth in the secret garden that morning, and in the midst of them came a delight more delightful than all, because it was more wonderful. Swiftly something flew across the wall and darted through the trees to a close grown corner, a little flare of red-breasted bird with something hanging from its beak. Dickon stood quite still and put his hand on Mary almost as if they had suddenly found themselves laughing in a church.

"We must not stir," he whispered. "We must scarcely breathe. I knew he was mate-hunting when I saw him last. It's Ben Weatherstaff's robin. He's building his nest. He'll stay here if we don't frighten him."

They settled down softly upon the grass and sat there without moving.

"We mustn't seem as if we were watching him too close," said Dickon. "He'd be out with us for good if he got the notion we were interfering now. He'll be a good bit different till all this is over. He's setting up housekeeping. He'll be shyer and readier to take things ill. He's got no time for visiting and gossiping. We must keep still a bit and try to look as if we were grass and trees and bushes. Then when he's got used to seeing us I'll chirp a bit and he'll know we'll not be in his way."

Mistress Mary was not at all sure that she knew, as Dickon seemed to, how to try to look like grass and trees and bushes. But he had said the queer thing as if it were the simplest and most natural thing in the world, and she felt it must be quite easy to him, and indeed she watched him for a few minutes carefully, wondering if it was possible for him to quietly turn green and put out branches and leaves. But he only sat wonderfully still, and when he spoke dropped his voice to such a softness that it was curious that she could hear him, but she could.

"It's part of the springtime, this nest-building is," he said. "I warrant it's been going on in the same way every year since the world was begun. They've got their way of thinking and doing things and a body had better not meddle. You can lose a friend in springtime easier than any other season if you're too curious."

"If we talk about him I can't help looking at him," Mary said as softly as possible. "We must talk of something else. There is something I want to tell you."

"He'll like it better if we talk of something else," said Dickon. "What is it you have got to tell me?"

"Well—do you know about Colin?" she whispered.

He turned his head to look at her.

"What do you know about him?" he asked.

"I've seen him. I have been to talk to him every day this week. He wants me to come. He says I'm making him forget about being ill and dying," answered Mary.

Dickon looked actually relieved as soon as the surprise died away from his round face.

"I am glad of that," he exclaimed. "I'm right down glad. It makes me easier. I knew I must say nothing about him and I don't like having to hide things."

"Don't you like hiding the garden?" said Mary.

"I'll never tell about it," he answered. "But I say to mother, 'Mother,' I say, 'I got a secret to keep. It's not a bad one, you know that. It's no worse than hiding where a bird's nest is. You don't mind it, do you?'"

Mary always wanted to hear about mother.

"What did she say?" she asked, not at all afraid to hear.
Dickon grinned sweet-temperedly.

"It was just like her, what she said," he answered. "She gave my head a bit of a rub and laughed and she said, 'Eh, lad, you can have all the secrets you like. I've known you twelve years.'"

"How did you know about Colin?" asked Mary.

"Everybody that knows about Master Craven knows there is a little lad that is a cripple, and they know Master Craven doesn't like him to be talked about. Folks are sorry for Master Craven because Mrs. Craven was such a pretty young lady and they were so fond of each other. Mrs. Medlock stops in our cottage whenever she goes to Thwaite and she doesn't mind talking to mother before us children, because she knows we have been brought up to be trustworthy. How did you find out about him? Martha was in fine trouble the last time she came home. She said you'd heard him fretting and you were asking questions and she didn't know what to say."

Mary told him her story about the midnight wuthering of the wind which had wakened her and about the faint far-off sounds of the complaining voice which had led her down the dark corridors with her candle and had ended with her opening of the door of the dimly lighted room with the carven four-posted bed in the corner. When she described the small ivory-white face and the strange black-rimmed eyes Dickon shook his head.

"They're just like his mother's eyes, only hers were always laughing, they say," he said. "They say as Mr. Craven can't bear to see him when he's awake and it's because his eyes are so like his mother's and yet looks so different in his miserable bit of a face."

"Do you think he wants him to die?" whispered Mary.

"No, but he wishes he'd never been born. Mother she says that's the worst thing on earth for a child. The ones that are not wanted scarcely ever thrive. Master Craven he'd buy anything that money could buy for the poor lad but he'd like to forget that he's on earth. For one thing, he's afraid he'll look at him some day and find he's grown hunchback."

"Colin's so afraid of it himself that he won't sit up," said Mary. "He says he's always thinking that if he should feel a lump coming he should go crazy and scream himself to death."

"Eh! He oughtn't lie there thinking things like that," said Dickon. "No lad could get well that thought them sort of things."

The fox was lying on the grass close by him looking up to ask for a pat now and then, and Dickon bent down and rubbed his neck softly and thought a few minutes in silence. Presently he lifted his head and looked round the garden.

"When first we got in here," he said, "it seemed like everything was grey. Look round now and tell me if you don't see a difference."

Mary looked and caught her breath a little.

"Why!" she cried, "the grey wall is changing. It is as if a green mist were creeping over it. It's almost like a green gauze veil."

"Aye," said Dickon. "And it'll be greener and greener till the grey's all gone. Can you guess what I was thinking?"

"I know it was something nice," said Mary eagerly. "I believe it was something about Colin."

"I was thinking that if he was out here he wouldn't be watching for lumps to grow on his back; he'd be watching for buds to break on the rose bushes, and he'd likely be healthier," explained Dickon. "I was wondering if we could ever get him in the humour to come out here and lie under the trees in his carriage."

"I've been wondering that myself. I've thought of it almost every time I've talked to him," said Mary. "I've wondered if he could keep a secret and I've wondered if we could bring him here without anyone seeing us. I thought perhaps you could push his carriage. The doctor said he must have fresh air and if he wants us to take him out no one dare disobey him. He won't go out for other people and perhaps they will be glad if he will go out with us. He could order the gardeners to keep away so they wouldn't find out."

Dickon was thinking very hard as he scratched Captain's back.

"It'd be good for him, I'll warrant," he said. "We'd not be thinking he'd better never been born. We'd be just two children watching a garden grow, and he'd be another. Two lads and a little lass just looking on at the springtime. I warrant it'd be better than doctor's stuff."

"He's been lying in his room so long and he's always been so afraid of his back that it has made him queer," said Mary. "He knows a good many things out of books but he doesn't know anything else. He says he has been too ill to notice things and he hates going out of doors and hates gardens and gardeners. But he likes to hear about this garden because it is a secret. I daren't tell him much but he said he wanted to see it."

"We'll have him out here sometime for sure," said Dickon. "I could push his carriage well enough. Have you noticed how the robin and his mate have been working while we've been sitting here? Look at him perched on that branch wondering where it'd be best to put that twig he's got in his beak."

He made one of his low whistling calls and the robin turned his head and looked at him inquiringly, still holding his twig. Dickon spoke to him as Ben Weatherstaff did, but Dickon's tone was one of friendly advice.

"Wherever you put it," he said, "it'll be alright. You knew how to build your nest before you came out of the egg. Get on with it, lad. You've got no time to lose."

"Oh, I do like to hear you talk to him!" Mary said, laughing delightedly. "Ben Weatherstaff scolds him and makes fun of him, and he hops about and looks as if he understood every word, and I know he likes it. Ben Weatherstaff says he is so conceited he would rather have stones thrown at him than not be noticed."

Dickon laughed too and went on talking.

"You know we won't trouble you," he said to the robin. "We are near being wild things ourselves. We are nest-building too, bless you. Look out you don't tell on us."

And though the robin did not answer, because his beak was occupied, Mary knew that when he flew away with his twig to his own corner of the garden the darkness of his dew-bright eye meant that he would not tell their secret for the world.

## CHAPTER XVI

### "I WON'T!" SAID MARY

They found a great deal to do that morning and Mary was late in returning to the house and was also in such a hurry to get back to her work that she quite forgot Colin until the last moment.

"Tell Colin that I can't come and see him yet," she said to Martha. "I'm very busy in the garden."

Martha looked rather frightened.

"Eh! Miss Mary," she said, "it may put him all out of humour when I tell him that."

But Mary was not as afraid of him as other people were and she was not a self-sacrificing person.

"I can't stay," she answered. "Dickon's waiting for me;" and she ran away.

The afternoon was even lovelier and busier than the morning had been. Already nearly all the weeds were cleared out of the garden and most of the roses and trees had been pruned or dug about. Dickon had brought a spade of his own and he had taught Mary to use all her tools, so that by this time it was plain that though the lovely wild place was not likely to become a "gardener's garden" it would be a wilderness of growing things before the springtime was over.

"There'll be apple blossoms and cherry blossoms overhead," Dickon said, working away with all his might. "And there'll be peach and plum trees in bloom against the walls, and the grass will be a carpet of flowers."

The little fox and the rook were as happy and busy as they were, and the robin and his mate flew backward and forward like tiny streaks of lightning. Sometimes the rook flapped his black wings and soared away over the tree-tops in the park. Each time he came back and perched near Dickon and cawed several times as if he were relating his adventures, and Dickon talked to him just as he had talked to the robin. Once when Dickon was so busy that he did not answer him at first, Soot flew on to his shoulders and gently tweaked his ear with his large beak. When Mary wanted to rest a little Dickon sat down with her under a tree and once he took his pipe out of his pocket and played the soft strange little notes and two squirrels appeared on the wall and looked and listened.

"You're a good bit stronger than you used to be," Dickon said, looking at her as she was digging. "You're beginning to look different, for sure."

Mary was glowing with exercise and good spirits.

"I'm getting fatter and fatter every day," she said quite exultantly. "Mrs. Medlock will have to get me some bigger dresses. Martha says my hair is growing thicker. It isn't so flat and stringy."

The sun was beginning to set and sending deep gold-coloured rays slanting under the trees when they parted.

"It'll be fine tomorrow," said Dickon. "I'll be at work by sunrise."

"So will I," said Mary.

She ran back to the house as quickly as her feet would carry her. She wanted to tell Colin about Dickon's fox cub and the rook and about what the springtime had been doing. She felt sure he would like to hear. So it was not very pleasant when she opened the door of her room, to see Martha standing waiting for her with a doleful face.

"What is the matter?" she asked. "What did Colin say when you told him I couldn't come?"

"Eh!" said Martha, "I wish you'd gone. He was going into one of his tantrums. There's been a lot to do all afternoon to keep him quiet. He would watch the clock all the time."

Mary's lips pinched themselves together. She was no more used to considering other people than Colin was and she saw no reason why an ill-tempered boy should interfere with the thing she liked best. She knew nothing about the pitifulness of people who had been ill and nervous and who did not know that they could control their tempers and need not make other people ill and nervous, too. When she had had a headache in India she had done her best to see that everybody else also had a headache or something quite as bad. And she felt she was quite right; but of course now she felt that Colin was quite wrong.

He was not on his sofa when she went into his room. He was lying flat on his back in bed and he did not turn his head toward her as she came in. This was a bad beginning and Mary marched up to him with her stiff manner.

"Why didn't you get up?" she said.

"I did get up this morning when I thought you were coming," he answered, without looking at her. "I made them put me back in bed this afternoon. My back ached and my head ached and I was tired. Why didn't you come?"

"I was working in the garden with Dickon," said Mary.

Colin frowned and condescended to look at her.

"I won't let that boy come here if you go and stay with him instead of coming to talk to me," he said.

Mary flew into a fine passion. She could fly into a passion without making a noise. She just grew sour and obstinate and did not care what happened.

"If you send Dickon away, I'll never come into this room again!" she retorted.

"You'll have to if I want you," said Colin.

"I won't!" said Mary.

"I'll make you," said Colin, "They shall drag you in."

"Shall they, Mr. Rajah!" said Mary fiercely. "They may drag me in but they can't make me talk when they get me here. I'll sit and clench my teeth and never tell you one thing. I won't even look at you. I'll stare at the floor!"

They were a nice agreeable pair as they glared at each other. If they had been two little street boys they would have sprung at each other and had a rough-and-tumble fight. As it was, they did the next thing to it.

"You are a selfish thing!" cried Colin.

"What are you?" said Mary. "Selfish people always say that. Any one is selfish who doesn't do what they want. You're more selfish than I am. You're the most selfish boy I ever saw."

"I'm not!" snapped Colin. "I'm not as selfish as your fine Dickon is! He keeps you playing in the dirt when he knows I am all by myself. He's selfish, if you like!"

Mary's eyes flashed fire.

"He's nicer than any other boy that ever lived!" she said. "He's—he's like an angel!" It might sound rather silly to say that but she did not care.

"A nice angel!" Colin sneered ferociously. "He's a common cottage boy off the moor!"

"He's better than a common Rajah!" retorted Mary. "He's a thousand times better!"

Because she was the stronger of the two she was beginning to get the better of him. The truth was that he had never had a fight with any one like himself in his life and, upon the whole, it was rather good for him, though neither he nor Mary knew anything about that. He turned his head on his pillow and shut his eyes and a big tear was squeezed out and ran down his cheek. He was beginning to feel pathetic and sorry for himself—not for anyone else.

"I'm not as selfish as you, because I'm always ill, and I'm sure there is a lump coming on my back," he said. "And I am going to die besides."

"You're not!" contradicted Mary unsympathetically.

He opened his eyes quite wide with indignation. He had never heard such a thing said before. He was at once furious and slightly pleased, if a person could be both at the same time.

"I'm not?" he cried. "I am! You know I am! Everybody says so."

"I don't believe it!" said Mary sourly. "You just say that to make people sorry. I believe you're proud of it. I don't believe it! If you were a nice boy it might be true—but you're too nasty!"

In spite of his invalid back Colin sat up in bed in quite a healthy rage.

"Get out of the room!" he shouted and he caught hold of his pillow and threw it at her. He was not strong enough to throw it far and it only fell at her feet, but Mary's face looked as pinched as a nutcracker.

"I'm going," she said. "And I won't come back!"

She walked to the door and when she reached it she turned round and spoke again.

"I was going to tell you all sorts of nice things," she said. "Dickon brought his fox and his rook and I was going to tell you all about them. Now I won't tell you a single thing!"

She marched out of the door and closed it behind her, and there to her great astonishment she found the trained nurse standing as if she had been listening and, more amazing still—she was laughing. She was a big handsome young woman who ought not to have been a trained nurse at all, as she could not bear invalids and she was always making excuses to leave Colin to Martha or anyone else who would take her place. Mary had never liked her, and she simply stood and gazed up at her as she stood giggling into her handkerchief.

"What are you laughing at?" she asked her.

"At you two young ones," said the nurse. "It's the best thing that could happen to the sickly pampered thing to have someone stand up to him that's as spoiled as himself;" and she laughed into her handkerchief again. "If he'd had a young vixen of a sister to fight with it would have been the saving of him."

"Is he going to die?"

"I don't know and I don't care," said the nurse. "Hysterics and temper are half what ails him."

"What are hysterics?" asked Mary.

"You'll find out if you work him into a tantrum after this—but at any rate you've given him something to have hysterics about, and I'm glad of it."

Mary went back to her room not feeling at all as she had felt when she had come in from the garden. She was cross and disappointed but not at all sorry for Colin. She had looked forward to telling him a great many things and she had meant to try to make up her mind whether it would be safe to trust him with the great secret. She had been beginning to think it would be, but now she had changed her mind entirely. She would never tell him and he could stay in his room and never get any fresh air and die if he liked! It would serve him right! She felt so sour and unrelenting that for a few minutes she almost forgot about Dickon and the green veil creeping over the world and the soft wind blowing down from the moor.

Martha was waiting for her and the trouble in her face had been temporarily replaced by interest and curiosity. There was a wooden box on the table and its cover had been removed and revealed that it was full of neat packages.

"Mr. Craven sent it to you," said Martha. "It looks as if it had picture-books in it."

Mary remembered what he had asked her the day she had gone to his room. "Do you want anything—dolls—toys—books?" She opened the package wondering if he had sent a doll, and also wondering what she should do with it if he had. But he had not sent one. There were several beautiful books such as Colin had, and two of them were about gardens and were full of pictures. There were two or three games and there was a beautiful little writing-case with a gold monogram on it and a gold pen and inkstand.

Everything was so nice that her pleasure began to crowd her anger out of her mind. She had not expected him to remember her at all and her hard little heart grew quite warm.

"I can write better than I can print," she said, "and the first thing I shall write with that pen will be a letter to tell him I am much obliged."

If she had been friends with Colin she would have run to show him her presents at once, and they would have looked at the pictures and read some of the gardening books and perhaps tried playing the games, and he would have enjoyed himself so much he would never once have thought he was going to die or have put his hand on his spine to see if there was a lump coming. He had a way of doing that which she could not bear. It gave her an uncomfortable frightened feeling because he always looked so frightened himself. He said that if he felt even quite a little lump someday he should know his hunch had begun to grow.

Something he had heard Mrs. Medlock whispering to the nurse had given him the idea and he had thought over it in secret until it was quite firmly fixed in his mind. Mrs. Medlock had said his father's back had begun to show its crookedness in that way when he was a child. He had never told anyone but Mary that most of his "tantrums" as they called them grew out of his hysterical hidden fear. Mary had been sorry for him when he had told her.

"He always began to think about it when he was cross or tired," she said to herself. "And he has been cross today. Perhaps—perhaps he has been thinking about it all afternoon."

She stood still, looking down at the carpet and thinking.

"I said I would never go back again—" she hesitated, knitting her brows—"but perhaps, just perhaps, I will go and see—if he wants me—in the morning. Perhaps he'll try to throw his pillow at me again, but—I think—I'll go."

## CHAPTER XVII

### A TANTRUM

She had got up very early in the morning and had worked hard in the garden and she was tired and sleepy, so as soon as Martha had brought her supper and she had eaten it, she was glad to go to bed. As she laid her head on the pillow she murmured to herself:

"I'll go out before breakfast and work with Dickon and then afterward—I believe—I'll go to see him."

She thought it was the middle of the night when she was awakened by such dreadful sounds that she jumped out of bed in an instant. What was it—what was it? The next minute she felt quite sure she knew. Doors were opened and shut and there were hurrying feet in the corridors and someone was crying and screaming at the same time, screaming and crying in a horrible way.

"It's Colin," she said. "He's having one of those tantrums the nurse called hysterics. How awful it sounds."

As she listened to the sobbing screams she did not wonder that people were so frightened that they gave him his own way in everything rather than hear them. She put her hands over her ears and felt sick and shivering.

"I don't know what to do. I don't know what to do," she kept saying. "I can't bear it."

Once she wondered if he would stop if she dared go to him and then she remembered how he had driven her out of the room and thought that perhaps the sight of her might make him worse. Even when she pressed her hands more tightly over her ears she could not keep the awful sounds out. She hated them so and was so terrified by them that suddenly they began to make her angry and she felt as if she should like to fly into a tantrum herself and frighten him as he was frightening her. She was not used to any one's tempers but her own. She took her hands from her ears and sprang up and stamped her foot.

"He ought to be stopped! Somebody ought to make him stop! Somebody ought to beat him!" she cried out.

Just then she heard feet almost running down the corridor and her door opened and the nurse came in. She was not laughing now by any means. She even looked rather pale.

"He's worked himself into hysterics," she said in a great hurry. "He'll do himself harm. No one can do anything with him. You come and try, like a good child. He likes you."

"He turned me out of the room this morning," said Mary, stamping her foot with excitement.

The stamp rather pleased the nurse. The truth was that she had been afraid she might find Mary crying and hiding her head under the bed clothes.

"That's right," she said. "You're in the right humour. You go and scold him. Give him something new to think of. Do go, child, as quick as ever you can."

It was not until afterward that Mary realized that the thing had been funny as well as dreadful—that it was funny that all the grown-up people were so frightened that they came to a little girl just because they guessed she was almost as bad as Colin himself.

She flew along the corridor and the nearer she got to the screams the higher her temper mounted. She felt quite wicked by the time she reached the door. She slapped it open with her hand and ran across the room to the four-posted bed.

"You stop!" she almost shouted. "You stop! I hate you! Everybody hates you! I wish everybody would run out of the house and let you scream yourself to death! You *will* scream yourself to death in a minute, and I wish you would!"

A nice sympathetic child could neither have thought nor said such things, but it just happened that the shock of hearing them was the best possible thing for this hysterical boy whom no one had ever dared to restrain or contradict.

He had been lying on his face beating his pillow with his hands and he actually almost jumped around, he turned so quickly at the sound of the furious little voice. His face looked dreadful, white and red and swollen, and he was gasping and choking; but savage little Mary did not care an atom.

"If you scream another scream," she said, "I'll scream too—and I can scream louder than you can and I'll frighten you, I'll frighten you!"

He actually had stopped screaming because she had startled him so. The scream which had been coming almost choked him. The tears were streaming down his face and he shook all over.

"I can't stop!" he gasped and sobbed. "I can't—I can't!"

"You can!" shouted Mary. "Half that ails you is hysterics and temper—just hysterics—hysterics—hysterics!" and she stamped each time she said it.

"I felt the lump—I felt it," choked out Colin. "I knew I should. I shall have a hunch on my back and then I shall die," and he began to squirm again and turned on his face and sobbed and wailed but he didn't scream.

"You didn't feel a lump!" contradicted Mary fiercely. "If you did it was only a hysterical lump. Hysterics makes lumps. There's nothing the matter with your horrid back—nothing but hysterics! Turn over and let me look at it!"

She liked the word "hysterics" and felt somehow as if it had an effect on him. He was probably like herself and had never heard it before.

"Nurse," she commanded, "come here and show me his back this minute!"

The nurse, Mrs. Medlock and Martha had been standing huddled together near the door staring at her, their mouths half open. All three had gasped with fright more than once. The nurse came forward as if she were half afraid. Colin was heaving with great breathless sobs.

"Perhaps he—he won't let me," she hesitated in a low voice.

Colin heard her, however, and he gasped out between two sobs:

"Sh—show her! She—she'll see then!"

It was a poor thin back to look at when it was bared. Every rib could be counted and every joint of the spine, though Mistress Mary did not count them as she bent over and examined them with a solemn savage little face. She looked so sour and old-fashioned that the nurse turned her head aside to hide the twitching of her mouth. There was just a minute's silence, for even Colin tried to hold his breath while Mary looked up and down his spine, and down and up, as intently as if she had been the great doctor from London.

"There's not a single lump there!" she said at last. "There's not a lump as big as a pin—except backbone lumps, and you can only feel them because you're thin. I've got backbone lumps myself, and they used to stick out as much as yours do, until I began to get fatter, and I am not fat enough yet to hide them. There's not a lump as big as a pin! If you ever say there is again, I shall laugh!"

No one but Colin himself knew what effect those crossly spoken childish words had on him. If he had ever had any one to talk to about his secret terrors—if he had ever dared to let himself ask questions—if he had had childish companions and had not lain on his back in the huge closed house, breathing an atmosphere heavy with the fears of people who were most of them ignorant and tired of him, he would have found out that most of his fright and illness was created by himself. But he had laid there and thought of himself and his aches and weariness for hours and days and months and years. And now that an angry unsympathetic little girl insisted obstinately that he was not as ill as he thought he was he actually felt as if she might be speaking the truth.

"I didn't know," ventured the nurse, "that he thought he had a lump on his spine. His back is weak because he won't try to sit up. I could have told him there was no lump there."

Colin gulped and turned his face a little to look at her.

"C-could you?" he said pathetically.

"Yes, sir."

"There!" said Mary, and she gulped too.

Colin turned on his face again and but for his long-drawn broken breaths, which were the dying down of his storm of sobbing, he lay still for a minute, though great tears streamed down his face and wet the pillow. Actually the tears meant that a curious great relief had come to him. Presently he turned and looked at the nurse again and strangely enough he was not like a Rajah at all as he spoke to her.

"Do you think—I could—live to grow up?" he said.

The nurse was neither clever nor soft-hearted but she could repeat some of the London doctor's words.

"You probably will if you will do what you are told to do and not give way to your temper, and stay out a great deal in the fresh air."

Colin's tantrum had passed and he was weak and worn out with crying and this perhaps made him feel gentle. He put out his hand a little toward Mary, and I am glad to say that, her own tantrum having passed, she was softened too and met him half-way with her hand, so that it was a sort of making up.

"I'll—I'll go out with you, Mary," he said. "I shan't hate fresh air if we can find—" He remembered just in time to stop himself from saying "if we can find the secret garden" and he ended, "I shall like to go out with you if Dickon will come and push my chair. I do so want to see Dickon and the fox and the crow."

The nurse remade the tumbled bed and shook and straightened the pillows. Then she made Colin a cup of beef tea and gave a cup to Mary, who really was very glad to get it after her excitement. Mrs. Medlock and Martha gladly slipped away, and after everything was neat and calm and in order the nurse looked as if she would very gladly slip away also. She was a healthy young woman who resented being robbed of her sleep and she yawned quite openly as she looked at Mary, who had pushed her big footstool close to the four-posted bed and was holding Colin's hand.

"You must go back and get your sleep," she said. "He'll drop off after a while—if he's not too upset. Then I'll lie down myself in the next room."

"Would you like me to sing you that song I learned from my Ayah?" Mary whispered to Colin.

His hand pulled hers gently and he turned his tired eyes on her appealingly.

"Oh, yes!" he answered. "It's such a soft song. I shall go to sleep in a minute."

"I will put him to sleep," Mary said to the yawning nurse. "You can go if you like."

"Well," said the nurse, with an attempt at reluctance. "If he doesn't go to sleep in half an hour you must call me."

"Very well," answered Mary.

The nurse was out of the room in a minute and as soon as she was gone Colin pulled Mary's hand again.

"I almost told," he said; "but I stopped myself in time. I won't talk and I'll go to sleep, but you said you had a whole lot of nice things to tell me. Have you—do you think you have found out anything at all about the way into the secret garden?"

Mary looked at his poor little tired face and swollen eyes and her heart relented.

"Ye-es," she answered, "I think I have. And if you will go to sleep I will tell you tomorrow."

His hand quite trembled.

"Oh, Mary!" he said. "Oh, Mary! If I could get into it I think I should live to grow up! Do you suppose that instead of singing the Ayah song—you could just tell me softly as you did that first day what you imagine it looks like inside? I am sure it will make me go to sleep."

"Yes," answered Mary. "Shut your eyes."

He closed his eyes and lay quite still and she held his hand and began to speak very slowly and in a very low voice.

"I think it has been left alone so long—that it has grown all into a lovely tangle. I think the roses have climbed and climbed and climbed until they hang from the branches and walls and creep over the ground—almost like a strange grey mist. Some of them have died but many—are alive and when the summer comes there will be curtains and fountains of roses. I think the ground is full of daffodils and snowdrops and lilies and iris working their way out of the dark. Now the spring has begun—perhaps—perhaps—"

The soft drone of her voice was making him stiller and stiller and she saw it and went on.

"Perhaps they are coming up through the grass—perhaps there are clusters of purple crocuses and gold ones—even now. Perhaps the leaves are beginning to break out and uncurl—and perhaps—the grey is changing and a green gauze veil is creeping—and creeping over—everything. And the birds are coming to look at it—because it is—so safe and still. And perhaps—perhaps—perhaps—" very softly and slowly indeed, "the robin has found a mate—and is building a nest."

And Colin was asleep.

## CHAPTER XVIII

### "YOU MUST NOT WASTE TIME"

Of course Mary did not wake up early the next morning. She slept late because she was tired, and when Martha brought her breakfast she told her that though Colin was quite quiet he was ill and feverish as he always was after he had worn himself out with a fit of crying. Mary ate her breakfast slowly as she listened.

"He says he wishes you would please go and see him as soon as you can," Martha said. "It's queer what a fancy he's taken to you. You did give it him last night for sure—didn't you? Nobody else would have dared to do it. Eh! Poor lad! He's been spoiled till salt won't save him. Mother says as the two worst things that can happen to a child is never to have his own way—or always to have it. She doesn't know

157

which is worse. You were in a fine temper yourself, too. But he said to me when I went into his room, 'Please ask Miss Mary if she'll please come and talk to me?' Think of him saying please! Will you go, Miss?"

"I'll run and see Dickon first," said Mary. "No, I'll go and see Colin first and tell him—I know what I'll tell him," with a sudden inspiration.

She had her hat on when she appeared in Colin's room and for a second he looked disappointed. He was in bed and his face was pitifully white and there were dark circles round his eyes.

"I'm glad you came," he said. "My head aches and I ache all over because I'm so tired. Are you going somewhere?"

Mary went and leaned against his bed.

"I won't be long," she said. "I'm going to Dickon, but I'll come back. Colin, it's—it's something about the secret garden."

His whole face brightened and a little colour came into it.

"Oh! Is it!" he cried out. "I dreamed about it all night. I heard you say something about grey changing into green, and I dreamed I was standing in a place all filled with trembling little green leaves—and there were birds on nests everywhere and they looked so soft and still. I'll lie and think about it until you come back."

In five minutes Mary was with Dickon in their garden. The fox and the crow were with him again and this time he had brought two tame squirrels.

"I came over on the pony this morning," he said. "Eh! He is a good little chap—Jump is! I brought these two in my pockets. This one's called Nut and the other one's called Shell."

When he said "Nut" one squirrel leaped on to his right shoulder and when he said "Shell" the other one leaped on to his left shoulder.

When they sat down on the grass with Captain curled at their feet, Soot solemnly listening on a tree and Nut and Shell nosing about close to them, it seemed to Mary that it would be scarcely bearable to leave such delightfulness, but when she began to tell her story somehow the look in Dickon's funny face gradually changed her mind. She could see he felt sorrier for Colin than she did. He looked up at the sky and all about him.

"Just listen to the birds—the world seems full of them—all whistling and piping," he said. "Look at them darting about, and hear them calling to each other. Come springtime it seems like all the world's calling. The leaves are uncurling so you can see them—and, my word, the nice smells that are about!" sniffing with his happy turned-up nose. "And that poor lad is lying shut up and seeing so little that he gets to thinking of things that set him screaming. Eh! We must get him out here—we must get him watching and listening and sniffing up the air and get him just soaked through with sunshine and we must not waste time."

"Yes, indeed, we must," she said. "I'll tell you what we'll do first," she proceeded. "He's taken a fancy to you. He wants to see you and he wants to see Soot and Captain. When I go back to the house to talk to him I'll ask him if you cannot come and see him tomorrow morning—and bring your creatures with you —and then— in a bit, when there's more leaves out, and a bud or two, we'll get him to come out and you'll push him in his chair and we'll bring him here and show him everything."

When she stopped she was quite proud of herself. She had never made a long speech before and she had remembered very well.

"You must talk a bit of Yorkshire like that to Master Colin," Dickon chuckled. "That'll make him laugh and there's nothing as good for ill folk as laughing. Mother says she believes that half an hour's good laugh every morning could cure a chap of typhus fever."

"I'm going to talk Yorkshire to him this very day," said Mary, chuckling herself.

The garden had reached the time when every day and every night it seemed as if Magicians were passing through it drawing loveliness out of the earth and the branches with wands. It was hard to go away and leave it all, particularly as Nut had actually crept on to her dress and Shell had scrambled down the trunk of the apple-tree they sat under and stayed there looking at her with inquiring eyes. But she went back to the house and when she sat down close to Colin's bed he began to sniff as Dickon did though not in such an experienced way.

"You smell like flowers and—and fresh things," he cried out quite joyously. "What is it you smell of? It's cool and warm and sweet all at the same time."

"It's the wind from the moor," said Mary. "It comes from sitting on the grass under a tree with Dickon and with Captain and Soot and Nut and Shell. It's the springtime and outdoors and sunshine that smells so great."

She said it as broadly as she could, and you do not know how broadly Yorkshire sounds until you have heard someone speak it. Colin began to laugh.

"What are you doing?" he said. "I never heard you talk like that before. How funny it sounds."

"I'm givin' thee a bit o' Yorkshire," answered Mary triumphantly. "I canna' talk as graidely as Dickon an' Martha can but tha' sees I can shape a bit. Doesn't tha' understand a bit o' Yorkshire when tha' hears it? An' tha' a Yorkshire lad thysel' bred an' born! Eh! I wonder tha'rt not ashamed o' thy face."

And then she began to laugh too and they both laughed until they could not stop themselves and they laughed until the room echoed and Mrs. Medlock opening the door to come in drew back into the corridor and stood listening amazed.

"Well, upon my word!" she said, quite astonished. "Whoever heard the like? Whoever on earth would have thought it!"

There was so much to talk about. It seemed as if Colin could never hear enough of Dickon and Captain and Soot and Nut and Shell and the pony whose name was Jump. Mary had run round into the wood with Dickon to see Jump. He was a tiny little shaggy moor pony with thick locks hanging over his eyes and with a pretty face and a nuzzling velvet nose. He was rather thin with living on moor grass but he was as tough and wiry as if the muscles in his little legs had been made of steel springs. He had lifted his head and whinnied softly the moment he saw Dickon and he had trotted up to him and put his head across his shoulder and then Dickon had talked into his ear and Jump had talked back in odd little whinnies and puffs and snorts. Dickon had made him give Mary his small front hoof and kiss her on her cheek with his velvet muzzle.

"Does he really understand everything Dickon says?" Colin asked.

"It seems as if he does," answered Mary. "Dickon says anything will understand if you're friends with it, but you have to be friends for sure."

Colin lay quiet a little while and his strange grey eyes seemed to be staring at the wall, but Mary saw he was thinking.

"I wish I was friends with things," he said at last, "but I'm not. I never had anything to be friends with, and I can't bear people."

"Can't you bear me?" asked Mary.

"Yes, I can," he answered. "It's very funny but I even like you."

"Ben Weatherstaff said I was like him," said Mary. "He said he'd warrant we'd both got the same nasty tempers. I think you are like him too. We are all three alike—you and I and Ben Weatherstaff. He said we were neither of us much to look at and we were as sour as we looked. But I don't feel as sour as I used to before I knew the robin and Dickon."

"Did you feel as if you hated people?"

"Yes," answered Mary without any affectation. "I should have detested you if I had seen you before I saw the robin and Dickon."

Colin put out his thin hand and touched her.

"Mary," he said, "I wish I hadn't said what I did about sending Dickon away. I hated you when you said he was like an angel and I laughed at you but—but perhaps he is."

"Well, it was rather funny to say it," she admitted frankly, "because his nose does turn up and he has a big mouth and his clothes have patches all over them and he

160

talks broad Yorkshire, but—but if an angel did come to Yorkshire and live on the moor—if there was a Yorkshire angel—I believe he'd understand the green things and know how to make them grow and he would know how to talk to the wild creatures as Dickon does and they'd know he was friends for sure."

"I shouldn't mind Dickon looking at me," said Colin; "I want to see him."

"I'm glad you said that," answered Mary, "because—because—"

Quite suddenly it came into her mind that this was the minute to tell him. Colin knew something new was coming.

"Because what?" he cried eagerly.

Mary was so anxious that she got up from her stool and came to him and caught hold of both his hands.

"Can I trust you? I trusted Dickon because birds trusted him. Can I trust you—for sure—*for sure*?" she implored.

Her face was so solemn that he almost whispered his answer.

"Yes—yes!"

"Well, Dickon will come to see you tomorrow morning, and he'll bring his creatures with him."

"Oh! Oh!" Colin cried out in delight.

"But that's not all," Mary went on, almost pale with solemn excitement. "The rest is better. There is a door into the garden. I found it. It is under the ivy on the wall."

If he had been a strong healthy boy Colin would probably have shouted "Hooray! Hooray! Hooray!" but he was weak and rather hysterical; his eyes grew bigger and bigger and he gasped for breath.

"Oh! Mary!" he cried out with a half sob. "Shall I see it? Shall I get into it? Shall I *live* to get into it?" and he clutched her hands and dragged her toward him.

"Of course you'll see it!" snapped Mary indignantly. "Of course you'll live to get into it! Don't be silly!"

And she was so natural and childish that she brought him to his senses and he began to laugh at himself and a few minutes afterward she was sitting on her stool again telling him not what she imagined the secret garden to be like but what it really was, and Colin's aches and tiredness were forgotten and he was listening enraptured.

"It is just what you thought it would be," he said at last. "It sounds just as if you had really seen it. You know I said that when you told me first."

Mary hesitated about two minutes and then boldly spoke the truth.

"I had seen it—and I had been in," she said. "I found the key and got in weeks ago. But I daren't tell you—I daren't because I was so afraid I couldn't trust you—*for sure*!"

## CHAPTER XIX

### "IT HAS COME!"

Of course Dr. Craven had been sent for the morning after Colin had had his tantrum. He was always sent for at once when such a thing occurred and he always found, when he arrived, a white shaken boy lying on his bed, sulky and still so hysterical that he was ready to break into fresh sobbing at the least word. In fact, Dr. Craven dreaded and detested the difficulties of these visits. On this occasion he was away from Misselthwaite Manor until afternoon.

"How is he?" he asked Mrs. Medlock rather irritably when he arrived. "He will break a blood-vessel in one of those fits someday. The boy is half insane with hysteria and self-indulgence."

"Well, sir," answered Mrs. Medlock, "you'll scarcely believe your eyes when you see him. That plain sour-faced child that's almost as bad as himself has just bewitched him. How she's done it there's no telling. The Lord knows she's nothing to look at and you scarcely ever hear her speak, but she did what none of us dare do. She just flew at him like a little cat last night, and stamped her feet and ordered him to stop screaming, and somehow she startled him so that he actually did stop, and this afternoon—well just come up and see, sir. It's past crediting."

The scene which Dr. Craven beheld when he entered his patient's room was indeed rather astonishing to him. As Mrs. Medlock opened the door he heard laughing and chattering. Colin was on his sofa in his dressing-gown and he was sitting up quite straight looking at a picture in one of the garden books and talking to the plain child who at that moment could scarcely be called plain at all because her face was so glowing with enjoyment.

"Those long spires of blue ones—we'll have a lot of those," Colin was announcing. "They're called Del-phin-iums."

"Dickon says they're larkspurs made big and grand," cried Mistress Mary. "There are clumps there already."

Then they saw Dr. Craven and stopped. Mary became quite still and Colin looked fretful.

"I am sorry to hear you were ill last night, my boy," Dr. Craven said a trifle nervously. He was rather a nervous man.

162

"I'm better now—much better," Colin answered, rather like a Rajah. "I'm going out in my chair in a day or two if it is fine. I want some fresh air."

Dr. Craven sat down by him and felt his pulse and looked at him curiously.

"It must be a very fine day," he said, "and you must be very careful not to tire yourself."

"Fresh air won't tire me," said the young Rajah.

As there had been occasions when this same young gentleman had shrieked aloud with rage and had insisted that fresh air would give him cold and kill him, it is not to be wondered at that his doctor felt somewhat startled.

"I thought you did not like fresh air," he said.

"I don't when I am by myself," replied the Rajah; "but my cousin is going out with me."

"And the nurse, of course?" suggested Dr. Craven.

"No, I will not have the nurse," so magnificently that Mary could not help remembering how the young native Prince had looked with his diamonds and emeralds and pearls stuck all over him and the great rubies on the small dark hand he had waved to command his servants to approach with salaams and receive his orders.

"My cousin knows how to take care of me. I am always better when she is with me. She made me better last night. A very strong boy I know will push my carriage."

Dr. Craven felt rather alarmed. If this tiresome hysterical boy should chance to get well he himself would lose all chance of inheriting Misselthwaite; but he was not an unscrupulous man, though he was a weak one, and he did not intend to let him run into actual danger.

"He must be a strong boy and a steady boy," he said. "And I must know something about him. Who is he? What is his name?"

"It's Dickon," Mary spoke up suddenly. She felt somehow that everybody who knew the moor must know Dickon. And she was right, too. She saw that in a moment Dr. Craven's serious face relaxed into a relieved smile.

"Oh, Dickon," he said. "If it is Dickon you will be safe enough. He's as strong as a moor pony, Dickon."

"And he's trustworthy," said Mary. "He's the most trustworthy lad in Yorkshire."

"Did Dickon teach you that?" asked Dr. Craven, laughing outright.

"I'm learning it as if it was French," said Mary rather coldly. "It's like a native dialect in India. Very clever people try to learn them. I like it and so does Colin."

"Well, well," he said. "If it amuses you perhaps it won't do you any harm. Did you take your bromide last night, Colin?"

"No," Colin answered. "I wouldn't take it at first and after Mary made me quiet she talked me to sleep—in a low voice—about the spring creeping into a garden."

"That sounds soothing," said Dr. Craven, more perplexed than ever and glancing sideways at Mistress Mary sitting on her stool and looking down silently at the carpet. "You are evidently better, but you must remember—"

"I don't want to remember," interrupted the Rajah, appearing again. "When I lie by myself and remember I begin to have pains everywhere and I think of things that make me begin to scream because I hate them so. If there was a doctor anywhere who could make you forget you were ill instead of remembering it I would have him brought here." And he waved a thin hand which ought really to have been covered with royal signet rings made of rubies. "It is because my cousin makes me forget that she makes me better."

Dr. Craven had never made such a short stay after a "tantrum"; usually he was obliged to remain a very long time and do a great many things. This afternoon he did not give any medicine or leave any new orders and he was spared any disagreeable scenes. When he went downstairs he looked very thoughtful and when he talked to Mrs. Medlock in the library she felt that he was a puzzled man.

"Well, sir," she ventured, "could you have believed it?"

"It is certainly a new state of affairs," said the doctor. "And there's no denying it is better than the old one."

"I believe Susan Sowerby's right—I do that," said Mrs. Medlock. "I stopped in her cottage on my way to Thwaite yesterday and had a bit of talk with her. And she says to me, 'Well, Sarah Ann, she may not be a good child, and she may not be a pretty one, but she's a child, and children need children.' We went to school together, Susan Sowerby and me."

"She's the best sick nurse I know," said Dr. Craven. "When I find her in a cottage I know the chances are that I shall save my patient."

Mrs. Medlock smiled. She was fond of Susan Sowerby.

"She's got a way with her, Susan has," she went on quite talkatively. "I've been thinking all morning of one thing she said yesterday. She said, 'Once when I was giving the children a bit of a preach after they'd been fighting I said to them all, "When I was at school my geography teacher told us that the world was shaped like an orange and I found out before I was ten that the whole orange doesn't belong to anybody. No one owns more than his bit of a quarter and there are times it seems like there are not enough quarters to go round. But don't you—none of you—think that you own the whole orange or you'll find out you're mistaken, and you won't find it out without hard knocks.' What children learn from children,' she says, 'is that there's no sense in grabbing at the whole orange—peel and all. If you do you'll likely not get more than the pips, and they're too bitter to eat.'"

"She's a shrewd woman," said Dr. Craven, putting on his coat.

"Well, she's got a way of saying things," ended Mrs. Medlock, much pleased. "Sometimes I've said to her, 'Eh! Susan, if you were a different woman and didn't talk such broad Yorkshire I've seen the times when I should have said you were clever.'"

That night Colin slept without once awakening and when he opened his eyes in the morning he lay still and smiled without knowing it—smiled because he felt so curiously comfortable. It was actually nice to be awake, and he turned over and stretched his limbs luxuriously. He felt as if tight strings which had held him had loosened themselves and let him go. He did not know that Dr. Craven would have said that his nerves had relaxed and rested themselves. Instead of lying and staring at the wall and wishing he had not awakened, his mind was full of the plans he and Mary had made yesterday, of pictures of the garden and of Dickon and his wild creatures. It was so nice to have things to think about. And he had not been awake more than ten minutes when he heard feet running along the corridor and Mary was at the door. The next minute she was in the room and had run across to his bed, bringing with her a waft of fresh air full of the scent of the morning.

"You've been out! You've been out! There's that nice smell of leaves!" he cried.

She had been running and her hair was loose and blown and she was bright with the air and pink-cheeked, though he could not see it.

"It's so beautiful!" she said, a little breathless with her speed. "You never saw anything so beautiful! It has *come*! I thought it had come that other morning, but it was only coming. It is here now! It has come, the spring! Dickon says so!"

"Has it?" cried Colin, and though he really knew nothing about it he felt his heart beat. He actually sat up in bed.

"Open the window!" he added, laughing half with joyful excitement and half at his own fancy. "Perhaps we may hear golden trumpets!"

And though he laughed, Mary was at the window in a moment and in a moment more it was opened wide and freshness and softness and scents and birds' songs were pouring through.

"That's fresh air," she said. "Lie on your back and draw in long breaths of it. That's what Dickon does when he's lying on the moor. He says he feels it in his veins and it makes him strong and he feels as if he could live forever and ever. Breathe it and breathe it."

She was only repeating what Dickon had told her, but she caught Colin's fancy.

"'Forever and ever'! Does it make him feel like that?" he said, and he did as she told him, drawing in long deep breaths over and over again until he felt that something quite new and delightful was happening to him.

Mary was at his bedside again.

"Things are crowding up out of the earth," she ran on in a hurry. "And there are flowers uncurling and buds on everything and the green veil has covered nearly all the grey and the birds are in such a hurry about their nests for fear they may be too late that some of them are even fighting for places in the secret garden. And the rose bushes look as thick as thick can be, and there are primroses in the lanes and woods, and the seeds we planted are up, and Dickon has brought the fox and the crow and the squirrels and a new-born lamb."

And then she paused for breath. The new-born lamb Dickon had found three days before lying by its dead mother among the gorse bushes on the moor. It was not the first motherless lamb he had found and he knew what to do with it. He had taken it to the cottage wrapped in his jacket and he had let it lie near the fire and had fed it with warm milk. It was a soft thing with a darling silly baby face and legs rather long for its body. Dickon had carried it over the moor in his arms and its feeding bottle was in his pocket with a squirrel, and when Mary had sat under a tree with its limp warmness huddled on her lap she had felt as if she were too full of strange joy to speak. A lamb—a lamb! A living lamb who lay on your lap like a baby!

She was describing it with great joy and Colin was listening and drawing in long breaths of air when the nurse entered. She started a little at the sight of the open window. She had sat stifling in the room many a warm day because her patient was sure that open windows gave people cold.

"Are you sure you are not chilly, Master Colin?" she inquired.

"No," was the answer. "I am breathing long breaths of fresh air. It makes you strong. I am going to get up to the sofa for breakfast and my cousin will have breakfast with me."

The nurse went away, concealing a smile, to give the order for two breakfasts. She found the servants' hall a more amusing place than the invalid's chamber and just now everybody wanted to hear the news from upstairs. There was a great deal of joking about the unpopular young recluse who, as the cook said, "had found his master, and good for him." The servants' hall had been very tired of the tantrums, and the butler, who was a man with a family, had more than once expressed his opinion that the invalid would be all the better "for a good hiding."

When Colin was on his sofa and the breakfast for two was put upon the table he made an announcement to the nurse in his most Rajah-like manner.

"A boy, and a fox, and a crow, and two squirrels, and a new-born lamb, are coming to see me this morning. I want them brought upstairs as soon as they come," he said.

"You are not to begin playing with the animals in the servants' hall and keep them there. I want them here."

The nurse gave a slight gasp and tried to conceal it with a cough.

"Yes, sir," she answered.

"I'll tell you what you can do," added Colin, waving his hand. "You can tell Martha to bring them here. The boy is Martha's brother. His name is Dickon and he is an animal charmer."

"I hope the animals won't bite, Master Colin," said the nurse.

"I told you he was a charmer," said Colin austerely. "Charmers' animals never bite."

"There are snake-charmers in India," said Mary; "and they can put their snakes' heads in their mouths."

"Goodness!" shuddered the nurse.

They ate their breakfast with the morning air pouring in upon them. Colin's breakfast was a very good one and Mary watched him with serious interest.

"You will begin to get fatter just as I did," she said. "I never wanted my breakfast when I was in India and now I always want it."

"I wanted mine this morning," said Colin. "Perhaps it was the fresh air. When do you think Dickon will come?"

He was not long in coming. In about ten minutes Mary held up her hand.

"Listen!" she said. "Did you hear a caw?"

Colin listened and heard it, the oddest sound in the world to hear inside a house, a hoarse "caw-caw."

"Yes," he answered.

"That's Soot," said Mary. "Listen again! Do you hear a bleat—a tiny one?"

"Oh, yes!" cried Colin, quite flushing.

"That's the new-born lamb," said Mary. "He's coming."

Dickon's moorland boots were thick and clumsy and though he tried to walk quietly they made a clumping sound as he walked through the long corridors. Mary and Colin heard him marching—marching, until he passed through the tapestry door on to the soft carpet of Colin's own passage.

"If you please, sir," announced Martha, opening the door, "if you please, sir, here's Dickon and his creatures."

Dickon came in smiling his nicest wide smile. The new-born lamb was in his arms and the little red fox trotted by his side. Nut sat on his left shoulder and Soot on his right and Shell's head and paws peeped out of his coat pocket.

Colin slowly sat up and stared and stared—as he had stared when he first saw Mary; but this was a stare of wonder and delight. The truth was that in spite of all he had heard he had not in the least understood what this boy would be like and that his fox and his crow and his squirrels and his lamb were so near to him and his friendliness that they seemed almost to be a part of him. Colin had never talked to a boy in his life and he was so overwhelmed by his own pleasure and curiosity that he did not even think of speaking.

But Dickon did not feel the least shy or awkward. He had not felt embarrassed because the crow had not known his language and had only stared and had not spoken to him the first time they met. Creatures were always like that until they found out about you. He walked over to Colin's sofa and put the new-born lamb quietly on his lap, and immediately the little creature turned to the warm velvet dressing-gown and began to nuzzle and nuzzle into its folds and butt its tight-curled head with soft impatience against his side. Of course no boy could have helped speaking then.

"What is it doing?" cried Colin. "What does it want?"

"It wants its mother," said Dickon, smiling more and more. "I brought it to you a bit hungry because I knew you'd like to see it feed."

He knelt down by the sofa and took a feeding-bottle from his pocket.

"Come on, little one," he said, turning the small woolly white head with a gentle brown hand.

"This is what you're after. You'll get more out of this than you will out of silk velvet coats. There now," and he pushed the rubber tip of the bottle into the nuzzling mouth and the lamb began to suck it with ravenous ecstasy.

After that there was no wondering what to say. By the time the lamb fell asleep questions poured forth and Dickon answered them all. He told them how he had found the lamb just as the sun was rising three mornings ago. He had been standing on the moor listening to a skylark and watching him swing higher and higher into the sky until he was only a speck in the heights of blue.

"I'd almost lost him but for his song and I was wondering how a chap could hear it when it seemed as if he'd get out of the world in a minute—and just then I heard something else far off among the gorse bushes. It was a weak bleating and I knew it was a new lamb that was hungry and I knew it wouldn't be hungry if it hadn't lost its mother somehow, so I set off searching Eh! I did have a look for it. I went in and out among the gorse bushes and round and round and I always seemed to take the wrong turning. But at last I saw a bit of white by a rock on top of the moor and I climbed up and found the little one half dead with cold and hunger."

While he talked, Soot flew solemnly in and out of the open window and cawed remarks about the scenery while Nut and Shell made excursions into the big trees outside and ran up and down trunks and explored branches. Captain curled up near Dickon, who sat on the hearth-rug from preference.

They looked at the pictures in the gardening books and Dickon knew all the flowers by their country names and knew exactly which ones were already growing in the secret garden.

"I couldn't have said that was their name," he said, pointing to one under which was written "Aquilegia," "but us calls that a columbine, and that one is a snapdragon and they both grow wild in hedges, but these are garden ones and they're bigger and grander. There's some big clumps of columbine in the garden. They'll look like a bed of blue and white butterflies fluttering when they're out."

"I'm going to see them," cried Colin. "I am going to see them!"

"Aye, that you must," said Mary quite seriously. "And you must not lose any time about it."

## CHAPTER XX

## "I SHALL LIVE FOREVER—AND EVER—AND EVER!"

But they were obliged to wait more than a week because first there came some very windy days and then Colin was threatened with a cold, which two things happening one after the other would no doubt have thrown him into a rage but there was so much careful and mysterious planning to do and almost every day Dickon came in, if only for a few minutes, to talk about what was happening on the moor and in the lanes and hedges and on the borders of streams. The things he had to tell about otters' and badgers' and water-rats' houses, not to mention birds' nests and field-mice and their burrows, were enough to make you almost tremble with excitement when you heard all the intimate details from an animal charmer and realized with what thrilling eagerness and anxiety the whole busy underworld was working.

"They're the same than us," said Dickon, "only they have to build their homes every year. And it keeps them so busy they scuffle to get them done."

The most absorbing thing, however, was the preparations to be made before Colin could be transported with sufficient secrecy to the garden. No one must see the chair-carriage and Dickon and Mary after they turned a certain corner of the shrubbery and entered upon the walk outside the ivied walls. As each day passed, Colin had become more and more fixed in his feeling that the mystery surrounding the garden was one of its greatest charms. Nothing must spoil that. No one must ever suspect that they had a secret. People must think that he was simply going out with Mary and Dickon because he liked them and did not object to their looking at him. They had long and quite delightful talks about their route. They would go up this path and down that one and cross the other and go round among the fountain flower-beds as if they were looking at the "bedding-out plants" the head gardener, Mr. Roach, had been having arranged. That would seem such a rational thing to do that no one would think it at all mysterious. They would turn into the shrubbery walks and lose themselves until they came to the long walls. It was almost as serious and elaborately thought out as the plans of march made by great generals in time of war.

Rumours of the new and curious things which were occurring in the invalid's apartments had of course filtered through the servants' hall into the stable yards and out among the gardeners, but notwithstanding this, Mr. Roach was startled one day when he received orders from Master Colin's room to the effect that he must report himself in the apartment no outsider had ever seen, as the invalid himself desired to speak to him.

"Well, well," he said to himself as he hurriedly changed his coat, "what's to do now? His Royal Highness that wasn't to be looked at calling up a man he's never set eyes on."

Mr. Roach was not without curiosity. He had never caught even a glimpse of the boy and had heard a dozen exaggerated stories about his uncanny looks and ways and his insane tempers. The thing he had heard most often was that he might die at any moment and there had been numerous fanciful descriptions of a humped back and helpless limbs, given by people who had never seen him.

"Things are changing in this house, Mr. Roach," said Mrs. Medlock, as she led him up the back staircase to the corridor on to which opened the hitherto mysterious chamber.

"Let's hope they're changing for the better, Mrs. Medlock," he answered.

"They couldn't well change for the worse," she continued; "and queer as it all is there're those who find their duties made a lot easier to stand up under. Don't you be surprised, Mr. Roach, if you find yourself in the middle of a menagerie and Martha Sowerby's Dickon more at home than you or me could ever be."

There really was a sort of Magic about Dickon, as Mary always privately believed. When Mr. Roach heard his name he smiled quite leniently.

"He'd be at home in Buckingham Palace or at the bottom of a coal mine," he said. "And yet it's not impudence, either. He's just fine, that lad."

It was perhaps well he had been prepared or he might have been startled. When the bedroom door was opened a large crow, which seemed quite at home perched on

170

the high back of a carven chair, announced the entrance of a visitor by saying "Caw—Caw" quite loudly. In spite of Mrs. Medlock's warning, Mr. Roach only just escaped being sufficiently undignified to jump backward.

The young Rajah was neither in bed nor on his sofa. He was sitting in an armchair and a young lamb was standing by him shaking its tail in feeding-lamb fashion as Dickon knelt giving it milk from its bottle. A squirrel was perched on Dickon's bent back attentively nibbling a nut. The little girl from India was sitting on a big footstool looking on.

"Here is Mr. Roach, Master Colin," said Mrs. Medlock.

The young Rajah turned and looked his servitor over—at least that was what the head gardener felt happened.

"Oh, you are Roach, are you?" he said. "I sent for you to give you some very important orders."

"Very good, sir," answered Roach, wondering if he was to receive instructions to fell all the oaks in the park or to transform the orchards into water-gardens.

"I am going out in my chair this afternoon," said Colin. "If the fresh air agrees with me I may go out every day. When I go, none of the gardeners are to be anywhere near the Long Walk by the garden walls. No one is to be there. I shall go out about two o'clock and everyone must keep away until I send word that they may go back to their work."

"Very good, sir," replied Mr. Roach, much relieved to hear that the oaks might remain and that the orchards were safe.

"Mary," said Colin, turning to her, "what is that thing you say in India when you have finished talking and want people to go?"

"You say, 'You have my permission to go,'" answered Mary.

The Rajah waved his hand.

"You have my permission to go, Roach," he said. "But, remember, this is very important."

"Caw—Caw!" remarked the crow hoarsely but not impolitely.

"Very good, sir. Thank you, sir," said Mr. Roach, and Mrs. Medlock took him out of the room.

Outside in the corridor, being a rather good-natured man, he smiled until he almost laughed.

"My word!" he said, "he's got a fine lordly way with him, hasn't he? You'd think he was a whole Royal Family rolled into one—Prince Consort and all."

171

"Eh!" protested Mrs. Medlock, "we've had to let him trample all over every one of us ever since he had feet and he thinks that's what folks were born for."

"Perhaps he'll grow out of it, if he lives," suggested Mr. Roach.

"Well, there's one thing pretty sure," said Mrs. Medlock. "If he does live and that Indian child stays here I'll warrant she teaches him that the whole orange does not belong to him, as Susan Sowerby says. And he'll be likely to find out the size of his own quarter."

Inside the room Colin was leaning back on his cushions.

"It's all safe now," he said. "And this afternoon I shall see it—this afternoon I shall be in it!"

Dickon went back to the garden with his creatures and Mary stayed with Colin. She did not think he looked tired but he was very quiet before their lunch came and he was quiet while they were eating it. She wondered why and asked him about it.

"What big eyes you've got, Colin," she said. "When you are thinking they get as big as saucers. What are you thinking about now?"

"I can't help thinking about what it will look like," he answered.

"The garden?" asked Mary.

"The springtime," he said. "I was thinking that I've really never seen it before. I scarcely ever went out and when I did go I never looked at it. I didn't even think about it."

"I never saw it in India because there wasn't any," said Mary.

Shut in and morbid as his life had been, Colin had more imagination than she had and at least he had spent a good deal of time looking at wonderful books and pictures.

"That morning when you ran in and said 'It's come! It's come!' you made me feel quite queer. It sounded as if things were coming with a great procession and big bursts and wafts of music. I've a picture like it in one of my books—crowds of lovely people and children with garlands and branches with blossoms on them, every one laughing and dancing and crowding and playing on pipes. That was why I said, 'Perhaps we shall hear golden trumpets' and told you to throw open the window."

"How funny!" said Mary. "That's really just what it feels like. And if all the flowers and leaves and green things and birds and wild creatures danced past at once, what a crowd it would be! I'm sure they'd dance and sing and flute and that would be the wafts of music."

They both laughed but it was not because the idea was laughable but because they both so liked it.

A little later the nurse made Colin ready. She noticed that instead of lying like a log while his clothes were put on he sat up and made some efforts to help himself, and he talked and laughed with Mary all the time.

"This is one of his good days, sir," she said to Dr. Craven, who dropped in to inspect him. "He's in such good spirits that it makes him stronger."

"I'll call in again later in the afternoon, after he has come in," said Dr. Craven. "I must see how the going out agrees with him. I wish," in a very low voice, "that he would let you go with him."

"I'd rather give up the case this moment, sir, than even stay here while it's suggested," answered the nurse with sudden firmness.

"I hadn't really decided to suggest it," said the doctor, with his slight nervousness. "We'll try the experiment. Dickon's a lad I'd trust with a new-born child."

The strongest footman in the house carried Colin downstairs and put him in his wheeled chair near which Dickon waited outside. After the manservant had arranged his rugs and cushions the Rajah waved his hand to him and to the nurse.

"You have my permission to go," he said, and they both disappeared quickly and it must be confessed giggled when they were safely inside the house.

Dickon began to push the wheeled chair slowly and steadily. Mistress Mary walked beside it and Colin leaned back and lifted his face to the sky. The arch of it looked very high and the small snowy clouds seemed like white birds floating on outspread wings below its crystal blueness. The wind swept in soft big breaths down from the moor and was strange with a wild clear scented sweetness. Colin kept lifting his thin chest to draw it in, and his big eyes looked as if it were they which were listening—listening, instead of his ears.

"There are so many sounds of singing and humming and calling out," he said. "What is that scent the puffs of wind bring?"

"It's gorse on the moor that's opening up," answered Dickon. "Eh! The bees are at it wonderfully today."

Not a human creature was to be caught sight of in the paths they took. In fact every gardener or gardener's lad had been witched away. But they wound in and out among the shrubbery and out and round the fountain beds, following their carefully planned route for the mere mysterious pleasure of it. But when at last they turned into the Long Walk by the ivied walls the excited sense of an approaching thrill made them, for some curious reason they could not have explained, begin to speak in whispers.

"This is it," breathed Mary. "This is where I used to walk up and down and wonder and wonder."

"Is it?" cried Colin, and his eyes began to search the ivy with eager curiousness. "But I can see nothing," he whispered. "There is no door."

"That's what I thought," said Mary.

Then there was a lovely breathless silence and the chair wheeled on.

"That is the garden where Ben Weatherstaff works," said Mary.

"Is it?" said Colin.

A few yards more and Mary whispered again.

"This is where the robin flew over the wall," she said.

"Is it?" cried Colin. "Oh! I wish he'd come again!"

"And that," said Mary with solemn delight, pointing under a big lilac bush, "is where he perched on the little heap of earth and showed me the key."

Then Colin sat up.

"Where? Where? There?" he cried, and his eyes were as big as the wolf's in Red Riding-Hood, when Red Riding-Hood felt called upon to remark on them. Dickon stood still and the wheeled chair stopped.

"And this," said Mary, stepping on to the bed close to the ivy, "is where I went to talk to him when he chirped at me from the top of the wall. And this is the ivy the wind blew back," and she took hold of the hanging green curtain.

"Oh! Is it—is it!" gasped Colin.

"And here is the handle, and here is the door. Dickon push him in—push him in quickly!"

And Dickon did it with one strong, steady, splendid push.

But Colin had actually dropped back against his cushions, even though he gasped with delight, and he had covered his eyes with his hands and held them there shutting out everything until they were inside and the chair stopped as if by magic and the door was closed. Not till then did he take them away and look round and round and round as Dickon and Mary had done. And over walls and earth and trees and swinging sprays and tendrils the fair green veil of tender little leaves had crept, and in the grass under the trees and the grey urns in the alcoves and here and there everywhere were touches or splashes of gold and purple and white and the trees were showing pink and snow above his head and there were fluttering of wings and faint sweet pipes and humming and scents and scents. And the sun fell warm upon his face like a hand with a lovely touch. And in wonder Mary and Dickon stood and stared at him. He looked so strange and different because a pink glow of colour had actually crept all over him—ivory face and neck and hands and all.

"I shall get well! I shall get well!" he cried out. "Mary! Dickon! I shall get well! And I shall live forever and ever and ever!"

## CHAPTER XXI

## BEN WEATHERSTAFF

One of the strange things about living in the world is that it is only now and then one is quite sure one is going to live forever and ever and ever. One knows it sometimes when one gets up at the tender solemn dawn-time and goes out and stands alone and throws one's head far back and looks up and up and watches the pale sky slowly changing and flushing and marvellous unknown things happening until the East almost makes one cry out and one's heart stands still at the strange unchanging majesty of the rising of the sun—which has been happening every morning for thousands and thousands and thousands of years. One knows it then for a moment or so. And one knows it sometimes when one stands by oneself in a wood at sunset and the mysterious deep gold stillness slanting through and under the branches seems to be saying slowly again and again something one cannot quite hear, however much one tries. Then sometimes the immense quiet of the dark blue at night with millions of stars waiting and watching makes one sure; and sometimes a sound of far-off music makes it true; and sometimes a look in some one's eyes.

And it was like that with Colin when he first saw and heard and felt the springtime inside the four high walls of a hidden garden. That afternoon the whole world seemed to devote itself to being perfect and radiantly beautiful and kind to one boy. Perhaps out of pure heavenly goodness the spring came and crowded everything it possibly could into that one place. More than once Dickon paused in what he was doing and stood still with a sort of growing wonder in his eyes, shaking his head softly.

"Eh! Isn't it amazing," he said. "I'm twelve going on thirteen and there're a lot of afternoons in thirteen years, but it seems to me like I have never seen one as amazing as this one here."

"Aye, it is a great one," said Mary, and she sighed for mere joy. "I'll warrant it's the greatest one ever in this world."

"Do you think," Said Colin with dreamy carefulness, "that it was made like this here all for my purpose?"

"My word!" cried Mary.

And delight reigned.

They drew the chair under the plum-tree, which was snow-white with blossoms and musical with bees. It was like a king's canopy, a fairy king's. There were flowering cherry-trees near and apple-trees whose buds were pink and white, and here and there one had burst open wide. Between the blossoming branches of the canopy bits of blue sky looked down like wonderful eyes.

Mary and Dickon worked a little here and there and Colin watched them. They brought him things to look at—buds which were opening, buds which were tight closed, bits of twig whose leaves were just showing green, the feather of a woodpecker which had dropped on the grass, the empty shell of some bird early hatched. Dickon pushed the chair slowly round and round the garden, stopping every other moment to let him look at wonders springing out of the earth or trailing down from trees. It was like being taken in state round the country of a magic king and queen and shown all the mysterious riches it contained.

"I wonder if we shall see the robin?" said Colin.

"You'll see him often enough after a bit," answered Dickon. "When the eggs hatch out the little chap will be keeping so busy it'll make his head swim. You'll see him flying backward and forward carrying worms almost as big as himself and that much noise going on in the nest when he gets there as fair flusters him so as he scarcely knows which big mouth to drop the first piece in. And gaping beaks and squawks on every side. Mother says that when she sees the work a robin has to keep them gaping beaks filled, she feels like she was a lady with nothing to do. She says she's seen the little chaps when it seemed like the sweat must be dropping off them, though folk can't see it."

This made them giggle so delightedly that they were obliged to cover their mouths with their hands, remembering that they must not be heard. Colin had been instructed as to the law of whispers and low voices several days before. He liked the mysteriousness of it and did his best, but in the midst of excited enjoyment it is rather difficult never to laugh above a whisper.

Every moment of the afternoon was full of new things and every hour the sunshine grew more golden. The wheeled chair had been drawn back under the canopy and Dickon had sat down on the grass and had just drawn out his pipe when Colin saw something he had not had time to notice before.

"That's a very old tree over there, isn't it?" he said.

Dickon looked across the grass at the tree and Mary looked and there was a brief moment of stillness.

"Yes," answered Dickon, after it, and his low voice had a very gentle sound.

Mary gazed at the tree and thought.

"The branches are quite grey and there's not a single leaf anywhere," Colin went on. "It's quite dead, isn't it?"

"Aye," admitted Dickon. "But the roses that have climbed all over it will nearly hide every bit of the dead wood when they're full of leaves and flowers. It won't look dead then. It'll be the prettiest of all."

Mary still gazed at the tree and thought.

"It looks as if a big branch had been broken off," said Colin. "I wonder how it was done."

"It's been done many years ago," answered Dickon. "Eh!" with a sudden relieved start and laying his hand on Colin. "Look at that robin! There he is! He's been foraging for his mate."

Colin was almost too late but he just caught sight of him, the flash of red-breasted bird with something in his beak. He darted through the greenness and into the close-grown corner and was out of sight. Colin leaned back on his cushion again, laughing a little.

"He's taking her tea to her. Perhaps it's five o'clock. I think I'd like some tea myself."

And so they were safe.

"It was Magic which sent the robin," said Mary secretly to Dickon afterward. "I know it was Magic." For both she and Dickon had been afraid Colin might ask something about the tree whose branch had broken off ten years ago and they had talked it over together and Dickon had stood and rubbed his head in a troubled way.

"We must look as if it wasn't any different from the other trees," he had said. "We could never tell him how it broke, poor lad. If he says anything about it we must— we must try to look cheerful."

"Aye, that we must," had answered Mary.

But she had not felt as if she looked cheerful when she gazed at the tree. She wondered and wondered in those few moments if there was any reality in that other thing Dickon had said. He had gone on rubbing his rust-red hair in a puzzled way, but a nice comforted look had begun to grow in his blue eyes.

"Mrs. Craven was a very lovely young lady," he had gone on rather hesitatingly. "And mother thinks maybe she's about Misselthwaite many a times looking after Master Colin, same as all mothers do when they're taken out of the world. They have to come back, you see. Maybe she's been in the garden and maybe it was her who set us to work, and told us to bring him here."

Mary had thought he meant something about Magic. She was a great believer in Magic. Secretly she quite believed that Dickon worked Magic, of course good Magic, on everything near him and that was why people liked him so much and wild creatures knew he was their friend. She wondered, indeed, if it were not possible that his gift had brought the robin just at the right moment when Colin asked that dangerous question. She felt that his Magic was working all the afternoon and making Colin look like an entirely different boy. It did not seem possible that he could be the crazy creature who had screamed and beaten and bitten his pillow. Even his ivory whiteness seemed to change. The faint glow of colour which had shown on his face and neck and hands when he first got inside the garden really never quite died away. He looked as if he were made of flesh instead of ivory or wax.

They saw the robin carry food to his mate two or three times, and it was so suggestive of afternoon tea that Colin felt they must have some.

"Go and make one of the men servants bring some in a basket to the rhododendron walk," he said. "And then you and Dickon can bring it here."

It was an agreeable idea, easily carried out, and when the white cloth was spread upon the grass, with hot tea and buttered toast and crumpets, a delightfully hungry meal was eaten, and several birds on domestic errands paused to inquire what was going on and were led into investigating crumbs with great activity. Nut and Shell whisked up trees with pieces of cake and Soot took the entire half of a buttered crumpet into a corner and pecked at and examined and turned it over and made hoarse remarks about it until he decided to swallow it all joyfully in one gulp.

The afternoon was dragging toward its mellow hour. The sun was deepening the gold of its lances, the bees were going home and the birds were flying past less often. Dickon and Mary were sitting on the grass, the tea basket was re-packed ready to be taken back to the house, and Colin was lying against his cushions with his heavy locks pushed back from his forehead and his face looking quite a natural colour.

"I don't want this afternoon to go," he said; "but I shall come back tomorrow, and the day after, and the day after, and the day after."

"You'll get plenty of fresh air, won't you?" said Mary.

"I'm going to get nothing else," he answered. "I've seen the spring now and I'm going to see the summer. I'm going to see everything grow here. I'm going to grow here myself."

"That you will," said Dickon. "We'll have you walking about here and digging same as other folk before long."

Colin flushed tremendously.

"Walk!" he said. "Dig! Shall I?"

Dickon's glance at him was delicately cautious. Neither he nor Mary had ever asked if anything was the matter with his legs.

"For sure you will," he said stoutly. "You— you've got legs of your own, same as other folks!"

Mary was rather frightened until she heard Colin's answer.

"Nothing really ails them," he said, "but they are so thin and weak. They shake so that I'm afraid to try to stand on them."

Both Mary and Dickon drew a relieved breath.

"When you stop being afraid you'll stand on them," Dickon said with renewed cheer. "And you'll stop being afraid in a bit."

"I shall?" said Colin, and he lay still as if he were wondering about things.

They were really very quiet for a little while. The sun was dropping lower. It was that hour when everything stills itself, and they really had had a busy and exciting afternoon. Colin looked as if he were resting luxuriously. Even the creatures had ceased moving about and had drawn together and were resting near them. Soot had perched on a low branch and drawn up one leg and dropped the grey film drowsily over his eyes. Mary privately thought he looked as if he might snore in a minute.

In the midst of this stillness it was rather startling when Colin half lifted his head and exclaimed in a loud suddenly alarmed whisper:

"Who is that man?"

Dickon and Mary scrambled to their feet.

"Man!" they both cried in low quick voices.

Colin pointed to the high wall.

"Look!" he whispered excitedly. "Just look!"

Mary and Dickon wheeled about and looked. There was Ben Weatherstaff's indignant face glaring at them over the wall from the top of a ladder! He actually shook his fist at Mary.

"If I weren't a bachelor, and you were a young of mine," he cried, "I'd give you a hiding!"

He mounted another step threateningly as if it were his energetic intention to jump down and deal with her; but as she came toward him he evidently thought better of it and stood on the top step of his ladder shaking his fist down at her.

"I never thought much of you!" he ranted. "I couldn't stand you the first time I set eyes on you. A scrawny buttermilk-faced young lass, always asking questions and poking your nose where it wasn't wanted. I never knew how you got so thick with me. If it hadn't been for the robin—"

"Ben Weatherstaff," called out Mary, finding her breath. She stood below him and called up to him with a sort of gasp. "Ben Weatherstaff, it was the robin who showed me the way!"

Then it did seem as if Ben really would scramble down on her side of the wall, he was so outraged.

"You young bad one!" he called down at her. "Laying your badness on a robin,—as if he was impudent enough for anything. Him showing you the way! Him! Eh! That young -,"—she could see his next words burst out because he was overpowered by curiosity—"however in this world did you get in?"

"It was the robin who showed me the way," she protested obstinately. "He didn't know he was doing it but he did. And I can't tell you from here while you're shaking your fist at me."

He stopped shaking his fist very suddenly at that very moment and his jaw actually dropped as he stared over her head at something he saw coming over the grass toward him.

At the first sound of his torrent of words Colin had been so surprised that he had only sat up and listened as if he were spellbound. But in the midst of it he had recovered himself and beckoned imperiously to Dickon.

"Wheel me over there!" he commanded. "Wheel me quite close and stop right in front of him!"

And this, if you please, this is what Ben Weatherstaff beheld and which made his jaw drop. A wheeled chair with luxurious cushions and robes which came toward him looking rather like some sort of State Coach because a young Rajah leaned back in it with royal command in his great black-rimmed eyes and a thin white hand extended haughtily toward him. And it stopped right under Ben Weatherstaff's nose. It was really no wonder his mouth dropped open.

"Do you know who I am?" demanded the Rajah.

How Ben Weatherstaff stared! His red old eyes fixed themselves on what was before him as if he were seeing a ghost. He gazed and gazed and gulped a lump down his throat and did not say a word.

"Do you know who I am?" demanded Colin still more imperiously. "Answer!"

Ben Weatherstaff put his gnarled hand up and passed it over his eyes and over his forehead and then he did answer in a queer shaky voice.

"Who you are?" he said. "Aye, that I do—with your mother's eyes staring at me out of that face. Lord knows how you came here. But you're the poor cripple."

Colin forgot that he had ever had a back. His face flushed scarlet and he sat bolt upright.

"I'm not a cripple!" he cried out furiously. "I'm not!"

"He's not!" cried Mary, almost shouting up the wall in her fierce indignation. "He's not got a lump as big as a pin! I looked and there was none there—not one!"

Ben Weatherstaff passed his hand over his forehead again and gazed as if he could never gaze enough. His hand shook and his mouth shook and his voice shook. He was an ignorant old man and a tactless old man and he could only remember the things he had heard.

"You— you haven't got a crooked back?" he said hoarsely.

"No!" shouted Colin.

"You— you haven't got crooked legs?" quavered Ben more hoarsely yet.

It was too much. The strength which Colin usually threw into his tantrums rushed through him now in a new way. Never yet had he been accused of crooked legs— even in whispers—and the perfectly simple belief in their existence which was revealed by Ben Weatherstaff's voice was more than Rajah flesh and blood could endure. His anger and insulted pride made him forget everything but this one moment and filled him with a power he had never known before, an almost unnatural strength.

"Come here!" he shouted to Dickon, and he actually began to tear the coverings off his lower limbs and disentangle himself. "Come here! Come here! This minute!"

Dickon was by his side in a second. Mary caught her breath in a short gasp and felt herself turn pale.

"He can do it! He can do it! He can do it! He can!" she gabbled over to herself under her breath as fast as ever she could.

There was a brief fierce scramble, the rugs were tossed on to the ground, Dickon held Colin's arm, the thin legs were out, and the thin feet were on the grass. Colin was standing upright—upright—as straight as an arrow and looking strangely tall— his head thrown back and his strange eyes flashing lightning.

"Look at me!" he flung up at Ben Weatherstaff. "Just look at me—you! Just look at me!"

"He's as straight as I am!" cried Dickon. "He's as straight as any lad in Yorkshire!"

What Ben Weatherstaff did Mary thought queer beyond measure. He choked and gulped and suddenly tears ran down his weather-wrinkled cheeks as he struck his old hands together.

"Eh!" he burst forth, "the lies folk tells! You're as thin as a rod and as white as a ghost, but there's not a knob on you. You'll make a man yet. God bless you!"

Dickon held Colin's arm strongly but the boy had not begun to falter. He stood straighter and straighter and looked Ben Weatherstaff in the face.

"I'm your master," he said, "when my father is away. And you are to obey me. This is my garden. Don't dare to say a word about it! You get down from that ladder and go out to the Long Walk and Miss Mary will meet you and bring you here. I want to talk to you. We did not want you, but now you will have to be in the secret. Be quick!"

Ben Weatherstaff's crabbed old face was still wet with that one queer rush of tears. It seemed as if he could not take his eyes from thin straight Colin standing on his feet with his head thrown back.

"Eh! Lad," he almost whispered. "Eh! My lad!" And then remembering himself he suddenly touched his hat gardener fashion and said, "Yes, sir! Yes, sir!" and obediently disappeared as he descended the ladder.

# CHAPTER XXII

## WHEN THE SUN WENT DOWN

When his head was out of sight Colin turned to Mary.

"Go and meet him," he said; and Mary flew across the grass to the door under the ivy.

Dickon was watching him with sharp eyes. There were scarlet spots on his cheeks and he looked amazing, but he showed no signs of falling.

"I can stand," he said, and his head was still held up and he said it quite grandly.

"I told you that you could as soon as you stopped being afraid," answered Dickon. "And you've stopped."

"Yes, I've stopped," said Colin.

Then suddenly he remembered something Mary had said.

"Are you making Magic?" he asked sharply.

Dickon's curly mouth spread in a cheerful grin.

"You're doing Magic yourself," he said. "It's same Magic that made these here work out of the earth," and he touched with his thick boot a clump of crocuses in the grass.

Colin looked down at them.

"Aye," he said slowly, "there couldn't be bigger Magic than that here—there couldn't be."

He drew himself up straighter than ever.

"I'm going to walk to that tree," he said, pointing to one a few feet away from him. "I'm going to be standing when Weatherstaff comes here. I can rest against the tree if I like. When I want to sit down I will sit down, but not before. Bring a rug from the chair."

He walked to the tree and though Dickon held his arm he was wonderfully steady. When he stood against the tree trunk it was not too plain that he supported himself against it, and he still held himself so straight that he looked tall.

When Ben Weatherstaff came through the door in the wall he saw him standing there and he heard Mary muttering something under her breath.

"What are you saying?" he asked rather testily because he did not want his attention distracted from the long thin straight boy figure and proud face.

But she did not tell him. What she was saying was this:

"You can do it! You can do it! I told you you could! You can do it! You can do it! You *can*!"

She was saying it to Colin because she wanted to make Magic and keep him on his feet looking like that. She could not bear that he should give in before Ben Weatherstaff. He did not give in. She was uplifted by a sudden feeling that he looked quite beautiful in spite of his thinness. He fixed his eyes on Ben Weatherstaff in his funny imperious way.

"Look at me!" he commanded. "Look at me all over! Am I a hunchback? Have I got crooked legs?"

Ben Weatherstaff had not quite got over his emotion, but he had recovered a little and answered almost in his usual way.

"Not at all," he said. "Nothing of the sort. What've you been doing with yourself? Hiding out of sight and letting folk think you were a cripple and half-witted?"

"Half-witted!" said Colin angrily. "Who thought that?"

"Lots of fools," said Ben. "The world's full of jackasses braying and they bray nothing but lies. What did you shut yourself up for?"

"Everyone thought I was going to die," said Colin shortly. "I'm not!"

And he said it with such decision Ben Weatherstaff looked him over, up and down, down and up.

"You – die?!" he said with dry exultation. "Nothing of the sort! You've got too much pluck in you. When I saw you put your legs on the ground in such a hurry I knew you were alright. Sit yourself down on the rug a bit young Master and give me your orders."

There was a queer mixture of grumpy tenderness and shrewd understanding in his manner. Mary had poured out speech as rapidly as she could as they had come down the Long Walk. The chief thing to be remembered, she had told him, was that Colin was getting well—getting well. The garden was doing it. No one must let him remember about having humps and dying.

The Rajah deigned to seat himself on a rug under the tree.

"What work do you do in the gardens, Weatherstaff?" he inquired.

"Anything I'm told to do," answered old Ben. "I'm kept on by favour—because she liked me."

"She?" said Colin.

"Your mother," answered Ben Weatherstaff.

"My mother?" said Colin, and he looked about him quietly. "This was her garden, wasn't it?"

"Aye, it was that!" and Ben Weatherstaff looked about him too. "She was very fond of it."

"It is my garden now, I am fond of it. I shall come here every day," announced Colin. "But it is to be a secret. My orders are that no one is to know that we come here. Dickon and my cousin have worked and made it come alive. I shall send for you sometimes to help—but you must come when no one can see you."

Ben Weatherstaff's face twisted itself in a dry old smile.

"I've come here before when no one saw me," he said.

"What!" exclaimed Colin. "When?"

"The last time I was here," rubbing his chin and looking round, "was about two years ago."

"But no one has been in it for ten years!" cried Colin. "There was no door!"

"I'm no one," said old Ben dryly. "And I didn't come through the door. I come over the wall. The rheumatism held me back the last two years."

"You came and did a bit of pruning!" cried Dickon. "I couldn't make out how it had been done."

"She was so fond of it—she was!" said Ben Weatherstaff slowly. "And she was such a pretty young thing. She said to me once, 'Ben,' she said laughingly, 'if ever I'm ill or if I go away you must take care of my roses.' When she did go away the orders were for no one to ever come near. But I came," with grumpy stubbornness. "Over the wall I came—until the rheumatism stopped me—and I did a bit of work once a year. She'd given her order first."

"It wouldn't be as beautiful if you hadn't done it," said Dickon. "I did wonder."

"I'm glad you did it, Weatherstaff," said Colin. "You'll know how to keep the secret."

"Aye, I'll know, sir," answered Ben. "And it'll be easier for a man with rheumatism to come in at the door."

On the grass near the tree Mary had dropped her trowel. Colin stretched out his hand and took it up. An odd expression came into his face and he began to scratch at the earth. His thin hand was weak enough but presently as they watched him—Mary with quite breathless interest—he drove the end of the trowel into the soil and turned some over.

"You can do it! You can do it!" said Mary to herself. "I tell you, you can!"

Dickon's round eyes were full of eager curiousness but he said not a word. Ben Weatherstaff looked on with interested face.

Colin persevered. After he had turned a few trowelfuls of soil he spoke exultantly to Dickon.

"You said that you'd have me walking about like other folk—and you said you'd have me digging. I thought you were just lying to please me. This is only the first day and I've walked—and here I am, digging."

Ben Weatherstaff's mouth fell open again when he heard him, but he ended by chuckling.

"Eh!" he said, "that sounds as if you'd got wits enough. You're a Yorkshire lad for sure. And you're digging, too. How'd you like to plant a bit of something? I can get you a rose in a pot."

"Go and get it!" said Colin, digging excitedly. "Quick! Quick!"

It was done quickly enough indeed. Ben Weatherstaff went his way forgetting rheumatics. Dickon took his spade and dug the hole deeper and wider than a new digger with thin white hands could make it. Mary slipped out to run and bring back a watering can. When Dickon had deepened the hole Colin went on turning the soft earth over and over. He looked up at the sky, flushed and glowing with the strangely new exercise, slight as it was.

"I want to do it before the sun goes quite—quite down," he said.

Mary thought that perhaps the sun held back a few minutes just on purpose. Ben Weatherstaff brought the rose in its pot from the greenhouse. He hobbled over the grass as fast as he could. He had begun to be excited, too. He knelt down by the hole and broke the pot from the mould.

"Here, lad," he said, handing the plant to Colin. "Set it in the earth yourself same as the king does when he goes to a new place."

The thin white hands shook a little and Colin's flush grew deeper as he set the rose in the mould and held it while old Ben made firm the earth. It was filled in and pressed down and made steady. Mary was leaning forward on her hands and knees. Soot had flown down and marched forward to see what was being done. Nut and Shell chattered about it from a cherry tree.

"It's planted!" said Colin at last. "And the sun is only slipping over the edge. Help me up, Dickon. I want to be standing when it goes. That's part of the Magic."

And Dickon helped him, and the Magic—or whatever it was—so gave him strength that when the sun did slip over the edge and end the strange lovely afternoon for them there he actually stood on his two feet—laughing.

## CHAPTER XXIII

## MAGIC

Dr. Craven had been waiting some time at the house when they returned to it. He had indeed begun to wonder if it might not be wise to send someone out to explore the garden paths. When Colin was brought back to his room the poor man looked him over seriously.

"You should not have stayed so long," he said. "You must not overexert yourself."

"I am not tired at all," said Colin. "It has made me well. Tomorrow I am going out in the morning as well as in the afternoon."

"I am not sure that I can allow it," answered Dr. Craven. "I am afraid it would not be wise."

"It would not be wise to try to stop me," said Colin quite seriously. "I am going."

Even Mary had found out that one of Colin's chief peculiarities was that he did not know in the least what a rude little brute he was with his way of ordering people about. He had lived on a sort of desert island all his life and as he had been the king of it. He had made his own manners and had had no one to compare himself with. Mary had indeed been rather like him herself and since she had been at Misselthwaite had gradually discovered that her own manners had not been of the kind which is usual or popular. Having made this discovery she naturally thought it of enough interest to communicate to Colin. So she sat and looked at him curiously for a few minutes after Dr. Craven had gone. She wanted to make him ask her why she was doing it and of course he did.

"What are you looking at me for?" he said.

"I'm thinking that I am rather sorry for Dr. Craven."

"So am I," said Colin calmly, but not without an air of some satisfaction. "He won't get Misselthwaite at all now I'm not going to die."

"I'm sorry for him because of that, of course," said Mary, "but I was thinking just then that it must have been very horrid to have had to be polite for ten years to a boy who was always rude. I would never have done it."

"Am I rude?" Colin inquired undisturbedly.

"If you had been his own boy and he had been a slapping sort of man," said Mary, "he would have slapped you."

"But he daren't," said Colin.

"No, he daren't," answered Mistress Mary, thinking the thing out quite without prejudice. "Nobody ever dared to do anything you didn't like—because you were going to die and things like that. You were such a poor thing."

"But," announced Colin stubbornly, "I am not going to be a poor thing. I won't let people think I'm one. I stood on my feet this afternoon."

"It is always having your own way that has made you so queer," Mary went on, thinking aloud.

Colin turned his head, frowning.

"Am I queer?" he demanded.

"Yes," answered Mary, "very. But you needn't be cross," she added impartially, "because so am I —and so is Ben Weatherstaff. But I am not as queer as I was before I began to like people and before I found the garden."

"I don't want to be queer," said Colin. "I am not going to be," and he frowned again with determination.

He was a very proud boy. He lay thinking for a while and then Mary saw his beautiful smile begin and gradually change his whole face.

"I shall stop being queer," he said, "If I go every day to the garden. There is Magic in there—good magic, you know, Mary. I am sure there is."

"So am I," said Mary.

"Even if it isn't real magic," Colin said, "we can pretend it is. *Something* is there—*something*!"

"It's Magic," said Mary, "but not black. It's as white as snow."

They always called it Magic and indeed it seemed like it in the months that followed—the wonderful months—the radiant months—the amazing ones. Oh! The things which happened in that garden! If you have never had a garden, you cannot understand, and if you have had a garden you will know that it would take a whole book to describe all that came to pass there. At first it seemed that green things would never cease pushing their way through the earth, in the grass, in the beds, even in the crevices of the walls. Then the green things began to show buds and the buds began to unfurl and show colour, every shade of blue, every shade of purple, every tint and hue of crimson. In its happy days flowers had been tucked away into every inch and hole and corner. Ben Weatherstaff had seen it done and had himself scraped out mortar from between the bricks of the wall and made pockets of earth for lovely clinging things to grow on. Iris and white lilies rose out of the grass in sheaves, and the green alcoves filled themselves with amazing armies of the blue and white flower lances of tall delphiniums or columbines or campanulas.

"She was so fond of them—she was," Ben Weatherstaff said. "She liked these things that were always pointing up to the blue sky, she used to tell. Not that she was one of them that looked down on the earth—not her. She just loved it but she said that the blue sky always looked so joyful."

The seeds Dickon and Mary had planted grew as if fairies had tended them. Satiny poppies of all tints danced in the breeze by the score, gaily defying flowers which had lived in the garden for years and which it might be confessed seemed rather to wonder how such new people had got there. And the roses—the roses! Rising out of the grass, tangled round the sun-dial, wreathing the tree trunks and hanging from their branches, climbing up the walls and spreading over them with long garlands falling in cascades—they came alive day by day, hour by hour. Fair fresh leaves, and buds—and buds—tiny at first but swelling and working Magic until they burst and uncurled into cups of scent delicately spilling themselves over their brims and filling the garden air.

Colin saw it all, watching each change as it took place. Every morning he was brought out and every hour of each day when it didn't rain he spent in the garden. Even grey days pleased him. He would lie on the grass "watching things growing," he said. If you watched long enough, he declared, you could see buds sprouting themselves. Also you could make the acquaintance of strange busy insect things running about on various unknown but evidently serious errands, sometimes carrying tiny scraps of straw or feather or food, or climbing blades of grass as if they were trees from whose tops one could look out to explore the country. A mole throwing up its mound at the end of its burrow and making its way out at last with the long-nailed paws which looked so like elfish hands, had absorbed him one whole morning. Ants' ways, beetles' ways, bees' ways, frogs' ways, birds' ways, plants' ways, gave him a new world to explore and when Dickon revealed them all and added foxes' ways, otters' ways, ferrets' ways, squirrels' ways, and trout's and water-rats' and badgers' ways, there was no end to the things to talk about and think over.

And this was not the half of the Magic. The fact that he had really once stood on his feet had set Colin thinking tremendously and when Mary told him of the spell she had worked he was excited and approved of it greatly. He talked of it constantly.

"Of course there must be lots of Magic in the world," he said wisely one day, "but people don't know what it is like or how to make it. Perhaps the beginning is just to say nice things are going to happen until you make them happen. I am going to try and experiment."

The next morning when they went to the secret garden he sent at once for Ben Weatherstaff. Ben came as quickly as he could and found the Rajah standing on his feet under a tree and looking very grand but also very beautifully smiling.

"Good morning, Ben Weatherstaff," he said. "I want you and Dickon and Miss Mary to stand in a row and listen to me because I am going to tell you something very important."

"Aye, aye, sir!" answered Ben Weatherstaff, touching his forehead. (One of the long concealed charms of Ben Weatherstaff was that in his boyhood he had once run away to sea and had made voyages. So he could reply like a sailor.)

"I am going to try a scientific experiment," explained the Rajah. "When I grow up I am going to make great scientific discoveries and I am going to begin now with this experiment."

"Aye, aye, sir!" said Ben Weatherstaff promptly, though this was the first time he had heard of great scientific discoveries.

It was the first time Mary had heard of them, either, but even at this stage she had begun to realize that, queer as he was, Colin had read about a great many singular things and was somehow a very convincing sort of boy. When he held up his head and fixed his strange eyes on you it seemed as if you believed him almost in spite of yourself though he was only ten years old—going on eleven. At this moment he was especially convincing because he suddenly felt the fascination of actually making a sort of speech like a grown-up person.

"The great scientific discoveries I am going to make," he went on, "will be about Magic. Magic is a great thing and scarcely any one knows anything about it except a few people in old books—and Mary a little, because she was born in India where there are fakirs. I believe Dickon knows some Magic, but perhaps he doesn't know he knows it. He charms animals and people. I would never have let him come to see me if he had not been an animal charmer—which is a boy charmer, too, because a boy is an animal. I am sure there is Magic in everything, only we have not sense enough to get hold of it and make it do things for us—like electricity and horses and steam."

This sounded so imposing that Ben Weatherstaff became quite excited and really could not keep still.

"Aye, aye, sir," he said and he began to stand up quite straight.

"When Mary found this garden it looked quite dead," the orator proceeded. "Then something began pushing things up out of the soil and making things out of nothing. One day things weren't there and another they were. I had never watched things before and it made me feel very curious. Scientific people are always curious and I am going to be scientific. I keep saying to myself, 'What is it? What is it?' It's something. It can't be nothing! I don't know its name so I call it Magic. I have never seen the sun rise but Mary and Dickon have and from what they tell me I am sure that is Magic too. Something pushes it up and draws it. Sometimes since I've been in the garden I've looked up through the trees at the sky and I have had a strange feeling of being happy as if something were pushing and drawing in my chest and making me breathe fast. Magic is always pushing and drawing and making things out of nothing. Everything is made out of Magic, leaves and trees, flowers and birds, badgers and foxes and squirrels and people. So it must be all around us. In this garden—in all the places. The Magic in this garden has made me stand up and know I am going to live to be a man. I am going to make the scientific experiment of trying to get some and put it in myself and make it push and draw me and make me strong. I don't know how to do it but I think that if you keep thinking about it and calling it perhaps it will come. Perhaps that is the first baby way to get it. When I was going to try to stand that first time Mary kept saying to herself as fast as she could, 'You can do it! You can do it!' and I did. I had to try myself at the same time, of course, but her Magic helped me—and so did Dickon's. Every morning and evening and as often in the daytime as I can remember I am going to say, 'Magic is in me! Magic is making me well! I am going to be as strong as Dickon, as strong as Dickon!' And you must all do it, too. That is my experiment. Will you help, Ben Weatherstaff?"

"Aye, aye, sir!" said Ben Weatherstaff. "Aye, aye!"

"If you keep doing it every day as regularly as soldiers go through drill we shall see what will happen and find out if the experiment succeeds. You learn things by saying them over and over and thinking about them until they stay in your mind forever and I think it will be the same with Magic. If you keep calling it to come to you and help you it will get to be part of you and it will stay and do things."

"I once heard an officer in India tell my mother that there were fakirs who said words over and over thousands of times," said Mary.

"I've heard Jem Fettleworth's wife say the same thing over thousands of times—calling Jem a drunken brute," said Ben Weatherstaff dryly. "Something always come of that, sure enough. He gave her a good hiding and went to the Blue Lion and got as drunk as a lord."

Colin drew his brows together and thought a few minutes. Then he cheered up.

"Well," he said, "you see something did come of it. She used the wrong Magic until she made him beat her. If she'd used the right Magic and had said something nice perhaps he wouldn't have got as drunk as a lord and perhaps—perhaps he might have bought her a new bonnet."

Ben Weatherstaff chuckled and there was shrewd admiration in his little old eyes.

"You're a clever lad as well as a straight-legged one, Master Colin," he said. "Next time I see Bess Fettleworth I'll give her a bit of a hint of what Magic will do for her. She'd be pleased if the scientific experiment worked—and so would Jem."

Dickon had stood listening to the lecture, his round eyes shining with curious delight. Nut and Shell were on his shoulders and he held a long-eared white rabbit in his arm and stroked and stroked it softly while it laid its ears along its back and enjoyed itself.

"Do you think the experiment will work?" Colin asked him, wondering what he was thinking. He so often wondered what Dickon was thinking when he saw him looking at him or at one of his "creatures" with his happy wide smile.

He smiled now and his smile was wider than usual.

"Aye," he answered, "that I do. It'll work the same as the seeds do when the sun shines on them. It'll work for sure. Shall we begin it now?"

Colin was delighted and so was Mary. Fired by recollections of fakirs and devotees in illustrations Colin suggested that they should all sit cross-legged under the tree which made a canopy.

"It will be like sitting in a sort of temple," said Colin. "I'm rather tired and I want to sit down."

"Eh!" said Dickon, "you mustn't begin by saying you're tired. You might spoil the Magic."

Colin turned and looked at him—into his innocent round eyes.

"That's true," he said slowly. "I must only think of the Magic."

It all seemed most majestic and mysterious when they sat down in their circle. Ben Weatherstaff felt as if he had somehow been led into appearing at a prayer-meeting. Ordinarily he was very fixed in being what he called "aging prayer-meetings" but this being the Rajah's affair, he did not resent it and was indeed inclined to be gratified at being called upon to assist. Mistress Mary felt solemnly enraptured. Dickon held his rabbit in his arm, and perhaps he made some charmer's signal no one heard, for when he sat down, cross-legged like the rest, the crow, the fox, the squirrels and the lamb slowly drew near and made part of the circle, settling each into a place of rest as if of their own desire.

"The 'creatures' have come," said Colin gravely. "They want to help us."

Colin really looked quite beautiful, Mary thought. He held his head high as if he felt like a sort of priest and his strange eyes had a wonderful look in them. The light shone on him through the tree canopy.

"Now we will begin," he said. "Shall we sway backward and forward, Mary, as if we were dervishes?"

"I cannot do no swaying backward and forward," said Ben Weatherstaff. "I've got rheumatism."

"The Magic will take them away," said Colin in a High Priest tone, "but we won't sway until it has done it. We will only chant."

"I cannot do no chanting," said Ben Weatherstaff a trifle testily. "They turned me out of the church choir the only time I ever tried it."

No one smiled. They were all too much in earnest. Colin's face was not even crossed by a shadow. He was thinking only of the Magic.

"Then I will chant," he said. And he began, looking like a strange boy spirit. "The sun is shining—the sun is shining. That is the Magic. The flowers are growing—the roots are stirring. That is the Magic. Being alive is the Magic—being strong is the Magic. The Magic is in me—the Magic is in me. It is in me—it is in me. It's in every one of us. It's in Ben Weatherstaff's back. Magic! Magic! Come and help!"

He said it a great many times—not a thousand times but quite a goodly number. Mary listened entranced. She felt as if it were at once queer and beautiful and she wanted him to go on and on. Ben Weatherstaff began to feel soothed into a sort of dream which was quite agreeable. The humming of the bees in the blossoms mingled with the chanting voice and drowsily melted into a doze. Dickon sat cross-legged with his rabbit asleep on his arm and a hand resting on the lamb's back. Soot had pushed away a squirrel and huddled close to him on his shoulder, the grey film dropped over his eyes. At last Colin stopped.

"Now I am going to walk round the garden," he announced.

Ben Weatherstaff's head had just dropped forward and he lifted it with a jerk.

"You have been asleep," said Colin.

"Nothing of the sort," mumbled Ben. "The sermon was good enough—but I'm bound to get out before the collection."

He was not quite awake yet.

"You're not in church," said Colin.

"Not me," said Ben, straightening himself. "Who said I were? I heard every bit of it. You said the Magic was in my back. The doctor calls it rheumatism."

The Rajah waved his hand.

"That was the wrong Magic," he said. "You will get better. You have my permission to go to your work. But come back tomorrow."

"I'd like to see you walk around the garden," grunted Ben.

It was not an unfriendly grunt, but it was a grunt. In fact, being a stubborn old party and not having entire faith in Magic he had made up his mind that if he were sent away he would climb his ladder and look over the wall so that he might be ready to hobble back if there were any stumbling.

The Rajah did not object to his staying and so the procession was formed. It really did look like a procession. Colin was at its head with Dickon on one side and Mary on the other. Ben Weatherstaff walked behind, and the "creatures" trailed after them, the lamb and the fox cub keeping close to Dickon, the white rabbit hopping along or stopping to nibble and Soot following with the solemnity of a person who felt himself in charge.

It was a procession which moved slowly but with dignity. Every few yards it stopped to rest. Colin leaned on Dickon's arm and privately Ben Weatherstaff kept a sharp lookout, but now and then Colin took his hand from its support and walked a few steps alone. His head was held up all the time and he looked very grand.

"The Magic is in me!" he kept saying. "The Magic is making me strong! I can feel it! I can feel it!"

It seemed very certain that something was upholding and uplifting him. He sat on the seats in the alcoves, and once or twice he sat down on the grass and several times he paused in the path and leaned on Dickon, but he would not give up until he had gone all round the garden. When he returned to the canopy tree his cheeks were flushed and he looked triumphant.

"I did it! The Magic worked!" he cried. "That is my first scientific discovery."

"What will Dr. Craven say?" broke out Mary.

"He won't say anything," Colin answered, "because he will not be told. This is to be the biggest secret of all. No one is to know anything about it until I have grown so strong that I can walk and run like any other boy. I shall come here every day in my chair and I shall be taken back in it. I won't have people whispering and asking questions and I won't let my father hear about it until the experiment has quite succeeded. Then sometime when he comes back to Misselthwaite I shall just walk into his study and say 'Here I am; I am like any other boy. I am quite well and I shall live to be a man. It has been done by a scientific experiment.'"

"He will think he is in a dream," cried Mary. "He won't believe his eyes."

Colin flushed triumphantly. He had made himself believe that he was going to get well, which was really more than half the battle, if he had been aware of it. And the thought which stimulated him more than any other was this imagining what his father would look like when he saw that he had a son who was as straight and strong as other fathers' sons. One of his darkest miseries in the unhealthy morbid past days had been his hatred of being a sickly weak-backed boy whose father was afraid to look at him.

"He'll be obliged to believe them," he said. "One of the things I am going to do, after the Magic works and before I begin to make scientific discoveries, is to be an athlete."

"We shall have you taking to boxing in a week or so," said Ben Weatherstaff. "You'll end up winning the Belt and being a champion prize-fighter of all England."

Colin fixed his eyes on him sternly.

"Weatherstaff," he said, "that is disrespectful. You must not take liberties because you are in the secret. However much the Magic works I shall not be a prize-fighter. I shall be a Scientific Discoverer."

"Ah pardon—ah pardon, sir," answered Ben, touching his forehead in salute. "I ought to have known it wasn't a joking matter," but his eyes twinkled and secretly he was immensely pleased. He really did not mind being snubbed since the snubbing meant that the lad was gaining strength and spirit.


# CHAPTER XXIV

## "LET THEM LAUGH"

The secret garden was not the only one Dickon worked in. Round the cottage on the moor there was a piece of ground enclosed by a low wall of rough stones. Early in the morning and late in the fading twilight and on all the days Colin and Mary did not see him, Dickon worked there planting or tending potatoes and cabbages, turnips and carrots and herbs for his mother. In the company of his "creatures" he did wonders there and was never tired of doing them, it seemed. While he dug or weeded he whistled or sang bits of Yorkshire moor songs or talked to Soot or Captain or the brothers and sisters he had taught to help him.

"We'd never get on as comfortably as we do," Mrs. Sowerby said, "if it wasn't for Dickon's garden. Anything'll grow for him. His potatoes and cabbages are twice the size of anyone else's and they've got a flavour like nobody else's."

When she found a moment to spare she liked to go out and talk to him. After supper there was still a long clear twilight to work in and that was her quiet time. She could sit upon the low rough wall and look on and hear stories of the day. She loved this time. There were not only vegetables in this garden. Dickon had bought penny packages of flower seeds now and then and sown bright sweet-scented things among gooseberry bushes and even cabbages and he grew borders of mignonette and pinks and pansies and things whose seeds he could save year after year or whose roots would bloom each spring and spread in time into fine clumps. The low wall was one of the prettiest things in Yorkshire because he had tucked moorland foxglove and ferns and rock-cress and hedgerow flowers into every crevice until only here and there glimpses of the stones were to be seen.

"All a chap's got to do to make them thrive, mother," he would say, "is to be friends with them for sure. They're just like the creatures. If they're thirsty give them a drink and if they're hungry give them a bit of food. They want to live like we do. If they died I should feel as if I'd been a bad lad and somehow treated them heartlessly."

It was in these twilight hours that Mrs. Sowerby heard of all that happened at Misselthwaite Manor. At first she was only told that "Master Colin" had taken a fancy to going out into the grounds with Miss Mary and that it was doing him good. But it was not long before it was agreed between the two children that Dickon's mother might "come into the secret." Somehow it was not doubted that she was "safe for sure."

So one beautiful still evening Dickon told the whole story, with all the thrilling details of the buried key and the robin and the grey haze which had seemed like deadness and the secret Mistress Mary had planned never to reveal. The coming of Dickon and how it had been told to him, the doubt of Master Colin and the final drama of his introduction to the hidden domain, combined with the incident of Ben Weatherstaff's angry face peering over the wall and Master Colin's sudden indignant strength, made Mrs. Sowerby's nice-looking face change colour several times.

"My word!" she said. "It was a good thing that little lass came to the Manor. It's been the making of her and the saving of him. Standing on his feet! And us all thinking he was a poor half-witted lad with not a straight bone in him."

She asked a great many questions and her blue eyes were full of deep thinking.

"What do they make of it at the Manor—him being so well and cheerful and never complaining?" she inquired.

"They don't know what to make of it," answered Dickon. "Every day that comes around his face looks different. It's filling out and doesn't look so sharp and the waxy colour is going. But he has to do his bit of complaining," with a highly entertained grin.

"What for, in Mercy's name?" asked Mrs. Sowerby.

Dickon chuckled.

"He does it to keep them from guessing what's happened. If the doctor knew he'd found out he could stand on his feet he'd likely write and tell Master Craven. Master Colin's saving the secret to tell himself. He's going to practise his Magic on his legs every day till his father comes back and then he's going to march into his room and show him he's as straight as other lads. But he and Miss Mary think it's best to do a bit of groaning and fretting now and then to throw folk off the scent."

Mrs. Sowerby was laughing a low comfortable laugh long before he had finished his last sentence.

"Eh!" she said, "that pair's enjoying themselves, I'll warrant. They'll get a good bit of play acting out of it and there's nothing children like as much as play acting. Let's hear what they do, Dickon lad."

Dickon stopped weeding and sat up on his heels to tell her. His eyes were twinkling with fun.

"Master Colin is carried down to his chair every time he goes out," he explained. "And he flies out at John, the footman, for not carrying him careful enough. He makes himself as helpless looking as he can and never lifts his head until we're out of sight of the house. And he grunts and frets a good bit when he's being settled into his chair. He and Miss Mary both got to enjoying it and when he groans and complains she'll say, 'Poor Colin! Does it hurt you so much? Are you as weak as that, poor Colin?'—but the trouble is that sometimes they can scarcely keep from bursting out laughing. When we get safe into the garden they laugh till they've no breath left to laugh with. And they have to stuff their faces into Master Colin's cushions to keep the gardeners from hearing, if any of them are about."

"The more they laugh the better for them!" said Mrs. Sowerby, still laughing herself. "Good healthy child laughing's better than pills any day of the year. That pair will plump up for sure."

"They are plumping up," said Dickon. "They're that hungry they don't know how to get enough to eat without raising suspicion. Master Colin says if he keeps sending for more food they won't believe he's an invalid at all. Miss Mary says she'll let him eat her share, but he says that if she goes hungry she'll get thin and they must both get fat at once."

Mrs. Sowerby laughed so heartily at the revelation of this difficulty that she quite rocked backward and forward in her blue cloak and Dickon laughed with her.

"I'll tell you what, lad," Mrs. Sowerby said when she could speak. "I've thought of a way to help them. When you go to them in the mornings, take a pail of good new milk and I'll bake them a crusty cottage loaf or some buns with currants in them, same as you children like. Nothing's as good as fresh milk and bread. Then they could take off the edge of their hunger while they were in their garden and the fine food they get indoors could polish off the corners."

"Eh! Mother!" said Dickon admiringly, "what a wonder you are! You always sees a way out of things. They were in quite in a state yesterday. They didn't see how they were to manage without ordering up more food—they felt that empty inside."

"They're two young ones growing fast, and health's coming back to both of them. Children like that feel like young wolves and food's flesh and blood to them," said Mrs. Sowerby. Then she smiled Dickon's own curving smile. "Eh! But they're enjoying themselves for sure," she said.

She was quite right, the comfortable wonderful mother creature—and she had never been more so than when she said their "play acting" would be their joy. Colin and Mary found it one of their most thrilling sources of entertainment. The idea of protecting themselves from suspicion had been unconsciously suggested to them first by the puzzled nurse and then by Dr. Craven himself.

"Your appetite is improving very much, Master Colin," the nurse had said one day. "You used to eat nothing, and so many things disagreed with you."

"Nothing disagrees with me now," replied Colin, and then seeing the nurse looking at him curiously he suddenly remembered that perhaps he ought not to appear too well just yet. "At least things don't so often disagree with me. It's the fresh air."

"Perhaps it is," said the nurse, still looking at him with a mystified expression. "But I must talk to Dr. Craven about it."

"How she stared at you!" said Mary when she went away. "As if she thought there must be something to find out."

"I won't have her finding out things," said Colin. "No one must begin to find out yet."

When Dr. Craven came that morning he seemed puzzled, also. He asked a number of questions, to Colin's great annoyance.

"You stay out in the garden a great deal," he suggested. "Where do you go?"

Colin put on his favourite air of dignified indifference to opinion.

"I will not let anyone know where I go," he answered. "I go to a place I like. Everyone has orders to keep out of the way. I won't be watched and stared at. You know that!"

"You seem to be out all day but I do not think it has done you harm—I do not think so. The nurse says that you eat much more than you have ever done before."

"Perhaps," said Colin, prompted by a sudden inspiration, "perhaps it is an unnatural appetite."

"I do not think so, as your food seems to agree with you," said Dr. Craven. "You are gaining flesh rapidly and your colour is better."

"Perhaps—perhaps I am bloated and feverish," said Colin, assuming a discouraging air of gloom. "People who are not going to live are often—different."

Dr. Craven shook his head. He was holding Colin's wrist and he pushed up his sleeve and felt his arm.

"You are not feverish," he said thoughtfully, "and such flesh as you have gained is healthy. If we can keep this up, my boy, we need not talk of dying. Your father will be very happy to hear of this remarkable improvement."

"I won't have him told!" Colin broke forth fiercely. "It will only disappoint him if I get worse again—and I may get worse this very night. I might have a raging fever. I feel as if I might be beginning to have one now. I won't have letters written to my father—I won't—I won't! You are making me angry and you know that is bad for me. I feel hot already. I hate being written about and being talked over as much as I hate being stared at!"

"Hush-h, my boy," Dr. Craven soothed him. "Nothing shall be written without your permission. You are too sensitive about things. You must not undo the good which has been done."

He said no more about writing to Mr. Craven and when he saw the nurse he privately warned her that such a possibility must not be mentioned to the patient.

"The boy is extraordinarily better," he said. "His advance seems almost abnormal. But of course he is doing now of his own free will what we could not make him do before. Still, he excites himself very easily and nothing must be said to irritate him."

Mary and Colin were much alarmed and talked together anxiously. From this time dated their plan of "play acting."

"I may be obliged to have a tantrum," said Colin regretfully. "I don't want to have one and I'm not miserable enough now to work myself into a big one. Perhaps I couldn't have one at all. That lump doesn't come in my throat now and I keep thinking of nice things instead of horrible ones. But if they talk about writing to my father I shall have to do something."

He made up his mind to eat less, but unfortunately it was not possible to carry out this brilliant idea when he wakened each morning with an amazing appetite and the table near his sofa was set with a breakfast of home-made bread and fresh butter, snow white eggs, raspberry jam and clotted cream. Mary always breakfasted with him and when they found themselves at the table—particularly if there were delicate slices of sizzling ham sending forth tempting odours from under a hot silver cover—they would look into each other's eyes in desperation.

"I think we shall have to eat it all this morning, Mary," Colin always ended by saying. "We can send away some of the lunch and a great deal of the dinner."

But they never found they could send away anything and the highly polished condition of the empty plates returned to the pantry awakened much comment.

"I do wish," Colin would say also, "I do wish the slices of ham were thicker, and one muffin each is not enough for anyone."

"It's enough for a person who is going to die," answered Mary when first she heard this, "but it's not enough for a person who is going to live. I sometimes feel as if I could eat three when those nice fresh heather and gorse smells from the moor come pouring in at the open window."

The morning that Dickon—after they had been enjoying themselves in the garden for about two hours—went behind a big rose-bush and brought forth two tin pails and revealed that one was full of rich new milk with cream on the top of it, and that the other held cottage-made currant buns folded in a clean blue and white napkin, buns so carefully tucked in that they were still hot, there was a riot of surprised joyfulness. What a wonderful thing for Mrs. Sowerby to think of! What a kind, clever woman she must be! How good the buns were! And what delicious fresh milk!

"Magic is in her just as it is in Dickon," said Colin. "It makes her think of ways to do things—nice things. She is a Magic person. Tell her we are grateful, Dickon—extremely grateful."

He was given to using rather grown-up phrases at times. He enjoyed them. He liked this so much that he improved upon it.

"Tell her she has been most generous and our gratitude is extreme."

And then forgetting his grandeur he fell to and stuffed himself with buns and drank milk out of the pail in abundant draughts in the manner of any hungry little boy who had been taking unusual exercise and breathing in moorland air and whose breakfast was more than two hours behind him.

This was the beginning of many agreeable incidents of the same kind. They actually awoke to the fact that as Mrs. Sowerby had fourteen people to provide food for she might not have enough to satisfy two extra appetites every day. So they asked her to let them send some of their shillings to buy things.

Dickon made the stimulating discovery that in the wood in the park outside the garden where Mary had first found him piping to the wild creatures there was a deep little hollow where you could build a sort of tiny oven with stones and roast potatoes and eggs in it. Roasted eggs were a previously unknown luxury and very hot potatoes with salt and fresh butter in them were fit for a woodland king—besides being deliciously satisfying. You could buy both potatoes and eggs and eat as many as you liked without feeling as if you were taking food out of the mouths of fourteen people.

Every beautiful morning the Magic was worked by the mystic circle under the plum-tree which provided a canopy of thickening green leaves after its brief blossom-time was ended. After the ceremony Colin always took his walking exercise and throughout the day he exercised his newly found power at intervals. Each day he grew stronger and could walk more steadily and cover more ground. And each day his belief in the Magic grew stronger—as well it might. He tried one experiment after another as he felt himself gaining strength and it was Dickon who showed him the best things of all.

"Yesterday," he said one morning after an absence, "I went to Thwaite for mother and near the Blue Cow Inn I seed Bob Haworth. He's the strongest chap on the moor. He's the champion wrestler and he can jump higher than any other chap and throw the hammer farther. He's gone all the way to Scotland for the sports some years ago. He's known me ever since I was a little one and he's a friendly sort and I asked him some questions. The gentry calls him an athlete and I thought of you, Master Colin, and I said, 'How did you make your muscles stick out that way, Bob? Did you do anything extra to make yourself so strong?' And he said 'Well, yes, lad, I did. A strong man in a show that came to Thwaite once showed me how to exercise my arms and legs and every muscle in my body.' And I said, 'Could a delicate chap make himself stronger with them, Bob?' and he laughed and said, 'Are you the delicate chap?' and I said, 'No, but I know a young gentleman who's getting well of a long illness and I wish I knew some tricks to tell him about.' I didn't say any names and he didn't ask none. He's friendly as I said and he stood up and showed me good-naturedly like, and I imitated what he did till I knew it by heart."

Colin had been listening excitedly.

"Can you show me?" he cried. "Will you?"

"Aye, to be sure," Dickon answered, getting up. "But he said you must do them gently at first and be careful not to tire yourself. Rest in between and take deep breaths and don't overdo it."

"I'll be careful," said Colin. "Show me! Show me! Dickon, you are the most Magic boy in the world!"

Dickon stood up on the grass and slowly went through a carefully practical but simple series of muscle exercises. Colin watched them with widening eyes. He could do a few while he was sitting down. Presently he did a few gently while he stood upon his already steadied feet. Mary began to do them also. Soot, who was watching the performance, became much disturbed and left his branch and hopped about restlessly because he could not do them too.

From that time on the exercises were part of the day's duties as much as the Magic was. It became possible for both Colin and Mary to do more of them each time they tried, and such appetites were the results that but for the basket Dickon put down behind the bush each morning when he arrived they would have been lost. But the little oven in the hollow and Mrs. Sowerby's bounties were so satisfying that Mrs. Medlock and the nurse and Dr. Craven became mystified again. You can trifle with your breakfast and seem to disdain your dinner if you are full to the brim with roasted eggs and potatoes and richly frothed new milk and oat-cakes and buns and heather honey and clotted cream.

"They are eating next to nothing," said the nurse. "They'll die of starvation if they can't be persuaded to take some nourishment. And yet see how they look."

"Look!" exclaimed Mrs. Medlock indignantly. "Eh! I'm baffled to death by them. They're a pair of young Satans. Bursting their jackets one day and the next turning up their noses at the best meals Cook can tempt them with. Not a mouthful of that lovely young fowl and bread sauce did they set a fork into yesterday—and the poor woman fair *invented* a pudding for them—and back it's sent. She almost cried. She's afraid she'll be blamed if they starve themselves into their graves."

Dr. Craven came and looked at Colin long and carefully. He wore an extremely worried expression when the nurse talked with him and showed him the almost untouched tray of breakfast she had saved for him to look at—but it was even more worried when he sat down by Colin's sofa and examined him. He had been called to London on business and had not seen the boy for nearly two weeks. When young things begin to gain health they gain it rapidly. The waxen tinge had left Colin's skin and a warm rose showed through it; his beautiful eyes were clear and the hollows under them and in his cheeks and temples had filled out. His once dark, heavy locks had begun to look as if they sprang healthily from his forehead and were soft and warm with life. His lips were fuller and of a normal colour. In fact as an imitation of a boy who was a confirmed invalid he was a disgraceful sight. Dr. Craven held his chin in his hand and thought him over.

"I am sorry to hear that you do not eat anything," he said. "That will not do. You will lose all you have gained—and you have gained amazingly. You ate so well a short time ago."

"I told you it was an unnatural appetite," answered Colin.

Mary was sitting on her stool nearby and she suddenly made a very queer sound which she tried so violently to repress that she ended by almost choking.

"What is the matter?" said Dr. Craven, turning to look at her.

Mary became quite severe in her manner.

"It was something between a sneeze and a cough," she replied with reproachful dignity, "and it got into my throat."

"But" she said afterward to Colin, "I couldn't stop myself. It just burst out because all at once I couldn't help remembering that last big potato you ate and the way your mouth stretched when you bit through that thick lovely crust with jam and clotted cream on it."

"Is there any way in which those children can get food secretly?" Dr. Craven inquired of Mrs. Medlock.

"There's no way unless they dig it out of the earth or pick it off the trees," Mrs. Medlock answered. "They stay out in the grounds all day and see no one but each other. And if they want anything different to eat from what's sent up to them they need only ask for it."

"Well," said Dr. Craven, "as long as going without food agrees with them we need not disturb ourselves. The boy is a new creature."

"So is the girl," said Mrs. Medlock. "She's begun to be downright pretty since she's filled out and lost her ugly little sour look. Her hair's grown thick and healthy looking and she's got a bright colour. The glummest, ill-natured little thing she used to be and now she and Master Colin laugh together like a pair of crazy young ones. Perhaps they're growing fat on that."

"Perhaps they are," said Dr. Craven. "Let them laugh."

## CHAPTER XXV

## THE CURTAIN

And the secret garden bloomed and bloomed and every morning revealed new miracles. In the robin's nest there were eggs and the robin's mate sat upon them keeping them warm with her feathery little breast and careful wings. At first she was very nervous and the robin himself was indignantly watchful. Even Dickon did not go near the close-grown corner in those days, but waited until by the quiet working of some mysterious spell he seemed to have conveyed to the soul of the little pair that in the garden there was nothing which was not quite like themselves—nothing which did not understand the wonderfulness of what was happening to them—the immense, tender, terrible, heart-breaking beauty and solemnity of eggs. If there had been one person in that garden who had not known through all his or her innermost being that if an egg were taken away or hurt the whole world would whirl round and crash through space and come to an end—if there had been even one who did not feel it and act accordingly there could have been no happiness even in that golden springtime air. But they all knew it and felt it and the robin and his mate knew they knew it.

At first the robin watched Mary and Colin with sharp anxiety. For some mysterious reason he knew he need not watch Dickon. The first moment he set his dew-bright black eye on Dickon he knew he was not a stranger but a sort of robin without beak or feathers. He could speak robin (which is a quite distinct language not to be mistaken for any other). To speak robin to a robin is like speaking French to a Frenchman. Dickon always spoke it to the robin himself, so the queer gibberish he used when he spoke to humans did not matter in the least. The robin thought he spoke this gibberish to them because they were not intelligent enough to understand feathered speech. His movements also were robin. They never startled one by being sudden enough to seem dangerous or threatening. Any robin could understand Dickon, so his presence was not even disturbing.

But at the outset it seemed necessary to be on guard against the other two. In the first place the boy creature did not come into the garden on his legs. He was pushed in on a thing with wheels and the skins of wild animals were thrown over him. That in itself was doubtful. Then when he began to stand up and move about he did it in a queer unaccustomed way and the others seemed to have to help him. The robin used to secrete himself in a bush and watch this anxiously, his head tilted first on one side and then on the other. He thought that the slow movements might mean that he was preparing to pounce, as cats do. When cats are preparing to pounce they creep over the ground very slowly. The robin talked this over with his mate a great deal for a few days but after that he decided not to speak of the subject because her terror was so great that he was afraid it might be injurious to the eggs.

When the boy began to walk by himself and even to move more quickly it was an immense relief. But for a long time—or it seemed a long time to the robin—he was a source of some anxiety. He did not act as the other humans did. He seemed very fond of walking but he had a way of sitting or lying down for a while and then getting up in a disconcerting manner to begin again.

One day the robin remembered that when he himself had been made to learn to fly by his parents he had done much the same sort of thing. He had taken short flights of a few yards and then had been obliged to rest. So it occurred to him that this boy was learning to fly—or rather to walk. He mentioned this to his mate and when he told her that the eggs would probably conduct themselves in the same way after they were fledged she was quite comforted and even became eagerly interested and derived great pleasure from watching the boy over the edge of her nest—though she always thought that the eggs would be much cleverer and learn more quickly. But then she said indulgently that humans were always more clumsy and slow than eggs and most of them never seemed really to learn to fly at all. You never met them in the air or on tree-tops.

After a while the boy began to move about as the others did, but all three of the children at times did unusual things. They would stand under the trees and move their arms and legs and heads about in a way which was neither walking nor running nor sitting down. They went through these movements at intervals every day and the robin was never able to explain to his mate what they were doing or trying to do. He could only say that he was sure that the eggs would never flap about in such a manner; but as the boy who could speak robin so fluently was doing the thing with them, birds could be quite sure that the actions were not of a dangerous nature. Of course neither the robin nor his mate had ever heard of the champion wrestler, Bob Haworth, and his exercises for making the muscles stand out like lumps. Robins are not like human beings; their muscles are always exercised from the first and so they develop themselves in a natural manner. If you have to fly about to find every meal you eat, your muscles do not become atrophied (atrophied means wasted away through want of use).

When the boy was walking and running about and digging and weeding like the others, the nest in the corner was brooded over by a great peace and content. Fears for the eggs became things of the past. Knowing that your eggs were as safe as if they were locked in a bank vault and the fact that you could watch so many curious things going on made setting a most entertaining occupation. On wet days the eggs' mother sometimes felt even a little dull because the children did not come into the garden.

But even on wet days it could not be said that Mary and Colin were dull. One morning when the rain streamed down unceasingly and Colin was beginning to feel a little restive, as he was obliged to remain on his sofa because it was not safe to get up and walk about, Mary had an inspiration.

"Now that I am a real boy," Colin had said, "my legs and arms and all my body are so full of Magic that I can't keep them still. They want to be doing things all the time. Do you know that when I wake up in the morning, Mary, when it's quite early and the birds are just shouting outside and everything seems just shouting for joy—even the trees and things we can't really hear—I feel as if I must jump out of bed and shout myself. And if I did it, just think what would happen!"

Mary giggled inordinately.

"The nurse would come running and Mrs. Medlock would come running and they would be sure you had gone crazy and they'd send for the doctor," she said.

Colin giggled himself. He could see how they would all look—how horrified by his outbreak and how amazed to see him standing upright.

"I wish my father would come home," he said. "I want to tell him myself. I'm always thinking about it—but we couldn't go on like this much longer. I can't stand lying still and pretending, and besides I look too different. I wish it wasn't raining today."

It was then Mistress Mary had her inspiration.

"Colin," she began mysteriously, "do you know how many rooms there are in this house?"

"About a thousand, I suppose," he answered.

"There're about a hundred no one ever goes into," said Mary. "And one rainy day I went and looked into ever so many of them. No one ever knew, though Mrs. Medlock nearly found me out. I lost my way when I was coming back and I stopped at the end of your corridor. That was the second time I heard you crying."

Colin started up on his sofa.

"A hundred rooms no one goes into," he said. "It sounds almost like a secret garden. Suppose we go and look at them. You could wheel me in my chair and nobody would know where we went."

"That's what I was thinking," said Mary. "No one would dare to follow us. There are galleries where you could run. We could do our exercises. There is a little Indian room where there is a cabinet full of ivory elephants. There are all sorts of rooms."

"Ring the bell," said Colin.

When the nurse came in he gave his orders.

"I want my chair," he said. "Miss Mary and I are going to look at the part of the house which is not used. John can push me as far as the picture-gallery because there are some stairs. Then he must go away and leave us alone until I send for him again."

Rainy days lost their terrors that morning. When the footman had wheeled the chair into the picture-gallery and left the two together in obedience to orders, Colin and Mary looked at each other delighted. As soon as Mary had made sure that John was really on his way back to his own quarters below stairs, Colin got out of his chair.

"I am going to run from one end of the gallery to the other," he said, "and then I am going to jump and then we will do Bob Haworth's exercises."

And they did all these things and many others. They looked at the portraits and found the plain little girl dressed in green brocade and holding the parrot on her finger.

"All these," said Colin, "must be my relations. They lived a long time ago. That parrot one, I believe, is one of my great, great, great, great aunts. She looks rather like you, Mary—not as you look now but as you looked when you came here. Now you are a great deal fatter and better looking."

"So are you," said Mary, and they both laughed.

They went to the Indian room and amused themselves with the ivory elephants. They found the rose-coloured brocade boudoir and the hole in the cushion the mouse had left but the mice had grown up and run away and the hole was empty. They saw more rooms and made more discoveries than Mary had made on her first pilgrimage. They found new corridors and corners and flights of steps and new old pictures they liked and weird old things they did not know the use of. It was a curiously entertaining morning and the feeling of wandering about in the same house with other people but at the same time feeling as if one were miles away from them was a fascinating thing.

"I'm glad we came," Colin said. "I never knew I lived in such a big queer old place. I like it. We will ramble about every rainy day. We shall always be finding new queer corners and things."

That morning they had found among other things such good appetites that when they returned to Colin's room it was not possible to send the luncheon away untouched.

When the nurse carried the tray downstairs she slapped it down on the kitchen dresser so that Mrs. Loomis, the cook, could see the highly polished dishes and plates.

"Look at that!" she said. "This is a house of mystery, and those two children are the greatest mysteries in it."

"If they keep that up every day," said the strong young footman John, "there'd be small wonder that he weighs twice as much today as he did a month ago. I should have to give up my place in time, for fear of doing my muscles an injury."

That afternoon Mary noticed that something new had happened in Colin's room. She had noticed it the day before but had said nothing because she thought the change might have been made by chance. She said nothing today but she sat and looked fixedly at the picture over the mantel. She could look at it because the curtain had been drawn aside. That was the change she noticed.

"I know what you want me to tell you," said Colin, after she had stared a few minutes. "I always know when you want me to tell you something. You are wondering why the curtain is drawn back. I am going to keep it like that."

"Why?" asked Mary.

"Because it doesn't make me angry any more to see her laughing. I awakened when it was bright moonlight two nights ago and felt as if the Magic was filling the room and making everything so splendid that I couldn't lie still. I got up and looked out of the window. The room was quite light and there was a patch of moonlight on the curtain and somehow that made me go and pull the cord. She looked right down at me as if she were laughing because she was glad I was standing there. It made me like to look at her. I want to see her laughing like that all the time. I think she must have been a sort of Magic person perhaps."

"You are so like her now," said Mary, "that sometimes I think perhaps you are her ghost made into a boy."

That idea seemed to impress Colin. He thought it over and then answered her slowly.

"If I were her ghost—my father would be fond of me," he said.

"Do you want him to be fond of you?" inquired Mary.

"I used to hate it because he was not fond of me. If he grew fond of me I think I should tell him about the Magic. It might make him more cheerful."

# CHAPTER XXVI

## "IT'S MOTHER!"

Their belief in the Magic was an abiding thing. After the morning's incantations Colin sometimes gave them Magic lectures.

"I like to do it," he explained, "because when I grow up and make great scientific discoveries I shall be obliged to lecture about them and so this is practise. I can only give short lectures now because I am very young, and besides Ben Weatherstaff would feel as if he was in church and he would go to sleep."

"The best thing about lecturing," said Ben, "is that a chap can get up and say what he pleases and no other chap can answer him back. I wouldn't mind lecturing a bit myself sometimes."

But when Colin held forth under his tree old Ben fixed devouring eyes on him and kept them there. He looked him over with critical affection. It was not so much the lecture which interested him as the legs which looked straighter and stronger each day, the boyish head which held itself up so well, the once sharp chin and hollow cheeks which had filled and rounded out and the eyes which had begun to hold the light he remembered in another pair. Sometimes when Colin felt Ben's earnest gaze meant that he was much impressed he wondered what he was reflecting on and once when he had seemed quite entranced he questioned him.

"What are you thinking about, Ben Weatherstaff?" he asked.

"I was thinking," answered Ben, "that I'd warrant you've gone up three or four pound this week. I was looking at your calves and your shoulders. I'd like to get you on a pair of scales."

"It's the Magic and—and Mrs. Sowerby's buns and milk and things," said Colin. "You see the scientific experiment has succeeded."

That morning Dickon was too late to hear the lecture. When he came he was ruddy with running and his funny face looked more twinkling than usual. As they had a good deal of weeding to do after the rains they fell to work. They always had plenty to do after a warm deep sinking rain. The moisture which was good for the flowers was also good for the weeds which thrust up tiny blades of grass and points of leaves which must be pulled up before their roots took too firm hold. Colin was as good at weeding as anyone in these days and he could lecture while he was doing it.

"The Magic works best when you work yourself," he said this morning. "You can feel it in your bones and muscles. I am going to read books about bones and muscles, but I am going to write a book about Magic. I am making it up now. I keep finding out things."

It was not very long after he had said this that he laid down his trowel and stood up on his feet. He had been silent for several minutes and they had seen that he was thinking out lectures, as he often did. When he dropped his trowel and stood upright it seemed to Mary and Dickon as if a sudden strong thought had made him do it. He stretched himself out to his tallest height and he threw out his arms exultantly. Colour glowed in his face and his strange eyes widened with joyfulness. All at once he had realized something to the full.

"Mary! Dickon!" he cried. "Just look at me!"

They stopped their weeding and looked at him.

"Do you remember that first morning you brought me in here?" he demanded.

Dickon was looking at him very hard. Being an animal charmer he could see more things than most people could and many of them were things he never talked about. He saw some of them now in this boy.

"Aye, that we do," he answered.

Mary looked hard too, but she said nothing.

"Just this minute," said Colin, "all at once I remembered it myself—when I looked at my hand digging with the trowel—and I had to stand up on my feet to see if it was real. And it *is* real! I'm *well*—I'm *well*!"

"Aye, that you are!" said Dickon.

"I'm well! I'm well!" said Colin again, and his face went quite red all over.

He had known it before in a way, he had hoped it and felt it and thought about it, but just at that minute something had rushed all through him—a sort of rapturous belief and realization and it had been so strong that he could not help calling out.

"I shall live forever and ever and ever!" he cried grandly. "I shall find out thousands and thousands of things. I shall find out about people and creatures and everything that grows—like Dickon—and I shall never stop making Magic. I'm well! I'm well! I feel—I feel as if I want to shout out something—something thankful, joyful!"

Ben Weatherstaff, who had been working near a rose-bush, glanced round at him.

"You might sing the Doxology," he suggested in his driest grunt. He had no opinion of the Doxology and he did not make the suggestion with any particular reverence.

But Colin was of an exploring mind and he knew nothing about the Doxology.

"What is that?" he inquired.

"Dickon can sing it for you, I'll warrant," replied Ben Weatherstaff.

Dickon answered with his all-perceiving animal charmer's smile.

"They sing it in church," he said. "Mother says she believes the skylarks sing it when they gets up in the morning."

"If she says that, it must be a nice song," Colin answered. "I've never been in a church myself. I was always too ill. Sing it, Dickon. I want to hear it."

Dickon was quite simple and unaffected about it. He understood what Colin felt better than Colin did himself. He understood by a sort of instinct so natural that he did not know it was understanding. He pulled off his cap and looked round still smiling.

"You must take off your cap," he said to Colin, "and so must you, Ben—and you must stand up, you know."

Colin took off his cap and the sun shone on and warmed his thick hair as he watched Dickon intently. Ben Weatherstaff scrambled up from his knees and bared his head too with a sort of puzzled half-resentful look on his old face as if he didn't know exactly why he was doing this remarkable thing.

Dickon stood out among the trees and rose bushes and began to sing in quite a simple matter-of-fact way and in a nice strong boy voice:

"Praise God from whom all blessings flow,

Praise Him all creatures here below,

Praise Him above ye Heavenly Host,

Praise Father, Son, and Holy Ghost.

Amen."

When he had finished, Ben Weatherstaff was standing quite still with his jaws set obstinately but with a disturbed look in his eyes fixed on Colin. Colin's face was thoughtful and appreciative.

"It is a very nice song," he said. "I like it. Perhaps it means just what I mean when I want to shout out that I am thankful to the Magic." He stopped and thought in a puzzled way. "Perhaps they are both the same thing. How can we know the exact names of everything? Sing it again, Dickon. Let us try, Mary. I want to sing it, too. It's my song. How does it begin? 'Praise God from whom all blessings flow'?"

And they sang it again, and Mary and Colin lifted their voices as musically as they could and Dickon's swelled quite loud and beautiful—and at the second line Ben Weatherstaff raspingly cleared his throat and at the third he joined in with such vigour that it seemed almost savage and when the "Amen" came to an end Mary observed that the very same thing had happened to him which had happened when he found out that Colin was not a cripple—his chin was twitching and he was staring and winking and his leathery old cheeks were wet.

"I never saw no sense in the Doxology before," he said hoarsely, "but I may change my mind in time. I should say you'd gone up five pound this week, Master Colin— five pound!"

Colin was looking across the garden at something attracting his attention and his expression had become a startled one.

"Who is coming in here?" he said quickly. "Who is it?"

The door in the ivied wall had been pushed gently open and a woman had entered. She had come in with the last line of their song and she had stood still listening and looking at them. With the ivy behind her, the sunlight drifting through the trees and dappling her long blue cloak, and her nice fresh face smiling across the greenery she was rather like a softly collared illustration in one of Colin's books. She had wonderful affectionate eyes which seemed to take everything in—all of them, even Ben Weatherstaff and the creatures and every flower that was in bloom. Unexpectedly as she had appeared, not one of them felt that she was an intruder at all. Dickon's eyes lit up like lamps.

"It's Mother—that's who it is!" he cried and he went across the grass at a run.

Colin began to move toward her, too, and Mary went with him. They both felt their pulses beat faster.

"It's Mother!" Dickon said again when they met half-way. "I knew you wanted to see her and I told her where the door was hidden."

Colin held out his hand with a sort of flushed royal shyness but his eyes quite devoured her face.

"Even when I was ill I wanted to see you," he said, "you and Dickon and the secret garden. I'd never wanted to see anyone or anything before."

The sight of his uplifted face brought about a sudden change in her own. She flushed and the corners of her mouth shook and a mist seemed to sweep over her eyes.

"Eh, dear lad!" she broke out tremulously. "Eh, dear lad!" as if she had not known she were going to say it. She did not say, "Master Colin," but just "dear lad" quite suddenly. She might have said it to Dickon in the same way if she had seen something in his face which touched her. Colin liked it.

"Are you surprised because I am so well?" he asked.

She put her hand on his shoulder and smiled the mist out of her eyes.

"Aye, that I am!" she said; "but that you're so like your mother made my heart jump."

"Do you think," said Colin a little awkwardly, "that will make my father like me?"

"Aye, for sure, dear lad," she answered and she gave his shoulder a soft quick pat. "He must come home—he must come home."

"Susan Sowerby," said Ben Weatherstaff, getting close to her. "Look at the lad's legs, will you? They were like drumsticks in stockings two months ago—and I heard folk tell that they were bandy and knock-kneed both at the same time. Look at them now!"

Susan Sowerby laughed a comfortable laugh.

"They're going to be fine strong lad's legs in a bit," she said. "Let him go on playing and working in the garden and eating hearty and drinking plenty of good sweet milk and there'll not be a finer pair in Yorkshire, thank God for it."

She put both hands on Mistress Mary's shoulders and looked her little face over in a motherly fashion.

"And you, too!" she said. "You've grown nearly as hearty as our Elizabeth Ellen. I'll warrant you're like your mother too. Our Martha told me that Mrs. Medlock heard she was a pretty woman. You'll be like a blush rose when you grow up, my little lass, bless you."

She did not mention that when Martha came home on her "day out" and described the plain sallow child she had said that she had no confidence whatever in what Mrs. Medlock had heard. "It doesn't stand to reason that a pretty woman could be the mother of such a foul little lass," she had added obstinately.

Mary had not had time to pay much attention to her changing face. She had only known that she looked "different" and seemed to have a great deal more hair and that it was growing very fast. But remembering her pleasure in looking at the Mem Sahib in the past she was glad to hear that she might some day look like her.

Susan Sowerby went round their garden with them and was told the whole story of it and shown every bush and tree which had come alive. Colin walked on one side of her and Mary on the other. Each of them kept looking up at her comfortable rosy face, secretly curious about the delightful feeling she gave them—a sort of warm, supported feeling. It seemed as if she understood them as Dickon understood his creatures. She stooped over the flowers and talked about them as if they were

211

children. Soot followed her and once or twice cawed at her and flew upon her shoulder as if it were Dickon's. When they told her about the robin and the first flight of the young ones she laughed a motherly little mellow laugh in her throat.

"I suppose learning to fly is like teaching children to walk, but I'm afraid I should be worried if mine had wings instead of legs," she said.

It was because she seemed such a wonderful woman in her nice moorland cottage way that at last she was told about the Magic.

"Do you believe in Magic?" asked Colin after he had explained about Indian fakirs. "I do hope you do."

"That I do, lad," she answered. "I never knew it by that name but what does the name matter? I warrant they call it a different name in France and a different one in Germany. The same thing that sets the seeds swelling and the sun shining made you a well lad and it's the Good Thing. It isn't like us poor fools think it matters which name we call it. The Big Good Thing doesn't stop to worry, bless you. It goes on making worlds by the million—worlds like ours. Never stop believing in the Big Good Thing and knowing the world's full of it—and call it what you like. You were singing to it when I came into the garden."

"I felt so joyful," said Colin, opening his beautiful strange eyes at her. "Suddenly I felt how different I was—how strong my arms and legs were, you know—and how I could dig and stand—and I jumped up and wanted to shout out something to anything that would listen."

"The Magic listened when you sung the Doxology. It would have listened to anything you'd sung. It was the joy that mattered. Eh, lad, lad—what's names to the Joy Maker," and she gave his shoulders a quick soft pat again.

She had packed a basket which held a regular feast this morning, and when the hungry hour came and Dickon brought it out from its hiding place, she sat down with them under their tree and watched them devour their food, laughing and quite gloating over their appetites. She was full of fun and made them laugh at all sorts of odd things. She told them stories in broad Yorkshire and taught them new words. She laughed as if she could not help it when they told her of the increasing difficulty there was in pretending that Colin was still a fretful invalid.

"You see we can't help laughing nearly all the time when we are together," explained Colin. "And it doesn't sound ill at all. We try to choke it back but it will burst out and that sounds worse than ever."

"There's one thing that comes into my mind so often," said Mary, "and I can scarcely ever hold in when I think of it suddenly. I keep thinking suppose Colin's face should get to look like a full moon. It isn't like one yet but he gets a tiny bit fatter every day—and suppose some morning it should look like one—what should we do!"

"Bless us all, I can see you have a good bit of play acting to do," said Susan Sowerby. "But you won't have to keep it up much longer. Master Craven will come home."

"Do you think he will?" asked Colin. "Why?"

Susan Sowerby chuckled softly.

"I suppose it would break your heart if he found out before you told him in your own way," she said. "You've lain awake nights planning it."

"I couldn't bear anyone else to tell him," said Colin. "I think about different ways every day. I think now I just want to run into his room."

"That'd be a fine start for him," said Susan Sowerby. "I'd like to see his face, lad. I would! He must come back—that he must."

One of the things they talked of was the visit they were to make to her cottage. They planned it all. They were to drive over the moor and lunch out of doors among the heather. They would see all the twelve children and Dickon's garden and would not come back until they were tired.

Susan Sowerby got up at last to return to the house and Mrs. Medlock. It was time for Colin to be wheeled back also. But before he got into his chair he stood quite close to Susan and fixed his eyes on her with a kind of bewildered adoration and he suddenly caught hold of the fold of her blue cloak and held it fast.

"You are just what I—what I wanted," he said. "I wish you were my mother—as well as Dickon's!"

All at once Susan Sowerby bent down and drew him with her warm arms close against the bosom under the blue cloak—as if he had been Dickon's brother. The quick mist swept over her eyes.

"Eh, dear lad!" she said. "Your own mother's in this very garden, I do believe. She couldn't keep out of it. Your father must come back to you —he must!"

## CHAPTER XXVII

## IN THE GARDEN

In each century since the beginning of the world wonderful things have been discovered. In the last century more amazing things were found out than in any century before. In this new century hundreds of things still more astounding will be brought to light. At first people refuse to believe that a strange new thing can be done, then they begin to hope it can be done, then they see it can be done—then it is done and all the world wonders why it was not done centuries ago. One of the new things people began to find out in the last century was that thoughts—just mere thoughts—are as powerful as electric batteries—as good for one as sunlight is, or as bad for one as poison. To let a sad thought or a bad one get into your mind is as dangerous as letting a scarlet fever germ get into your body. If you let it stay there after it has got in you may never get over it as long as you live.

As long as Mistress Mary's mind was full of disagreeable thoughts about her dislikes and sour opinions of people and her determination not to be pleased by or interested in anything, she was a yellow-faced, sickly, bored and wretched child. Circumstances, however, were very kind to her, though she was not at all aware of it. They began to push her about for her own good. When her mind gradually filled itself with robins, and moorland cottages crowded with children, with queer crabbed old gardeners and common little Yorkshire housemaids, with springtime and with secret gardens coming alive day by day, and also with a moor boy and his creatures, there was no room left for the disagreeable thoughts which affected her liver and her digestion and made her yellow and tired.

As long as Colin shut himself up in his room and thought only of his fears and weakness and his detest of people who looked at him and reflected hourly on humps and early death, he was a hysterical half-crazy little hypochondriac who knew nothing of the sunshine and the spring and also did not know that he could get well and could stand upon his feet if he tried to do it. When new beautiful thoughts began to push out the old hideous ones, life began to come back to him, his blood ran healthily through his veins and strength poured into him like a flood. His scientific experiment was quite practical and simple and there was nothing weird about it at all. Much more surprising things can happen to anyone who, when a disagreeable or discouraged thought comes into his mind, just has the sense to remember in time and push it out by putting in an agreeable determinedly courageous one. Two things cannot be in one place.

"Where you tend a rose, my lad, A thistle cannot grow."

While the secret garden was coming alive and two children were coming alive with it, there was a man wandering about certain far-away beautiful places in the Norwegian fiords and the valleys and mountains of Switzerland and he was a man who for ten years had kept his mind filled with dark and heart-broken thinking. He had not been courageous; he had never tried to put any other thoughts in the place of the dark ones. He had wandered by blue lakes and thought them; he had lain on mountain-sides with sheets of deep blue gentians blooming all about him and flower breaths filling all the air and he had thought them. A terrible sorrow had fallen upon him when he had been happy and he had let his soul fill itself with blackness and had refused obstinately to allow any rift of light to pierce through.

He had forgotten and deserted his home and his duties. When he travelled about, darkness so brooded over him that the sight of him was a wrong done to other people because it was as if he poisoned the air about him with gloom. Most strangers thought he must be either half mad or a man with some hidden crime on his soul.

He was a tall man with a drawn face and crooked shoulders and the name he always entered on hotel registers was, "Archibald Craven, Misselthwaite Manor, and Yorkshire, England."

He had travelled far and wide since the day he saw Mistress Mary in his study and told her she might have her "bit of earth." He had been in the most beautiful places in Europe, though he had remained nowhere more than a few days. He had chosen the quietest and remotest spots. He had been on the tops of mountains whose heads were in the clouds and had looked down on other mountains when the sun rose and touched them with such light as made it seem as if the world were just being born.

But the light had never seemed to touch himself until one day when he realized that for the first time in ten years a strange thing had happened. He was in a wonderful valley in the Austrian Tyrol and he had been walking alone through such beauty as might have lifted any man's soul out of shadow. He had walked a long way and it had not lifted his. But at last he had felt tired and had thrown himself down to rest on a carpet of moss by a stream. It was a clear little stream which ran quite merrily along on its narrow way through the luscious damp greenness. Sometimes it made a sound rather like very low laughter as it bubbled over and round stones. He saw birds come and dip their heads to drink in it and then flick their wings and fly away. It seemed like a thing alive and yet its tiny voice made the stillness seem deeper. The valley was very, very still.

As he sat gazing into the clear running of the water, Archibald Craven gradually felt his mind and body both grow quiet, as quiet as the valley itself. He wondered if he were going to sleep, but he was not. He sat and gazed at the sunlit water and his eyes began to see things growing at its edge. There was one lovely mass of blue forget-me-nots growing so close to the stream that its leaves were wet and at these he found himself looking as he remembered he had looked at such things years ago. He was actually thinking tenderly how lovely it was and what wonders of blue its hundreds of little blossoms were. He did not know that just that simple thought was slowly filling his mind—filling and filling it until other things were softly pushed aside.

It was as if a sweet clear spring had begun to rise in a stagnant pool and had risen and risen until at last it swept the dark water away. But of course he did not think of this himself. He only knew that the valley seemed to grow quieter and quieter as he sat and stared at the bright delicate blueness. He did not know how long he sat there or what was happening to him, but at last he moved as if he were awakening and he got up slowly and stood on the moss carpet, drawing a long, deep, soft breath and wondering at himself. Something seemed to have been unbound and released in him, very quietly.

"What is it?" he said, almost in a whisper, and he passed his hand over his forehead. "I almost feel as if—I were alive!"

I do not know enough about the wonder of undiscovered things to be able to explain how this had happened to him. Neither does anyone else yet. He did not understand at all himself—but he remembered this strange hour months afterward when he was at Misselthwaite again and he found out quite by accident that on this very day Colin had cried out as he went into the secret garden:

"I am going to live forever and ever and ever!"

The singular calmness remained with him the rest of the evening and he slept a new reposeful sleep; but it was not with him very long. He did not know that it could be kept. By the next night he had opened the doors wide to his dark thoughts and they had come trooping and rushing back. He left the valley and went on his wandering way again. But, strange as it seemed to him, there were minutes—sometimes half-hours—when, without his knowing why, the black burden seemed to lift itself again and he knew he was a living man and not a dead one. Slowly—slowly—for no reason that he knew of—he was "coming alive" with the garden.

As the golden summer changed into the deeper golden autumn he went to the Lake of Como. There he found the loveliness of a dream. He spent his days upon the crystal blueness of the lake or he walked back into the soft thick verdure of the hills and tramped until he was tired so that he might sleep. But by this time he had begun to sleep better, he knew, and his dreams had ceased to be a terror to him.

"Perhaps," he thought, "my body is growing stronger."

It was growing stronger but—because of the rare peaceful hours when his thoughts were changed—his soul was slowly growing stronger, too. He began to think of Misselthwaite and wonder if he should not go home. Now and then he wondered vaguely about his boy and asked himself what he should feel when he went and stood by the carved four-posted bed again and looked down at the sharply chiselled ivory-white face while it slept and the black lashes rimmed so startlingly the close-shut eyes. He shrank from it.

One marvel of a day he had walked so far that when he returned the moon was high and full and all the world was purple shadow and silver. The stillness of lake and shore and wood was so wonderful that he did not go into the villa he lived in. He walked down to a little bowered terrace at the water's edge and sat upon a seat and breathed in all the heavenly scents of the night. He felt the strange calmness stealing over him and it grew deeper and deeper until he fell asleep.

He did not know when he fell asleep and when he began to dream; his dream was so real that he did not feel as if he were dreaming. He remembered afterward how intensely wide awake and alert he had thought he was. He thought that as he sat and breathed in the scent of the late roses and listened to the lapping of the water at his feet he heard a voice calling. It was sweet and clear and happy and far away. It seemed very far, but he heard it as distinctly as if it had been at his very side.

"Archie! Archie! Archie!" it said, and then again, sweeter and clearer than before, "Archie! Archie!"

He thought he sprang to his feet not even startled. It was such a real voice and it seemed so natural that he should hear it.

"Lilias! Lilias!" he answered. "Lilias, where are you?"

"In the garden," it came back like a sound from a golden flute. "In the garden!"

And then the dream ended. But he did not awaken. He slept soundly and sweetly all through the lovely night. When he did awake at last it was brilliant morning and a servant was standing staring at him. He was an Italian servant and was accustomed, as all the servants of the villa were, to accepting without question any strange thing his foreign master might do. No one ever knew when he would go out or come in or where he would choose to sleep or if he would roam about the garden or lie in the boat on the lake all night. The man held a salver with some letters on it and he waited quietly until Mr. Craven took them.

When he had gone away Mr. Craven sat a few moments holding them in his hand and looking at the lake. His strange calm was still upon him and something more—a lightness as if the cruel thing which had been done had not happened as he thought—as if something had changed. He was remembering the dream—the real—real dream.

"In the garden!" he said, wondering at himself. "In the garden! But the door is locked and the key is buried deep."

When he glanced at the letters a few minutes later he saw that the one lying at the top of the rest was an English letter and came from Yorkshire. It was directed in a plain woman's hand but it was not a hand he knew. He opened it, scarcely thinking of the writer, but the first words attracted his attention at once.

"*Dear Sir:*
"I am Susan Sowerby that was so bold to speak to you once on the moor. It was about Miss Mary I spoke. I will make bold to speak again. Please, sir, I would come home if I were you. I think you would be glad to come and—if you will excuse me, sir—I think your lady would ask you to come if she was here.
                                        "Your obedient servant,
                                        "Susan Sowerby."


Mr. Craven read the letter twice before he put it back in its envelope. He kept thinking about the dream.

"I will go back to Misselthwaite," he said. "Yes, I'll go at once."

And he went through the garden to the villa and ordered Pitcher to prepare for his return to England.

In a few days he was in Yorkshire again, and on his long railroad journey he found himself thinking of his boy as he had never thought in all the ten years past. During those years he had only wished to forget him. Now, though he did not intend to think about him, memories of him constantly drifted into his mind. He remembered the black days when he had raved like a madman because the child was alive and the mother was dead. He had refused to see it, and when he had gone to look at it at last it had been such a weak wretched thing that everyone had been sure it would die in a few days. But to the surprise of those who took care of it the days passed and it lived and then everyone believed it would be a deformed and crippled creature.

He had not meant to be a bad father, but he had not felt like a father at all. He had supplied doctors and nurses and luxuries, but he had shrunk from the mere thought of the boy and had buried himself in his own misery. The first time after a year's absence he returned to Misselthwaite and the small miserable looking thing languidly and indifferently lifted to his face the great grey eyes with black lashes round them, so like and yet so horribly unlike the happy eyes he had adored, he could not bear the sight of them and turned away pale as death. After that he scarcely ever saw him except when he was asleep, and all he knew of him was that he was a confirmed invalid, with a vicious, hysterical, half-insane temper. He could only be kept from furies dangerous to himself by being given his own way in every detail.

All this was not an uplifting thing to recall, but as the train whirled him through mountain passes and golden plains the man who was "coming alive" began to think in a new way and he thought long and steadily and deeply.

"Perhaps I have been all wrong for ten years," he said to himself. "Ten years is a long time. It may be too late to do anything—quite too late. What have I been thinking of?"

Of course this was the wrong Magic—to begin by saying "too late." Even Colin could have told him that. But he knew nothing of Magic—either black or white. This he had yet to learn. He wondered if Susan Sowerby had taken courage and written to him only because the motherly creature had realized that the boy was much worse—was fatally ill. If he had not been under the spell of the curious calmness which had taken possession of him he would have been more wretched than ever. But the calm had brought a sort of courage and hope with it. Instead of giving way to thoughts of the worst he actually found he was trying to believe in better things.

"Could it be possible that she sees that I may be able to do him good and control him?" he thought. "I will go and see her on my way to Misselthwaite."

But when on his way across the moor he stopped the carriage at the cottage, seven or eight children who were playing about gathered in a group and bobbing seven or eight friendly and polite curtsies told him that their mother had gone to the other side of the moor early in the morning to help a woman who had a new baby. "Our

Dickon," they volunteered, was over at the Manor working in one of the gardens where he went several days each week.

Mr. Craven looked over the collection of sturdy little bodies and round red-cheeked faces, each one grinning in its own particular way, and he awoke to the fact that they were a healthy likable lot. He smiled at their friendly grins and took a golden sovereign from his pocket and gave it to "our Elizabeth Ellen" who was the oldest.

"If you divide that into eight parts there will be half a crown for each of you," he said.

Then amid grins and chuckles and bobbing of curtsies he drove away, leaving ecstasy and nudging elbows and little jumps of joy behind.

The drive across the wonderfulness of the moor was a soothing thing. Why did it seem to give him a sense of home-coming which he had been sure he could never feel again—that sense of the beauty of land and sky and purple bloom of distance and a warming of the heart at drawing nearer to the great old house which had held those of his blood for six hundred years? How he had driven away from it the last time, shuddering to think of its closed rooms and the boy lying in the four-posted bed with the brocaded hangings. Was it possible that perhaps he might find him changed a little for the better and that he might overcome his shrinking from him? How real that dream had been—how wonderful and clear the voice which called back to him, "In the garden—in the garden!"

"I will try to find the key," he said. "I will try to open the door. I must—though I don't know why."

When he arrived at the Manor the servants who received him with the usual ceremony noticed that he looked better and that he did not go to the remote rooms where he usually lived attended by Pitcher. He went into the library and sent for Mrs. Medlock. She came to him somewhat excited and curious and flustered.

"How is Master Colin, Medlock?" he inquired.

"Well, sir," Mrs. Medlock answered, "he's—he's different, in a manner of speaking."

"Worse?" he suggested.

Mrs. Medlock really was flushed.

"Well, you see, sir, "she tried to explain," Neither Dr. Craven, nor the nurse, nor I can exactly make him out."

"Why is that?"

"To tell the truth, sir, Master Colin might be better and he might be changing for the worse. His appetite, sir, is past understanding—and his ways—"

"Has he become more—more peculiar?" her master asked, knitting his brows anxiously.

"That's it, sir. He's growing very peculiar—when you compare him with what he used to be. He used to eat nothing and then suddenly he began to eat something enormous—and then he stopped again all at once and the meals were sent back just as they used to be. You never knew, sir, perhaps, that out of doors he never would let himself be taken. The things we've gone through to get him to go out in his chair would leave a body trembling like a leaf. He'd throw himself into such a state that Dr. Craven said he couldn't be responsible for forcing him. Well, sir, just without warning—not long after one of his worst tantrums he suddenly insisted on being taken out every day by Miss Mary and Susan Sowerby's boy Dickon that could push his chair. He took a fancy to both Miss Mary and Dickon, and Dickon brought his tame animals, and, if you'll credit it, sir, out of doors he will stay from morning until night."

"How does he look?" was the next question.

"If he took his food natural, sir, you'd think he was putting on flesh—but we're afraid it may be a sort of bloat. He laughs sometimes in a queer way when he's alone with Miss Mary. He never used to laugh at all. Dr. Craven is coming to see you at once, if you'll allow him. He never was as puzzled in his life."

"Where is Master Colin now?" Mr. Craven asked.

"In the garden, sir. He's always in the garden—though not a human creature is allowed to go near for fear they'll look at him."

Mr. Craven scarcely heard her last words.

"In the garden," he said, and after he had sent Mrs. Medlock away he stood and repeated it again and again. "In the garden!"

He had to make an effort to bring himself back to the place he was standing in and when he felt he was on earth again he turned and went out of the room. He took his way, as Mary had done, through the door in the shrubbery and among the laurels and the fountain beds. The fountain was playing now and was encircled by beds of brilliant autumn flowers. He crossed the lawn and turned into the Long Walk by the ivied walls. He did not walk quickly, but slowly, and his eyes were on the path. He felt as if he were being drawn back to the place he had so long forsaken, and he did not know why. As he drew near to it his step became still slower. He knew where the door was even though the ivy hung thick over it—but he did not know exactly where it lay—that buried key.

So he stopped and stood still, looking about him, and almost the moment after he had paused he started and listened—asking himself if he were walking in a dream.

The ivy hung thick over the door, the key was buried under the shrubs, no human being had passed that portal for ten lonely years—and yet inside the garden there were sounds. They were the sounds of running scuffling feet seeming to chase round and round under the trees, they were strange sounds of lowered suppressed voices—exclamations and smothered joyous cries.

It seemed actually like the laughter of young things, the uncontrollable laughter of children who were trying not to be heard but who in a moment or so—as their excitement mounted—would burst forth. What in heaven's name was he dreaming of—what in heaven's name did he hear? Was he losing his reason and thinking he heard things which were not for human ears? Was it that the far clear voice had meant?

And then the moment came, the uncontrollable moment when the sounds forgot to hush themselves. The feet ran faster and faster—they were nearing the garden door—there was quick strong young breathing and a wild outbreak of laughing shouts which could not be contained—and the door in the wall was flung wide open, the sheet of ivy swinging back, and a boy burst through it at full speed and, without seeing the outsider, dashed almost into his arms.

Mr. Craven had extended them just in time to save him from falling as a result of his unseeing dash against him, and when he held him away to look at him in amazement at his being there he truly gasped for breath.

He was a tall boy and a handsome one. He was glowing with life and his running had sent splendid colour leaping to his face. He threw the thick hair back from his forehead and lifted a pair of strange grey eyes—eyes full of boyish laughter and rimmed with black lashes like a fringe. It was the eyes which made Mr. Craven gasp for breath.

"Who—What? Who!" he stammered.

This was not what Colin had expected—this was not what he had planned. He had never thought of such a meeting. And yet to come dashing out—winning a race—perhaps it was even better. He drew himself up to his very tallest. Mary, who had been running with him and had dashed through the door too, believed that he managed to make himself look taller than he had ever looked before—inches taller.

"Father," he said, "I'm Colin. You can't believe it. I scarcely can myself. I'm Colin."

Like Mrs. Medlock, he did not understand what his father meant when he said hurriedly:

"In the garden! In the garden!"

"Yes," hurried on Colin. "It was the garden that did it—and Mary and Dickon and the creatures—and the Magic. No one knows. We kept it to tell you when you came. I'm well, I can beat Mary in a race. I'm going to be an athlete."

He said it all so like a healthy boy—his face flushed, his words tumbling over each other in his eagerness—that Mr. Craven's soul shook with unbelieving joy.

Colin put out his hand and laid it on his father's arm.

"Aren't you glad, Father?" he ended.

"Aren't you glad? I'm going to live forever and ever and ever!"

Mr. Craven put his hands on both the boy's shoulders and held him still. He knew he dared not even try to speak for a moment.

"Take me into the garden, my boy," he said at last. "And tell me all about it."

And so they led him in.

The place was a wilderness of autumn gold and purple and violet blue and flaming scarlet and on every side were sheaves of late lilies standing together—lilies which were white or white and ruby. He remembered well when the first of them had been planted that just at this season of the year their late glories should reveal themselves. Late roses climbed and hung and clustered and the sunshine deepening the hue of the yellowing trees made one feel that one stood in an embowered temple of gold. The newcomer stood silent just as the children had done when they came into its greyness. He looked round and round.

"I thought it would be dead," he said.

"Mary thought so at first," said Colin. "But it came alive."

Then they sat down under their tree—all but Colin, who wanted to stand while he told the story.

It was the strangest thing he had ever heard, Archibald Craven thought, as it was poured forth in headlong boy fashion. Mystery and Magic and wild creatures, the weird midnight meeting—the coming of the spring—the passion of insulted pride which had dragged the young Rajah to his feet to defy old Ben Weatherstaff to his face. The odd companionship, the play acting, the great secret so carefully kept. The listener laughed until tears came into his eyes and sometimes tears came into his eyes when he was not laughing. The Athlete, the Lecturer, the Scientific Discoverer was a laughable, lovable, healthy young human thing.

"Now," he said at the end of the story, "it need not be a secret any more. I dare say it will frighten them nearly into fits when they see me—but I am never going to get into the chair again. I shall walk back with you, Father—to the house."

Ben Weatherstaff's duties rarely took him away from the gardens, but on this occasion he made an excuse to carry some vegetables to the kitchen and being invited into the servants' hall by Mrs. Medlock to drink a glass of beer he was on the spot—as he had hoped to be—when the most dramatic event Misselthwaite Manor had seen during the present generation actually took place.

One of the windows looking upon the courtyard gave also a glimpse of the lawn. Mrs. Medlock, knowing Ben had come from the gardens, hoped that he might have caught sight of his master and even by chance of his meeting with Master Colin.

"Did you see either of them, Weatherstaff?" she asked.

Ben took his beer-mug from his mouth and wiped his lips with the back of his hand.

"Aye, that I did," he answered with a shrewdly significant air.

"Both of them?" suggested Mrs. Medlock.

"Both of them," returned Ben Weatherstaff. "Thank you kindly, ma'am, I could sip up another mug of it."

"Together?" said Mrs. Medlock, hastily overfilling his beer-mug in her excitement.

"Together, ma'am," and Ben gulped down half of his new mug at one gulp.

"Where was Master Colin? How did he look? What did they say to each other?"

"I didn't hear that," said Ben, "by only being on the step-ladder looking over the wall. But I'll tell you this. There've been things going on around this house people know nothing about. And what you'll find out soon."

And it was not two minutes before he swallowed the last of his beer and waved his mug solemnly toward the window which took in through the shrubbery a piece of the lawn.

"Look there," he said, "if you're curious. Look what's coming across the grass."

When Mrs. Medlock looked she threw up her hands and gave a little shriek and every man and woman servant within hearing bolted across the servants' hall and stood looking through the window with their eyes almost falling out of their heads.

Across the lawn came the Master of Misselthwaite and he looked as many of them had never seen him. And by his side with his head up in the air and his eyes full of laughter walked as strongly and steadily as any boy in Yorkshire—Master Colin!

**THE END**

# Dictionary of Abstract Words – becoming Picture Words

**a**:   1 one; one kind of [I want to buy a book for you.]

**about**:   1 having to do with [Here is a book about cooking. I want to talk about him.]
   2 more or less [She's about nine years old]

**after**: (adverb)   1 behind in place or time; coming next  [Please turn left after the petrol station.]
2 behind in time [Shall we meet after school?]

**again**: (adverb)   1 once more; a second time [I enjoyed your book so much that I may read it again.]   2 back into a former place or condition; as before [He came to our hotel again.]

**ago**: (adjective) gone by; before now [They were married ten years ago.]   (adverb) in the past [That happened long ago.]

**all**: (adjective)   1 the whole of or the whole amount of [He gave her all the money.]   2 every one of [All the students passed the exam.]

**almost**: (adverb) 1 very nearly but not completely [Sue is almost six years old.] 2 in addition; too; besides [She sang and also played the piano for us.]

**already**: (adverb) 1 by a specified time [The children were already asleep.]   2 so soon [Are you leaving already?]

**also**: in addition; too [He could sing and also play the guitar.]

**although**: (conjunction) 1 in spite of the fact that; though [Although it's raining we will go to our picnic] 2 however; and yet [They will probably lose, although nobody seems to think so]

**always**:   1 at all times; at every time [He is always polite.]
2 all the time [Oxygen is always present in the air.]   3 forever [I will always love her.]

**among**: in the middle of; in the company of [He was among them.]

**an**:   one; one kind of [Have you ever seen an elephant?]. Use **"a"** before a word that begins with a consonant sound. Use **"an"** before a word that begins with a vowel sound.

**and**:   1 also; in addition; as well as [I would like bread and butter.]

2 added to; plus [6 and 3 equals 9.]

**another**:   1 one more [Have another piece of cake.]

2 a different one; not the same [Exchange the movie for another one.]

**any**: 1 one, no matter which one, out of three or more;   [Take any fruit you like.]
2 some, no matter how many or what kind [Do you have any roses?]

**anyhow**:   no matter what else is true; just the same; anyway [You may know this poem, but study it anyhow.]

**anyway**: no matter what happens; in any case [I'm to London anyway.]

**around:** located or situated on every side; to face the opposite direction [They walked around the building twice.]

**as**: 1 to the same amount or degree; equally [Are you as tall as your brother?] 2 because; since [As I am tired, I'll stay home.]

3 in the role or manner of [He poses as a friend. The table can serve as a desk.]

**at**: 1 on, in, near, or by [Are they at home?]

2 to or toward [Look at her. Aim at the target.]   3 attending [Paul was at the party.]

**away**:   1 from one place to another [The boy ran away from home.]
        2 not here; absent [She is away for the day]

**back**: 1 at the rear or back [the back wheel of my car].
        2 to the place that it came from [Throw the ball back.]

**be**:   1 to live or exist [Lincoln will be a doctor. Let it be.]
        2 to stay or continue [I will be here until Monday.]
   • First Person singular: **am** – I live [I'm not at home.]
   • Second Person singular: **are** – you live [You are my best friend]
   • Third Person singular: **is** – he/she/it lives or exists [He's a great singer. Why is it not produced anymore?]
   • First, Second and Third Person plural: **are** – we/you/they live or exist [We are not welcome. You are all too late. They're my family]
   • Present Participle First, Second and Third Person: **being** – living, existing [I'm being polite.]
   • Past Tense First and Third Person singular: **was** – lived, existed [She was not feeling well.]
   • Second Person singular/ First, Second and Third Person plural: **were** – you, we, they live/exist [You were right to come along. They were not dressed properly.]
   • Past Participle First, Second and Third Person: **been** – have lived/existed.

**because**:  for the reason that; since [I'm late because I slept in.]

**become**:  to come to be [I become ill at the sight of it.]
   • **became**: came to be; happened  [What became of that movie star?]
   • **becoming**: coming to be [She's becoming quite well known]
   • **becomes**: he/she/it comes to be [My sister becomes a lawyer.]

**before**: 1 ahead of [The valley stretched before us.]
        2 happening earlier than; previous to [Will you finish before noon?]

**between**: 1 in the space that separates [a lake between the U.S. and Canada]
        2 in the time that separates [The doctor has office hours between one and five o'clock.]

**both:** refers to two people or things, regarded and identified together [Both children were treated equally.]

**but**: 1 except; other than [Nobody came but me.]
        2 yet; however [The story is long, but it is never dull.]

**buy - bought - bought:** to purchase or obtain in exchange for payment [I bought him a book.]

**by:**   1 near or beside [Come and sit by the fire.]
2 in or during [We travelled by night.]
3 through the means or work of [I like to travel by car. We've read books by Shakespeare.]

**can:**  1 know how to [I can speak Russian.]   2 is able to [The baby can walk.]
  **could:** -  1 he/she/it was able to or knew how to [She could read every word.]
       2. showing less force or sureness [You could be right.  I could do it tomorrow.]
  **can't:**   cannot [He can't understand you.]

**catch - caught - caught:** capture; intercept and hold [Show me how to catch butterflies!]

**come:**   to move from "there" to "here" [The dogs come to me quickly when I call them.]
  1. **comes:** he/she/it moves, arrives  [She comes home late.]
  2. **coming:** moving from "there" to "here"; arriving [Don't worry, I'm coming]
  3. **came:**  moved from "there" to "here"; arrived [He came too late.]

**do:**  Do can be both a main verb and a helping verb.
  • **do:** (main verb) 1 to carry out or perform [Please do the dishes.]   2 to work at; have as an occupation [What does he do for a living?]
  • **do:** (helping verb) 1 to ask a question [Do you want to eat now?]
  • **don't:**  do not [I don't know the answer.]
  • **did:** carried out; performed [I did my homework.]
  • **done:** have carried out; have performed [We have done it already.]
  • **doing:** carrying out; performing [What are you doing here?]
  • **does:** he/she/it carries out; performs [She does all the work around here.]

**down:**   1 from a higher to a lower place [If you can't jump down, climb down.]
       2 being in a low position or on the ground, floor, or bottom; not up [The shades are down. The sun is down.]

**each:**  every one of two or more things, thought of separately [Each of my pets is special.]

**either:**  1 one or the other of two [You may use either door.]
       2 both one and the other; each [She had a tool in either hand.]

**else:**  1 not the same; different or other [I thought you were someone else.]
       2 in addition; more [Do you want anything else?]

**even:**  1 though it may seem unlikely; indeed [Even a child could do it.]
       2 by comparison [She knows even less about music than I do.]
       3 flat, level, or smooth [an even surface].
       4 capable of being divided by two without remainder [2, 4, 6 and 8 are even numbers.]

**ever:**  1 at any time [Have you ever seen a ghost?]
       2 at all times; always [They lived happily ever after.]

**every:**  all or each one of the people or things that are part of a group; each with no exceptions [Every student must take the test.]

**everything**:    every thing that there is [Did you bring everything for the picnic?]

**few**:  not many [There are few good men left.]

**for**:    1 meant to be received by or used in [I have got a present for you.].    2 to the distance of; as far as [Every day we walk for two miles.]    3 as long as; through the time of [The movie runs for an hour.]

**from**:    1 beginning at [ They ran from Sydney to Newcastle].    2 made, sent, or said by [I got a letter from my friend in Spain.]    3 out of the whole of [Subtract 2 from 4.]

**front**:    1 the part that faces forward; most important side [The front of the house usually faces the street.]    2 in, on, near, or facing the front [the front door; the front page of a newspaper]

**full**:  holding or containing as much as possible; filled [a full jar]

**get**:  1 to become the owner of by receiving, buying, or earning; to gain or obtain [We get a new car.]    2 to go and bring [Get your books.]
2. **got**: received; arrived at; reached [They got home early.]
3. **gotten/got**:  have received; have bought; have gained [I've got one hundred dollar.]
4. **gets**: he/she/it receives, buys, gets [She gets an allowance]
5. **getting**: receiving, buying, earning [We are getting a puppy.]

**go**:  1 to move along or pass from one place, point, or person to another [I must go to the hospital today.]
2. **goes**: he/she/it moves along; belongs [The broom goes in the cupboard.]
3. **went**: moved along; passed from one place to another [He went to New York last night.]
4. **gone**: have moved along; have/has ceased [Is your pain gone?]

**have**:    to be the owner of; possess [We have a new car.]
  • **have**: (helping verb) 1 present perfect tense [They have gone to Italy.]
  • **have to:** need to; must [We have to go.]
  • **had:** was the owner of; possessed [He had a great smile.]
  • **has:** he/she/it is the owner of; possesses [My cat has sharp claws.]
  • **having:** being the owner of; possessing; experiencing [Are you having a good time?]

**he:**  the man, boy, or male animal that is being talked about [Jim thought he was right.]

**he's**: he is [He's a really nice person.] 2 he has [He's got a lot of time.]

**her:**  the form of she as an object:    1 after certain verbs [The dog bit her.]    2 after prepositions [I gave the tapes to her.]
**her:**  done by her or having to do with her [She enjoys her work.]
**hers:**  the one or the ones that belong to her [I know that this book is hers.]

**here:**  at or in this place [Who lives here?]

**him:**  The form of he as an object:    1 after certain verbs [The dog bit him.] 2 after prepositions [I came over to talk to him.]

**his**: the one or the ones that belong to him [I know that this place is his.]

**his**: done by him or having to do with him [his work; his shoes.]

**how**: 1 in what way [How do you start the motor?] 2 in what condition [How is your mother today?]

**I**: the person who is speaking [I like sushi.]

**I'm**: I am [I'm sorry to disappoint you.]

**if**: in case that; supposing that: 1 likely [If I like it, I will buy it.]
2. not likely [If I was rich, I would buy the painting.]
3. in case I had; not possible [If I had won the lottery, I would have moved to Italy.]

**in**: 1 contained by [There are five fish in the bowl.]
2 living or located at [They are in Chicago.]

**into**: 1 to the inside of [Let's go into the house.]
2 to the form or condition of [I got into trouble.]

**isn't**: is not.

**it**: the thing or animal that is being talked about [I saw the letter and opened it.]

**it's**: it is [It's all right; I'm not hurt.]

**its**: 1 the one or the ones that belong to it [The ribbon of the dress was its.]
2 done by it or having to do with it [Every plant has its particular needs.]

**just**: 1 right or fair [a just decision]. 2 neither more nor less than; exactly [It's just two o'clock now.] 3 no more than; only [I'm just teasing you.]

**know - knew - known**: to be aware of through observation, inquiry or information [I knew the boy from school.]

**last**: 1 being or coming after all others [the last month of the year; the last word in an argument]. 2 after all others [Our team came in last.] 3 to go on; continue [The play lasts for only an hour.]

**leave**: 1 to go away from [I always leave the house at 8 a.m.] 2 to let stay or be [Leave the door open.]
- **leaves:** he/she/it goes away from [She leaves the place in a good condition.]
- **leaving:** going away from [Why are you leaving us?]
- **left:** went away from [All children have left the house.]
- **left:** on or to the side that is toward the west when a person faces north [the left hand; a left turn]

**least**: 1 a superlative of little. 2 smallest in size, amount, or importance [He didn't show the least interest in going.]

**less**: 1 a comparative of little. 2 not so much; smaller in size or amount [drink less soda; take less time]

**let:**  to give permission to; allow [They let me help.]

**lets:**  he/she/it gives permission to [He often lets me work here.]

**let's:**  let us [Let's go now!]

**letting:**  giving permission to; allowing [We are letting the dogs play outside.]

**like:**  1 similar to; somewhat the same as [He has hands like claws].  2 fond of or pleased with [I think that they like each other.]
  • **likes:** (verb) to be fond of or pleased with; enjoy [She likes dogs.]
  • **liked:** was fond of or pleased with; enjoyed [The girl liked her new room.]
  **3** **liking:**  being fond of; enjoying [Are you liking the ice cream?]

**little:** small in size, amount or degree [Melany's little sister didn't come along.]

**make:**  1 to bring into being; build, create, produce, or put together [Let's make a fire.]
  • **makes:** he/she/it builds, creates, produces [She makes breakfast for him.]
  • **making:** building, creating, producing [We are making plans for Sunday.]
  • **made:** built, created, produced [He made plans to go to New Mexico.]

**many:**  a large number of; not few [many boxes; many times]

**may:**  1 can or is likely to [I may stay home.  It may rain.]  2 is allowed or has permission to [You may go now.]
  **might:** (past tense of 'may') expresses a possibility [She might be going overseas.].

**maybe:**  it may be; perhaps. [Maybe they come over later.]

**me:**  the form of 'I' as the object 1. After a verb [The dog bit me.]  2 after a preposition [He gave the form to me.]

**mine:**  the one or the ones that belong to me [I know this book is mine.]

**more:**  greater in amount or degree or in number [He has more free time than I do. We need more helpers.]

**most:**  1 superlative of much or many.  2 greatest in amount or degree or in number [Who won the most money? Most people like summer.]

**much:**  1 great in amount or degree [Children give me much joy.]  2 to a great degree or extent [I feel much happier.]

**my:**  done by me or having to do with me [my work; my shoes]

**neither:**  1 not one or the other of two; not either [Neither boy went to the park.] 2 not either - often used in phrases with nor [I'll buy neither roses nor tulips.]

**never:**  at no time; not ever [I never saw her again.]

**no:**  not so; the opposite of yes. [I have no money left.]

**none**:  not one or not any [None of these books is new. None of the cake was eaten.]

**nor**:  and not; and not either [I know neither Ben nor Frank.]

**not**:  in no way; to no degree [Do not talk.  They are not happy.]

**now**:  1 at this moment; at the present time [We are eating now.]

**of**:  1 belonging to; connected to [Three pages of my book are missing.]
2 about; concerning [Think of me when I'm away.]

**off**:  1 away; to or at some other place [The button fell off.]
2 so that it is no longer working or on [Turn the light off.]

**on**:  1 held up by or attached to [a picture on the wall].
• Supported by a surface [Put the vase on the table.]
3 having as its location [a house on Main Street].
4 in action; working or acting [The radio is on.]

**one**:  1 being a single thing or unit [one vote].   2 one or anything [What can one do about it?]

**only**: without any others of the same kind [I am an only child.]

**onto**:  to a position on [The cat climbed onto the roof.]

**or**:  1 the second of two choices or possibilities [Do you want milk or cocoa?]
2 the last of a series of choices [Is the light green, yellow, or red?]

**other**:   1 not this one or the one just mentioned, but a different one [Stand on one foot and lift the other one.]   2 additional; extra [I have no other shoes.]

**others**: (plural of other) different ones [We are staying with the others.]

**otherwise**:   1 in some other way; differently [He liked the movie, but I felt otherwise.]
2 or else [I'm tired; otherwise I would join you.]

**ought**: to be forced by what is right, wise or necessary; to be expected to [He ought to do his homework]

**our**:  done by us or having to do with us [our work; our cars].

**ours**:  the one or the ones that belong to us [The corner block is ours.]

**out**:  away from or beyond a certain position, place, or situation [Open the window and look out. Spit it out.]

**over**:   1 in, at, or to a place above; higher than [Hang the picture over the fireplace.]
2 so as to cover [Put a blanket over my legs.]

**possible**:  able to be done or achieved, but not certain [Is it possible to learn a new language in three weeks?]

**put**: to cause to be in a certain place or position; place [Put soap in the water. Put the books side by side.]

**quite**: to the utmost or to a certain extent or degree; fairly; comparatively [Are you quite sure that you want to come?]

**rather**: 1. indicates one's preference in a particular matter [I would rather drink water than wine.] 2. to a certain or significant degree [She was rather tired.]

**really**: in fact; indeed [She was a really nice girl.]

**run**: to go by moving the legs faster than in walking. When a person runs, both feet are off the ground at the same time for a moment with each step.
  **runs**: he/she/it moves fast [The dog runs towards you.]
  **running**: moving faster than walking [We were running on the beach.]
  **ran**: moved faster than walking [He ran quickly down the street.]

**same**: 1 being the very one [She is the same girl who runs on this track every day.]
  2 alike in some way; similar [He has the same bike as Martin.]

**say - said - said**: use words to convey information, an opinion or feeling; to voice or speak [He said that he won't be coming.]

**seem**: appear to or giving the impression of being something or having a particular quality [The children seem to enjoy themselves.]

**see**: to be aware of through the eyes; have or use the sense of sight [I don't see very well.]
  **sees**: he/she/it has the sense of sight [My friend sees him all the time.]
  **seeing**: being aware of through the eyes [I am seeing a bird outside.]
  **seen**: have been aware through the eyes [They have seen the horrors of war.]
  **saw**: was aware through the eyes; looked [We saw the movie twice.]

**she**: the woman, girl, or female animal that is being talked about [Annette thought she heard a noise.]

**she's**: she is [She's a beautiful girl.]
  2 she has [She's got a lot of time.]

**shall**: Shall is used with other verbs to show future time of 'I' and 'we' [I shall leave tomorrow. Shall we eat?]
  **should**: 1 something expected [He should be on time for dinner.]
  2 to talk about something that one ought to do [I should lose weight.]

**so**: 1 to the degree or amount that has been expressed [Why are you so late?]
  2 as a result; therefore [He couldn't swim and so was drowned.]

**some**: 1 a few; a little [Can you buy me some sweets?]
  2 being a certain group of persons or things that are not named or not known [Some people were playing ball.]

**soon**: 1 in a short time from now [Spring will soon be here.]
   2 fast or quickly [as soon as possible]

**stand**:   to be on one's feet without moving [Stand by your desk.]
   **stands**: is on one's feet without moving [He stands up for the ladies.]
   **standing**: being on one's feet without moving [People are standing in a line.]
   **stood**: was on your feet without moving [She stood still for minutes.]

**still**: 1 without moving [They stood still for a minute.]
   2 in a greater amount or degree [She became angrier still.]

**such**: 1 of the same kind or similar [Such rugs are expensive.]
   2 so much or so great [We had such fun that nobody left.]

**sure**:   1 convinced; feeling no doubt [I am sure it will be fun.]
   •   not capable of failing; safe or certain [a sure cure; a sure friend]

**take**:   1 to get hold of; grasp [Take my hand as we cross the street.]
   **takes**: gets hold of; grasps [He takes lunch to school.]
   **taking**: getting hold of; grasping; needing [He's taking his time.]
   **took**: got hold of; captured [The soldiers took the town.]

**than**:   1 compared to.  This word is used before the second part of a comparison [I am taller than you.]   2 besides; except [What could I do other than stop?]

**that**:   1 the person or thing  being talked about [That man is called Josef.]
   2 the thing farther away or different in some way [I prefer that dress to this one.]

**the**: 1 referring to a particular person or thing [I want the cake with the cherry on top.]
   2 that one which is here or which has been mentioned [The day is hot.  The story ended.]

**their**:  done by them or having to do with them [their work; their shoe.]

**theirs**: belonging to them [The house is theirs.]

**them**:  the form of they that is used:   1 after certain verbs [The dog bit them. I saw them.]
2 after prepositions [Give it to them.]

**then**:   1 at that time [We were young then.]   2 after that; next [The party ended, and then we left.]

**there**:   1 at or in that place [Who lives there?]

**there's**: there is [There's a puppy in the room.]

**these**: plural of this. [These pills put me to sleep.]

**they**: the people or things being talked about [They loved the present you sent.]

**they're**:   they are. [They're not fit to play.]

**this**:   1 the one here [This is Juan.]   2 the thing that is present or nearer [This is prettier than that.]

**though**: in spite of the fact that; although [Though it rained, we walked.]

**those**:  plural of that. [You can wear those boots instead.]

**through**:  in one side and out the other side of; from end to end of [The nail went through the board.  We drove through the tunnel.]

**throw**: to send with some force through the air [Don't throw things around.].
   **threw**: past tense of throw [He threw the shoes at her.]

**to**:  1 in the direction of [Turn to the right.]
   2 shows the infinitive form of a verb [Mary will learn to listen.]

**too**:  1 in addition; also [He came too.]   2 more than enough [This hat is too big.]

**two**: the cardinal number between one and three; 2.  [She brought two suitcases.]

**unless**:   except when or if [I won't go unless you do.]

**until**:   up to the time of; till [Wait until noon.]

**up**:   1 to, in, or on a higher place or position [She climbed up. The sun comes up at dawn.]
2 to a larger amount or size; to a greater degree [Electricity went up in price. My ankle swelled up.]

**upon**:  on or up and on [He put the box upon the table.]

**us**:  the form of we that is used:   1 after certain verbs [The dog bit us.  He saw us. Tell us the truth.]   2 after prepositions [Tell the story to us.  The song was written by us.]

**very**:   1 in a high degree; to a great extent [very cold; very funny; very sad]

**we**: the persons speaking or writing [We like candy.  Are we still friends?]

**we're**:  we are. [We're very happy here.]

**what**:   1 which thing, happening, or condition? [What did he ask? What is your name?]

**when**:  at what time? [When did they leave?]

**where**:  in or at what place? [Where is the car?]

**whether**:   1 if it is true or likely that [I don't know whether I can go.]
2 in either case that [It makes no difference whether he comes or not.]

**which**:   1 what person or thing? [Which will you choose?]

**while**: 1 a period of time [I waited a short while.]
   2 during the time that [I read a book while I waited.]

**who**:   what or which person or persons? [Who helped you? I know who lives here.]

**whom**: which person or people? [To whom are you writing?]

**who's**:   1 who is [Who's your boss?]  2 who has [Who's got the money?]
**whose**:  the one or the ones that belong to whom [Whose are these cups?]

**why**:   for what reason, cause, or purpose? [Why did he go?]

**will**:   1 to decide or choose [Let her do as she wills.]
Will is also used with other verbs to show future time. [We will leave next week. Will you please save some dessert for me?]

**within**:   in the inner part of; inside [Stay within the house.]

**without**: free from; not having [He only eats food without preservatives.]

**would**:  1 past tense of will [They thought they would enjoy the circus, but they didn't like it.]
2 used to [My granny would take me to the movies.]
3 to talk about something that depends on something else [I would have helped if you had asked me.]   2 to ask something in a polite way [Would you please leave?]

**with**:   1 in the company of [Come with me.]
2 as part of; into [Mix blue with yellow to get green]

**within**:   in the inner part of; inside [Stay within the house.]

**without**:  free from; not having [a person without a worry; a cup without a saucer]

**won't**:   will not [She won't hire him.]

**would**: – see 'will'

**write - wrote - written:** mark words, letters or symbols on a surface [He wrote her a poem.]

**yet**: 1 up to now; so far [He has not gone yet.]

**you**:   1 the person or persons that are being spoken to. [You are a good friend.  I saw you both. He borrowed the eggs from you.]

**your**: done by you or having to do with you [I admire your work.]

**you're**:   you are [You're not a friend of mine.]

**yours**: the one or the ones that belong to you [I know that this animal is yours. Yours costs more than ours.]

Made in the USA
Monee, IL
06 November 2020